Writing for your Life

L#3

Writing for your Life #3

edited by

Sybil Steinberg and Jonathan Bing

**with an introduction by
Sybil Steinberg**

PUSHCART

ISBN 0-916366-29-4 (hb)
ISBN 1-888889-02-0 (pb)

For information address Pushcart Press,
PO Box 380, Wainscott, NY 11975

Distributed by W. W. Norton & Co., New York, N.Y.

CONTENTS

INTRODUCTION

Much like the proud parent of an outstanding offspring, I am gratified when, at industry gatherings, editors, agents, publishers, even authors themselves, confess that the *Publishers Weekly* Interview is the first section they turn to in the magazine every week. Over the last fifteen years I've come to realize that each interview has the allure of a human interest story, revealing the author at home or in an office redolent of personality. There is often an undercurrent of suspense that springs from the frank sharing of experiences that most readers would not otherwise be aware of. We think of these pieces as dispatches from the writers' world, glimpses of the arduous process that must be made to seem magical and effortless by the time a book reaches a reader's hands, mind and heart.

Whether one reads a single profile at a time, or several at each sitting, certain hallmarks of the trade seem to prevail. Most writers speak of the daunting relationship between storyteller (or historian or essayist) and the blank sheet of paper, or as it frequently occurs lately, the humming computer screen.

And however different their literary pursuits, many of the same challenges pertain: how they can find the courage to jettison a bad start, muster the discipline to rise before dawn to catch the muse before other obligations intervene, or endure the chagrin (and financial pressure) of disappointing sales. Invariably, there is one common thread: the writers' relationships with dedicated editors—or the lack thereof. There are poignant examples of the orphaned feeling a writer suffers when a beloved editor leaves the publishing house but the contract says the writer must stay; and more happily, expressions of gratitude for a long editor-author relationship in calm waters.

This volume also reflects the fact that English-language literature now firmly includes the voices of many traditions.

Salman Rushdie writes about England and India through eyes that know both cultures. André Brink's work reflects the turmoil of South

Africa. The poetry of Seamus Heaney is steeped in Ireland, as are the novels of Roddy Doyle. Mavis Gallant and Annie Ernaux offer distinctive views of France. Albert Murray and Dorothy West reflect the black experience from widely divergent vantage points; Jamaica Kincaid's view is refracted through a Caribbean culture. Sherman Alexie is inspired by his Native American background. The Chicano protagonists of Ana Castillo and Rudolfo Anaya come from the barrio. Gus Lee knows the stresses of Asian Americans. Mario Puzo inhabits the world of Italian immigrants and their descendants. Ursula Hegi recreates Germany, where she was born. Tom Keneally roams the globe, but his native Australia informs his imagination. Gay lives can be glimpsed through the works of Andrew Holleran and Mark Doty.

And America's multifarious regional voices are heard in works as varied as the continent's topography, from E. Annie Proulx's and Tobias Wolff's and James Carroll's experiences of New England to Rick Bass's and Stephen Ambrose's evocations of the Western landscape; Barry Lopez starts there and wanders to the Arctic. The South of Doris Betts and of Winston Groom are different places; yet they are the same.

And most striking, there's the relationship between art and life that many readers suspect but find confirmed in those instances where the rapport between author and interviewer allows discussion of the interaction between fact and fiction. John Updike, Julia Alvarez, Mona Simpson and Connie May Fowler are among the fiction writers who have transformed the circumstances of their lives into something larger, in fashioning stories of people who live through many of their creators' experiences and find universal resonance. Jimmy Breslin and Michael Korda were moved by existential events to reveal their deepest feelings in memoirs.

There is one significant addition to *Writing for Your Life #3*. Jonathan Bing's name now joins mine as co-editor of this book, as reflects his position on the magazine. Jon's enormous contributions in editing the interviews every week have been evident to the readers of *Publishers Weekly;* and he has contributed in equal measure to the editing of this volume. We both thank Gary Ink, *PW*'s librarian, for his contributions.

SYBIL STEINBERG
Publishers Weekly

Writing for your Life

#3

SHERMAN ALEXIE

As a 24-year-old student at Washington State University, Sherman Alexie, a Spokane/Coeur d'Alene Indian, set down his career goals at the insistence of a friend: 1) to publish 10 books by age 30; 2) to see a book on the silver screen by 35; and 3) to receive a major literary prize by 40.

With *Indian Killer*, his third prose work, a tragic thriller about the ravages of cultural dilution and dissolution, out from Grove/Atlantic, and *The Summer of Black Widows*, his seventh collection of poetry, imminent from Hanging Loose Press, the first goal will be achieved. Three of Alexie's books—his first short-story collection, *The Lone Ranger and Tonto Fistfight in Heaven* (Atlantic Monthly, 1993); his novel *Reservation Blues* (Atlantic Monthly, 1994); and *Indian Killer*—are the subjects of ongoing film negotiations. As for a major literary award, if review acclaim from such established masters as Reynolds Price, Leslie Marmon Silko and Frederick Bausch, not to mention inclusion in the recent "Best of Young American Novelists" issue of *Granta*, means anything, Alexie could well win his prize.

When asked how sudden success has affected him, Alexie flashes a quick smile and quips: "I like room service." The remark—even coming from a sometime stand-up comic—is revealing. Self-described as "mouthy, opinionated and arrogant," Alexie betrays no squeamishness about the mix of art and commerce. He loves the limelight, and his readings are known for their improvisational energy, costume changes and singing. Six years sober after a six-year binge that began the day he entered college, he explains: "Today, I get high, I get drunk off of public readings. I'm good at it. It comes from being a debater in high school, but also, crucially, it comes from the oral tradition of my own culture. It's in performance that the two cultures become one." Then he laughs, adding: "The most terrifying phrase in the world is when an Indian man grabs a microphone and says 'I have a few words to say.'"

1

Alexie has more than a few words to say. His memory runs deep. Whether cast in poetry or prose, his work offers a devastating and deeply human portrait of contemporary Indian life. Meeting an interviewer in the modest Seattle apartment where he lives with his wife of two years, Diane, a beautiful, private woman of Hidatsa/Ho Chunk/ Pottawatomi descent, Alexie proves to be affable and generous, ready to sit down around the kitchen table and talk about his life and art.

Tall, handsome, his long black hair tied in a ponytail, dressed casually in a beige knit shirt and khakis, Alexie, who played basketball in high school, has a shooting guard's easy movements and soft touch. One would never suspect that he was born hydrocephalic, endured a brain operation at six months that should have left him mentally retarded—if not dead—and for his first seven years was beset with seizures and medicated with regular doses of lithium, phenobarbital and other sedatives.

The son of Sherman Sr. and Lillian Alexie (his father is Coeur d'Alene, his mother Spokane), Alexie was born and reared in Wellpinit, the only town on the Spokane Indian Reservation—a place he describes as a landscape of "HUD shacks and abandoned cars"— which lies some 50 miles northwest of Spokane, Wash. Alcoholism, a central concern of Alexie's work, afflicted his family, but there was love in the house, along with a mix of traditional and contemporary culture. "I've come to realize my parents did a damn good job, considering the cards they were dealt," he says.

Then there was his maternal grandmother, Etta Adams, who died when Alexie was eight, and who appears as the eternal, wise and practical Big Mom in *Reservation Blues*. "She was one of the great spiritual leaders of the Spokane tribe," Alexie says, "one of the most powerful figures to visit the Northwest, and in her last days thousands came to pay their respects." The need for female strength and wisdom is a primary theme of Alexie's, sounded early on in "Indian Boy Love Songs," four poems collected in *The Business of Fancydancing* (Hanging Loose, 1992).

Alexie began reading in earnest at an early age. Because he was unable to participate in the wild athleticism of a young male Indian's rites of passage, books became his world. "I knew what a paragraph was before I could read the words," he says, claiming that at age six, he began working his way through *The Grapes of Wrath*. Steinbeck's final image of a starving man being breast-fed is fixed in his mind: "Ah, so *that's* the way a story's supposed to end," he recalls telling himself.

2

"With that kind of huge moment, which is the way the stories we tell ourselves end." Through grade and high school, he devoured every book in the school libraries, reading and re-reading Steinbeck until the copies fell apart in his hands. "I was a total geek," Alexie recalls, "which automatically made me an outcast, so in order to succeed I had to be smarter than everybody else. My sense of competitiveness came out that way. I was fierce in the classroom. I humiliated everybody and had my nose broken five times after school for being the smart kid."

Alexie's view of Indian life acquired more complexity when, in 1981, he enrolled at an all-white high school in Reardan, a reservation border town unfriendly to Indians. With his world turned upside-down, he became the "perfect Reardan kid": an honor student and class president and the only ponytail on the crewcut Reardan Indians basketball team. "I kept my mouth shut and became a good white Indian," he acknowledges. "All those qualities that made me unpopular on the reservation made me popular at Reardan. It got to the point where I don't think they saw me as Indian."

The hard work and conformity earned Alexie a scholarship to Gonzaga University in Spokane, where he enrolled with vague intentions of becoming a doctor or lawyer—"the usual options for a bright brown kid"—and promptly fell apart. Feeling lost, lacking a life plan, he began drinking heavily. His misery found consolation in poetry, which he began to read avidly—Keats, Yeats, Dickinson, Whitman. "I didn't see myself in them," he says, "so I felt like I was doing anthropology, like I was studying white people. Obviously, something was drawing me in that I couldn't intellectualize or verbalize, and then I realized that the poems *weren't* just about white people. They were about everybody. I also realized that the poets were outcasts too," he chuckles.

After two years, Alexie packed his bags and left Gonzaga for the University of Washington. Newly arrived in Seattle, he was robbed and soon found himself back in Wellpinit, on the verge of joining the long history of young Indians who come home to a slow death by alcohol. Waking one morning on the steps of the Assembly of God Church, hung over, his pants wet, he staggered home to mail off an application to WSU in Pullman. It was a poetry class at WSU taught by Alex Kuo that finally helped him to get his bearings as a writer, he recalls.

The boozing didn't stop, but the words poured out. Kuo, who became a father figure to Alexie, gave him a copy of the anthology *Songs of This Earth on Turtle's Back*. "In an instant I saw myself in literature," Alexie recalls. A line from an Adrian C. Louis poem called

"Elegy for the Forgotten Oldsmobile" changed his life forever: "O Uncle Adrian! I'm in the reservation of my own mind." "I started crying. That was my whole life. Forget Steinbeck, forget Keats. I just kept saying that line over and over again. I sat down and started writing poems. And they came. It was scary."

Under Kuo's guidance, his first-semester manuscript became his first book, *I Would Steal Horses,* which was published by Slipstream in 1992. With Native poets such as Louis and Simon Ortiz, Joy Harjo and Linda Hogan as models, he began to write his own story in his own voice. Lyrical, angry, poignant, socially engaged, the poems found their way into small literary magazines such as Brooklyn's *Hanging Loose.* Eventually, Hanging Loose Press brought out *The Business of Fancydancing,* which received a strong critical reception and has sold 11,000 copies, an astounding number for a book of poems from a small press. Serendipitously, the letter accepting the manuscript for publication arrived the day Alexie decided to quit drinking.

During his student days, and at Kuo's urging, Alexie began to experiment with prose—some of which appeared in *Fancydancing.* Other fictions were later collected in *The Lone Ranger and Tonto Fistfight in Heaven,* half of which was written in a four-month burst when agents, alert to his poetry, began calling with requests for fiction.

A friend introduced Alexie to Nancy Stauffer, who remains his agent to this day. "Nancy's really been good at helping me develop a career," he says. "We really have a plan. We're not just going book to book. First and foremost, I want to be a better writer, and I want a larger audience." In short order, Alexie found himself with a two-book, six-figure contract with Morgan Entrekin at the Atlantic Monthly Press at a time when, he says, he "didn't even have an idea for a novel."

The idea did come, in the guise of *Reservation Blues,* a novel that imagines legendary bluesman Robert Johnson arriving on a reservation seeking redemption from "a woman," in this case Big Mom. Johnson's magic guitar carries four young Indians off the reservation and into the world of rock and roll. The book explores differences between reservation and urban Indians and the effects of the church on traditional people, among other themes. It's a bleak novel that's leavened by Alexie's signature black humor. "I'm not trying to be funny," he explains. "I don't sit down to write something funny. In my everyday life I'm funny, and when I write, it comes out. Laughter is a ceremony; it's the way people cope."

There isn't much laughter in *Indian Killer,* which depicts John Smith, an Indian without a tribal affiliation. Adopted off the reservation and reared by a white couple, he becomes a suspect in a string of scalping murders that terrorize Seattle. Tangent to Smith is a host of characters, including a racist talk-show host, a white professor of Native American studies and a defiant female Indian activist, all of whom are struggling with their sense of identity. The picture is of a man divided by culture, a culture divided by its tragic history, a city divided by race, and a nation at war with itself. And it is a vision Alexie paints with excruciating clarity.

The perception of being an outcast among outcasts contributes to Alexie's complex portrait of reservation life, a view rife with ironies and a sense of complicity that has come under fire from Indian writers for its apparent emphasis on hopelessness, alcoholism and suicide. "I write what I know," he says, "and I don't try to mythologize myself, which is what some seem to want, and which some Indian women and men writers are doing, this Earth Mother and Shaman Man thing, trying to create these 'authentic, traditional' Indians. We don't live our lives that way."

Well aware that his poems and novels have angered Indians and whites alike, Alexie enjoys walking a kind of cultural highwire. "I use a racial criterion in my literary critiques," he says. "I have a very specific commitment to Indian people, and I'm very tribal in that sense. I want us to survive *as* Indians."

That said, Alexie's Indian characters are never guileless victims. Echoing Big Mom, who continually reminds her neighbors in *Reservation Blues* that their fate is in their own hands, he explains: "It's a two-way street. The system sets you up to fail, and then, somehow, you choose to be part of it."

DOUG MARX
September 16, 1996

JULIA ALVAREZ

In 1991, Julia Alvarez made a resounding splash on the literary scene
with her first novel, *How the Garcia Girls Lost Their Accents,* whose
narrators, the four vibrant and distinctive Garcia siblings, captivated
readers and critics. Like their author, the characters emigrated to
middle-class Queens, N.Y., from the Dominican Republic, and the
novel provided a keen look at the island social structure they wistfully
remember and the political turmoil they escaped.

The second-oldest sister, Yolanda, now a well-known author, is the
protagonist of Alvarez's third novel, *¡Yo!,* out from Algonquin. Alvarez brings to Yo's portrait an empathy of shared experiences, anxieties and hopes.

In 1960 at the age of 10, Alvarez fled the Dominican Republic with
her parents and three sisters (her father was involved in the underground against the dictator Raphael Trujillo). She has since roamed
this country, teaching writing in far-flung schools and communities,
before finally putting down roots in Middlebury, Vt., and writing two
books of poetry and three novels, including 1994's *In the Time of the
Butterflies* (Algonquin).

A recent exhibit at the New York Public Library, "The Hand of the
Poet from John Donne to Julia Alvarez," displayed snapshots of the author in the Dominican Republic (she travels there at least once a year),
riding horseback, dancing the merengue and obstreperously bartering
for plantains. When *PW* catches up with Alvarez, it is in the rare-book
room of the Middlebury College library, where a standing-room-only
audience has gathered to hear her read from the new novel. Brushing
unruly, dark bangs from her lively face, her voice inflected by a faint
Latin twang, she shows few signs of the butterflies fluttering in her
stomach, induced by the prospect of reciting her work on her own turf.

"I couldn't sleep last night before this reading," she confesses, later
ushering *PW* into the living room of her secluded ranch house, which
is brimming with plants, cacti and photographs of her extended fam-

ily. Alvarez, who first came to Middlebury to attend the Breadloaf Writers' Conference as an undergraduate in the late 1960s and is now a tenured professor of English, has lived here permanently since 1988, and it is here that she met her husband, an ophthalmologist. Yet she expresses ambivalence at the thought of becoming something of a local fixture.

"I see myself marginally in the academic community, which I think in part is good for a writer, because it keeps you on your toes," she says. "When I first moved here, people would come up to me and say things that I hadn't told them. Or remark upon things that I didn't know they knew. I didn't realize that everything's connected. There's no anonymity. The good part of that is, as a friend said, 'Julia, you've always wanted roots. But now you realize that once there are roots, there are worms in the soil.' "

In conversation, Alvarez is an ebullient blend of insecurities, tart anecdotes and spitfire judgments, often punctuated by a deep, chesty laugh. Scooping up an obese marmalade cat named Lucia, she babbles half in English and half in Spanish into its fur, then offers us a glass of wine and sits crosslegged on a leather ottoman, recalling the tumult of a childhood bifurcated by conflicting cultural milieus.

"I grew up in that generation of women thinking I would keep house. Especially with my Latino background, I wasn't even expected to go to college," she says. "I had never been raised to have a public voice."

Herself the second-oldest, Alvarez was sent to boarding school in her early teens under the protective wing of her older sister. "My parents were afraid of public school. I think they were just afraid in general of this country. So I went away to school and was on the move and not living at home since I was 13 years old."

Like many political refugees, Alvarez soon found the displacements of language and geography to be the stuff of art. As an adolescent, she says, the act of writing helped to allay the pain of acculturation and the stigma of being an outsider. "I came late into the language but I came early into the profession. In high school, I fell in love with how words can make you feel complete in a way that I hadn't felt complete since leaving the island. Early on, I fell in love with books, which I didn't have at all growing up. In the Dominican Republic, I was a nonreader in what was basically an oral culture and I hated books, school, anything that had to do with work."

Alvarez went to Connecticut College, but after winning the school's poetry prize, she departed for Breadloaf and Middlebury, where she earned her B.A. in 1971. After an M.F.A. at Syracuse University, she lit out for the heartland, taking a job with the Kentucky Arts Commission as a traveling poet-in-residence. For two years, Alvarez traversed the back roads of the Bluegrass State, with *Leaves of Grass* as her Baedeker. "I would just pack up my car. I had a little Volkswagen. My whole car was a file system. Everything I owned was in there.

"In some communities I'd give workshops or talk at night in the local church. I loved it. I felt like the Whitman poem where he travels throughout the country and now will do nothing but listen. I was listening. I was seeing the inside of so many places and so many people, from the Mennonites of southern Kentucky to the people of Appalachia who thought I had come to do something with poultry."

When that job ended, other teaching jobs beckoned, and Alvarez careened around the country for more than a decade. "I was a migrant poet," she laughs. "I would go anywhere."

With no fixed address, Alvarez gradually assembled her first collection of poetry, which Breadloaf director Bob Pack placed with Grove. Aptly called *Homecomings,* it featured a 33-sonnet sequence called "33," which portrays the emotional vertigo Alvarez suffered on her 33rd birthday, facing middle age without a secure job, a family of her own or a career blueprint to sustain her. Alvarez nevertheless greeted the book's publication, in 1984, with great trepidation. "It was scary," she says. "I thought 'Oh, my God, what if my parents read this? There are love affairs in here. Maybe I can go out and buy all the copies.' "

She has since reprinted *Homecomings* and issued another book of verse with Dutton (*The Other Side,* 1995). Now, however, she writes poetry less frequently than fiction. "I think what's hard for me about writing poetry is that it is so naked," Alvarez explains. In retrospect, it's not surprising that her emergence as a novelist coincided with her first tenure-track job at Middlebury. *How the Garcia Girls Lost Their Accents*, a novel displaying a historical sweep and mobility of voice not found in her poetry, was a natural next step after years of rootlessness.

"It used to turn me off, the idea of writing something bigger than a poem," she reflects. "But you grow as a writer and you start to imagine other possibilities."

Susan Bergholz, certainly the most influential agent of Latino fiction, whose clients include Ana Castillo, Sandra Cisneros and Denise Chávez, has represented Alvarez since placing *Garcia Girls* with Shannon Ravenel at Algonquin. As Alvarez remembers, Bergholz approached her at a reading she gave in New York after winning a 1986

G.E. Foundation Award for Younger Writers. "She was interested in my work, so I sent her a bunch of things. She really plugged away at that stuff, sending it around and talking to people and finally she landed Shannon. I'm very grateful to Susan as the person who really fought that battle for me, which—because of my background and because of my self-doubt—I probably would not have fought for myself."

Yet when *Garcia Girls* first reached Ravenel, "there was no book there," Alvarez says. "I sent portions of it to Shannon and she said: 'There's a bigger story here you're trying to tell.' "

Today Alvarez can't imagine publishing with a larger house at any price, provided that Ravenel stays put. "Shannon helped form me as a writer. She often helps me to think of how to put my books together. Sometimes, I'll say, 'our book' and she'll say, 'Julia, it's your book.' Maybe a place could initially offer you more money or more razzmatazz. But I was 41 when *Garcia Girls* came out. If I were writing to make a whole lot of money, I would have given this craft up a long time ago. I'm doing the writing because it's the way I understand my life. It's what I do and I want a place that is sympatico to that."

Alvarez's trajectory as a novelist has hardly followed a predictable scheme. Her second novel revisits the last days of the Trujillo regime and retells the story of the three Mirabal sisters, Patricia, Minerva and Maria Teresa—actual political dissidents called Las Mariposas (the Butterflies)—who in 1960 were murdered by Trujillo's henchmen. The event galvanized the political insurrection that led to Trujillo's assassination in 1961. "It's always been a story I wanted to tell. But I didn't know how to do it. They seemed to me such enormous, mythical figures. I didn't know how to touch them and make them real. I thought it would be a sacrilege even to do that in some people's eyes. But I knew it was a story I wanted to tell."

Alvarez had previously tackled the subject in an essay in a small press book on heroic women, but in returning to the island to research the novel, she made an astonishing discovery: there were, in fact, four sisters, and the eldest, Dédé, had survived and was still living in the Dominican Republic. Alvarez interviewed Dédé and began to piece together the minutiae of the sisters' lives. "I understand the politics of a four-daughter family with no boys in a Latino culture," she notes.

All of Alvarez's novels are constructed from multiple viewpoints, ranging freely from sassy gossip to animated autobiography, but always concealing a forceful political undercurrent. She attributes her interest in voice to the storytelling traditions of Dominican life. "We didn't have TV, we didn't have books. It was just what people did. That was our newspaper."

Yo, of course, means "I" in Spanish, but Alvarez has shrewdly left the self at the center of the novel absent. Yolanda isn't granted a voice in the novel. Instead, Alvarez builds the book around the memories of those who have suffered the manipulations of the budding author. The liberty a writer takes with her family and background is a subject of increasing importance to Alvarez as her books grow more popular. "My sisters had a hard time with *Garcia Girls.* But I think they're proud of me, and I think the books have helped them understand their lives better. Sometimes they will remember something that I think I invented. Now it's almost like the stories in that book are part of the memory pool."

In 1993, *Vanity Fair* ran a splashy profile of Alvarez, Castillo, Cisneros and Chávez (all are indeed friends) under the rubric "Los Girlfriends," portraying a cliquish set of Latino writers sharing the same literary concerns and themes. It's precisely such hype and labeling that ¡*Yo!* set out to interrogate. "One thing I didn't like about it from the beginning, which didn't have to do with the people involved, is I thought how I would feel if I was a Latino writer and I saw *the* Girlfriends and these are the [only] Latino writers. I felt there should have been 100 writers on either side of us. Not that I think it was a terrible thing. I just wonder and worry about what all of this publicity and labeling comes to."

Discussing the extravagant antics of book marketing, the 22-city tour she is about to embark on and the persistent film interest in her work (*Butterflies* has been optioned to Phoenix Pictures), Alvarez grows antsy. "As you talk, I realize I am always that immigrant. This, too, I am experiencing and watching. But I don't put faith in it. In a minute, it can be swept away." She needn't worry. Once an author without an address, a language or a homeland to call her own, Alvarez now has a loyal readership that in years to come will undoubtedly only grow larger.

JONATHAN BING
December 16, 1996

10

STEPHEN AMBROSE

As a writer who has devoted his professional life to the study of military history and the lives of notable American leaders, Stephen E. Ambrose has a keen eye for decisive moments, those make-or-break events in a person's life in which good luck can be as important as sound judgment.

The 60-year-old Mississippi scholar's 18 books have included multi-volume biographies of Dwight D. Eisenhower and Richard M. Nixon, a penetrating study of the parallel lives led by Gen. George Armstrong Custer and Chief Crazy Horse, and a riveting narrative of the Allied invasion of Normandy on June 6, 1944. *Undaunted Courage* (Simon & Schuster) is an absorbing account of the Lewis and Clark expedition commissioned by Thomas Jefferson two centuries ago, and it takes full advantage of recent scholarship on the intrepid band of soldiers that Meriwether Lewis and William Clark led across the American West.

"I always try to look at whatever I'm writing about as both a biographer and a historian," Ambrose tells us during a cordial tour of the large office he maintains behind Merry Weather, his modern house in Bay St. Louis, Miss., an Old South community an hour's drive east of New Orleans on the Gulf of Mexico. On the walls and shelves is a variety of photographs, maps, posters, antique firearms, busts, statuettes and knicknacks, all related in one way or another to the various books he has written over the past 34 years.

"I find that people who make key decisions, whether they're political or military, are not just fascinating characters in their own right, but so consequential. The impact of the individual on the situation—from squad level through high command in wartime on to the White House—is the same. The mistake that a person makes at a critical time, or the right choice that is made, is a very important part of how I try to meld history and biography. For my own part, I think that the two disciplines are one."

11

Significantly, Ambrose cites an encounter from his own youth as an example of how chance events can profoundly determine the future. In 1962, Louisiana State University Press published his first book, a biography of Army Gen. Henry W. Halleck, President Lincoln's wartime chief of staff. "I doubt that they ran off a thousand copies, but one of them found its way to Dwight Eisenhower," Ambrose says between deep drags from one of the Marlboro Lights he smokes with undisguised satisfaction. "Talk about a life-changing incident; Ike phoned one day and asked me to visit him at his farm in Gettysburg." After a lengthy chat, the Supreme Commander of Allied Forces in Europe during WWII and the former two-term President of the U.S. offered Ambrose, then 28, an opportunity to assist in the editing of his papers, and to write his authorized biography. "I asked Ike, 'Why me?' and he said, 'I read your book on Halleck.' He really could have knocked me over with that."

With a Ph.D. in history from the University of Wisconsin, Ambrose was at that time an assistant professor at the University of New Orleans. In 1964, he received a teaching appointment at Johns Hopkins University in Maryland, where Eisenhower's brother, Milton, was president, and where a team of scholars had been assembled to edit the general's papers.

The arrangement kept him within close driving distance of Gettysburg, where he was able to conduct numerous personal interviews with Eisenhower. "Ike had the most fabulous ability to concentrate," Ambrose recalls. "He would lock his eyes right on me and put his mind fully on every question I asked. There was never a look at the watch, never a straightening of the clothes, never a call for coffee."

The first five volumes of the *The Papers of Dwight David Eisenhower* were published in 1967 by Johns Hopkins University Press; 15 volumes have appeared thus far in the series. Ambrose's first biography of Eisenhower, *The Supreme Commander: The War Years of General Dwight D. Eisenhower,* was published by Doubleday in 1970, the same year he returned to the University of New Orleans and became a full professor. The move from an academic press to a trade house was made without the assistance of an agent, for a simple reason Ambrose explains: "It's pretty easy when you've got exclusive access to General Eisenhower."

Ambrose published two more books about Ike with Doubleday. When his editor there, John Ware, left to form his own literary agency, Ambrose went with him as a prize client. An auction for his next book was promptly announced, with the winning bid tendered by Alice E. Mayhew, v-p and editorial director of Simon & Schuster. "It was by far the biggest advance I'd ever gotten." In 1983, *Eisenhower: Soldier, General of the Army, President-Elect, 1890–1952*, the first of 11 books Ambrose has published with Mayhew, was released to widespread acclaim. So strong is his relationship with Mayhew that he dismissed his agent years ago and negotiates all of his publishing contracts himself.

"I admire her so much," he says, making no bones about the fact that he writes with the single-minded idea of trying to please Alice Mayhew. "She's my target audience. She's fast-track New York, extraordinarily bright, very opinionated and terrifically good at what she does. Mostly, what I learn from her is what works and what doesn't. She can pick out the superfluous paragraph, or sentence, or word better than anybody, but she never tries to tell me what to say. She's an absolute genius."

Ambrose credits Mayhew with persuading him to write a series of books about Richard Nixon, a man he told her he "detested" when she broached the idea. "She said, 'There's no Nixon biography, and you're the perfect person to do it.' I said, 'Alice, I don't want to spend maybe five years with that son of a bitch,' and she said, 'Steve, where could you find a greater challenge?' She kind of caught me with that line." In due course, Ambrose furnished for her approval *Nixon: The Education of a Politician, 1913–1962* (1987), *Nixon: The Triumph of a Politician, 1962–1972* (1989) and *Nixon: The Ruin and Recovery of a Politician, 1973–1990* (1991).

He admits to never liking Nixon, whom he did not meet in person until after the three books were written. But he came to admire and respect him, "which was the biggest surprise of my whole writing career," recalls Ambrose, who has voiced his chagrin over the creative license taken in *Nixon*, Oliver Stone's recent film about the late president's life. "If Stone wants to say this is history, then damn it, he has an obligation to honor the integrity of the past," he observes.

In the midst of these numerous successes came work on a novel that recreated the Lewis and Clark expedition through the imagined recollections of one of the enlisted men who participated. Ambrose declines to say why it was never published as a novel. "Alice told me to go back to writing what I do well."

The result of that advice is *Undaunted Courage: Meriwether Lewis, Thomas Jefferson, and the Opening of the American West*, a book Ambrose flatly declares to be a "labor of love."

Asked to explain the genesis of the project, Ambrose declares, "As a rule, I find my subjects by getting a curiosity, and once I get that curiosity, the only way to satisfy it is to write my own book." In 1975, Ambrose and his wife, Moira, decided that they would spend the nation's bicentennial with their five children at Lemhi Pass in the Rocky Mountains, where Meriwether Lewis was the first non-native American to cross the Continental Divide in August 1805. What most whetted Ambrose's interest was the gift of an early edition of the journals kept by Lewis and Clark on the two-and-a-half-year expedition.

"I am embarrassed to say that I had never read Lewis and Clark before that. I took one look and said, "Wow, I've just got to go.' We began making plans immediately." After their first trip in 1976, the Ambroses have returned every year since. "Every summer we managed to get back to Montana or Idaho, or the Dakotas, or Oregon or Kansas to follow some part of the trail." The family has canoed 165 miles down the Missouri River, backpacked through the wilderness, horsebacked along the Lolo Trail and turned in at night at various Lewis and Clark campsites. Three Ambrose children attended the University of Montana and now live in the state. Last year, when Ambrose took early retirement from the University of New Orleans, he bought a summer house in Helena.

Although the inspiration to write about Lewis and Clark can be traced back 20 years, Ambrose says other, more pressing projects always got in the way. Of particular urgency was his desire to finish *D-Day, June 6, 1944: The Climactic Battle of World War II* in time to coincide with the 50th anniversary of the Normandy invasion. That book drew heavily on 1400 oral histories compiled by the Eisenhower Center for American Studies, which Ambrose has directed since its establishment at the University of New Orleans in 1983.

"When I finally finished the D-Day book, I decided it was time to concentrate on Lewis and Clark. I started by looking at what my strengths are. I know a lot about the U.S. Army. I know the Washington scene, which is virtually the same today as it was 200 years ago. I know how to write a biography, and I am a serious student of what qualities go into making a great leader. I decided the best approach was to focus on one of the captains." What elevates Meriwether Lewis above most of his contemporaries, Ambrose emphasizes, is leadership, the very quality which has been the focus of his life's work. "To command with distinction is a rare talent, and studying it has been a passion for me."

In 1992, Ambrose received a fan letter from another eminent military commander, Gen. Colin Powell, then Chairman of the Joint Chiefs of Staff. Powell had just read *Band of Brothers,* Ambrose's engaging book about the valiant exploits of the elite 101st Airborne company in Europe during WWII. The letter began a relationship that continues to this day. Last year, Ambrose championed Powell as a candidate for the presidency and spoke publicly in his behalf.

When Powell announced last fall that he would not seek elective office, Ambrose was disappointed. But he remains hopeful about a future candidacy. "Powell is a genuinely great man. He's a great leader, and in my opinion the best man America has produced in this century. He has the qualities of leadership that are unique and blessed. I don't use the word 'unique' the way the television reporters do. I judge this by his character, by his personality and by his experience. This is my deepest belief: Colin Powell is going to be President of the United States, and it's going to be a great day for us, and a great day for the world."

A native of Illinois, Ambrose did his undergraduate study at the University of Wisconsin and played football for three Badger teams during the 1950s. When he goes outside with *PW* to shoot some photographs at Merry Weather, Ambrose wears a crimson and white jacket with a big 'W' sewn on the chest. "I was the last Big 10 player to play a full 60-minute game," he says proudly.

"I was left guard on offense, a middle linebacker on defense, and if I had been 10 pounds heavier, I'd have taken a shot at the pros. If I'd have done that, my life would have taken an entirely different course, and I doubt very much that I would have written any books. Call that another example of good fortune. I firmly believe that history is chance, just like evolution. It's not survival of the fittest, it's survival of the luckiest."

NICHOLAS A. BASBANES
January 23, 1996

Rudolfo Anaya

From the large, east-facing windows of his home high on the mesa west of Albuquerque, N.M., Rudolfo Anaya commands a sweeping panorama of the Rio Grande Valley. The city where this legendary 57-year-old Chicano author has lived his varied and prolific literary life spreads out below, threaded by the sinuous *bosque*, the forest of giant cottonwoods that flanks the Great River.

"River of dreams, river of cruel history, river of borders, river that was home," Anaya calls this artery of water, so vital to the arid landscape of New Mexico, in his novel *Alburquerque*. It is a region that, with its unique, centuries-old culture—part Spanish, part Native American—he has made inimitably his own.

Anaya's father was a *vaquero* from Pastura, a horseman who worked cattle and sheep on the big ranches of this region; his mother came from a farming family in the Hispanic village of Puerto de Luna in the Pecos Valley. The windswept wildness and solitude of the *llano*, the plains, and the settled domesticity of the farm—"Those are the two halves of my nature," says Anaya, a short, wiry man, quiet and reserved, with curly, graying hair and a thick mustache reminiscent of Pancho Villa's that dominates his strong, rugged features, the face of the *ranchero* he might well have become.

"Much is in the blood," he continues in his soft, resonant voice, "because the blood has memory, memory that has been imprinted, encoded, from the past—the whispers of the blood are stories. The rational mind works in tandem with that information; in fact, its job is to bring that to light, to tell us who we are." Beyond the valley and the city's eastern sprawl, the Sandia Mountains rise in a sheer escarpment that marks the point of the sun's daily rebirth, an event that has deep spiritual significance for Anaya.

The sun is indeed the central symbol of *Zia Summer*, the new novel from Warner Books—and this versatile writer's first outing in the murder-mystery genre. The Zia is an ancient Pueblo Indian sun symbol, and it provides key clues in Anaya's tale of Albuquerque PI Sonny Baca, who, in solving the murder of his cousin, confronts a terrorist cult and the threat posed by the transport and disposal of nuclear waste.

Zia Summer is the second of a planned quartet of seasonal novels that began in 1992 with Anaya's *Alburquerque* (the original spelling of the city's name), whose protagonist, a young barrio boxer in search of his true Chicano identity, helps thwart a grandiose real-estate development scheme that threatens the traditional life of the region's old Hispanic and Indian communities.

Sonny Baca will return in *Rio Grande Fall,* the already-completed third book in this series. That mystery deals with, among other matters, the pressing social problem of homelessness, Anaya says. He prefers not to speak of the final novel of his quartet, which is now in progress, beyond noting that Sonny will once again do battle with the eco-terrorist villain he first encountered in *Zia Summer.*

But, underpinning Anaya's most recent novels—with their new emphasis on contemporary social issues and the more accessible style he says he's consciously adopted—are the themes he has consistently probed since his first book, the seminal Chicano coming-of-age novel *Bless Me, Ultima,* appeared in 1972: spirituality and healing; Chicano tradition and myth; the sacredness of the land; the role of shaman-like figures as mentors and guides; and the quest for personal, communal and cultural identity.

Though published by a small academic press, *Bless Me, Ultima* sold more than 300,000 copies in 21 printings before Warner finally brought out the first hardcover edition in 1994. Told with lyric magic realism, steeped in the traditional lifeways and folklore of New Mexico's rural Latino culture, the novel established Anaya's reputation as one of the founding fathers of Chicano literature.

Addressing matters that mirror not only Anaya's own life but also the experience of Chicanos throughout the Southwest, his next novel, *Heart of Aztlan* (Editorial Justo Publications, 1976) brought a rural *Nuevo Mexicano* family to Albuquerque and depicted their painful struggle to maintain the values of their Mexican-American culture within the new context of the urban barrio. His third novel, *Tortuga* (Editorial Justo, 1979), examined pain, loss and healing in a different way—through the experience of a boy hospitalized with a severe back injury like the one Anaya himself endured as a teenager, the result of a diving accident.

"I think of myself as a novelist," Anaya muses, "but from the beginning, I wanted to try many things." In the dozen years between *Tortuga* and *Alburquerque*, he published a volume of short stories, *The Silence of the Llano* (Quinto Sol, 1982), two novellas and several plays; produced a book-length Chicano mock-epic poem and the travel journal *A Chicano in China* (Univ. of New Mexico, 1986); and wrote a steady stream of essays. One of his children's stories of that period, *The Farolitos of Christmas,* is due out from Hyperion, and Warner has just released a wide-ranging anthology, *The Anaya Reader.*

This productive career has brought Anaya more than a score of honors, among them the Premio Quinto Sol national Chicano literary award for *Bless Me, Ultima,* the PEN-West Fiction Award for *Alburquerque,* and a National Endowment for the Arts fellowship. His lectures and readings have taken him throughout the U.S. and far abroad—a long way from the tiny village of Pastura on the plains of east-central New Mexico, where he was born, and the nearby Pecos River town of Santa Rosa, where he grew up.

Anaya's family left rural New Mexico when he was in the eighth grade and moved to Albuquerque, where he attended high school and went on to study English and American literature at the University of New Mexico, earning a bachelor's degree in 1963, then an M.A. in 1968. Though he began writing *Bless Me, Ultima* in 1963, he was also teaching in the Albuquerque public schools and attending graduate school part-time; he spent seven years perfecting that book. He was working, he says, "in a vacuum," not yet involved with the Chicano movement then gaining momentum in the Southwest, of which he would soon become one of the most eloquent voices.

"With as much literature as I'd read and studied," Anaya recalls, "when it came time to treat my own experience, other novels in the American experience didn't work as models. I had to find my own voice, my own expression, my own forms, working with my own materials, values, culture. What I set out to do—which is what every writer does—was to create a universe, one that had its roots in the *Nuevo Mexicano* experience. I just plunged into the material and tried to give it form, structure. I wanted to take those people I had known and make them breathe again."

History would show that he succeeded masterfully, but getting this new work out—couched in the bilingual style that Anaya pioneered and has pursued throughout his career—proved, to say the least, difficult.

"It was *extremely* hard," he says. "I sent the book to dozens of trade publishers over a couple of years and found no interest at all. The mainstream publishers weren't taking anything Chicano and we had nowhere to go. For us, living in a bilingual world, it was very normal to allow Spanish into a story written in English—it's a process that reflects our spoken language—but in approaching mainstream publishers I was always called on it. Without the small academic, ethnic and university presses, we'd never have gotten our work published intact."

Keeping faith in his work through those years of rejection, Anaya ultimately gleaned the address of one such obscure press, Quinto Sol Publications in Berkeley, Calif., from a magazine, and sent off his manuscript—which was accepted immediately and published in 1972.

But, even as his reputation as the "godfather" of the Chicano novel grew, Anaya would continue to publish exclusively with small presses for over two decades. In 1992, he met New York literary agent Susan Bergholz and, in part because of her longstanding advocacy of Latino writers, signed with her—the first and only agent he's ever had. Together, they developed a proposal for a package of books, a mix of old and new work, and, by late 1993, Bergholz had settled a series of contracts with Warner for the publication of illustrated hardcover, paperback and Spanish editions of *Bless Me, Ultima* and a paperback edition of *Alburquerque* in 1994, as well as *The Anaya Reader* and the three novels featuring Sonny Baca. That major recognition at last placed Anaya, after 20 years, squarely in the world of mainstream publishing, with access to the broad public he's always wanted.

Throughout his career, Anaya supported his family and his writing through work as a teacher and academic counselor. From 1974 until his retirement in 1993, he was a professor at the University of New Mexico, specializing in creative writing and Chicano literature—a field in which his own widely anthologized work has become standard fare. That long commitment to education connects with the idea of mentorship that is a consistent theme in his writing (most of his protagonists have spiritual guides) and that is, he says, "in a sense, the role of the writer."

Anaya has provided a groundbreaking model for a whole generation of Latino writers, and his UNM students have included Chicana novelist and playwright Denise Chávez. "There seems to be a new wave in Chicano literature and visual art—it's booming, and Chicanos are coming into their own," Anaya says, with one of the grins that frequently light up his face, hints of the humor that pervades his work. "Any community, to be known, needs many voices to describe it, and that's what's happening."

For two or three hours each weekday morning, Anaya, working on his computer, continues to add his voice to that vibrant chorus, pursuing his life's work in the adobe home he and Patricia—his wife of 29 years, who is also a writer—designed for themselves two decades ago. In his small study, a glass door faces the Rio Grande Valley, and one book-lined wall bears a row of *santos,* the statues of saints that are so much a part of *Nuevo Mexicano* life.

"The place where I work is very important, hard to duplicate," he says. "It's where all the characters gather; they're used to this little room." For Anaya, the process of fiction is "part meditation, part bringing up ideas that have been fermenting, but a lot of it involves characters speaking to you and forcing you to write their stories. There's no preconceived story line—the characters come alive and say: Here's my story."

In this "centered, sacred space," Anaya will typically draft a novel within a year, then revise extensively through five or six drafts—each of them read by Patricia, his "frontline editor"—as he hones language, fills out characters, sharpens his focus. "What I've wanted to do is compose the Chicano worldview—the synthesis that shows our true *mestizo* identity—and clarify it for my community and for myself," Anaya says. "Writing for me is a way of knowledge, and what I find illuminates my life."

WILLIAM CLARK
June 5, 1995

RICK BASS

Montana has bred, or attracted, more than its share of writers, but few have craved its isolation or valued its wildness with the passion of Rick Bass. "Do I want more society or less? I think the question is going in the wrong direction," he says. "In our society it's going to be hard to get *enough* remoteness, or enough time with one's self. I wouldn't be so cornball as to say I think all the great lessons that lie ahead of us are to be found in the woods, but the more time I spend here, the more I'm impressed with the way we *ignore* what's in the woods."

It's a cool spring day when we track him down in the Yaak Valley, a remote pocket of northwestern Montana where he and his wife, the artist Elizabeth Hughes, have lived since 1987. He's waving from the porch of a handsome new house they've just moved into. Two weeks ago, Elizabeth gave birth to their second daughter, Lowry; Mary Katherine was born in 1991. Bounding around the woods are the two pups, Ann and Homer, whom readers will recall from *Oil Notes,* now in their middle years; also his bird dog, a young German pointer named Colter. Bass himself is compact and muscular. His eyebrows bunch as he talks, his gaze narrows into a squint as if he were eyeing something far across the meadow. He laughs readily, and to our northern ears his Texas accent has a softly pleasing cadence.

Bass's life is awash with writing projects. His second collection of short stories, *In the Loyal Mountains,* has just been issued by Houghton Mifflin, and the publication of *The Lost Grizzlies,* his longest nonfiction book, is imminent. Meantime, he produces a relentless flow of personal essays on natural history and environmental issues for magazines such as *Audubon, Men's Journal* and *Outside.* And there are more stories, more novellas and the novel he's been amassing for years, *Where the Sea Used to Be.*

The 10 short stories in the new book will be familiar to Bass's faithful—they've been turning up regularly in the major story venues for several years, including *Best American Short Stories, The Pushcart Prize* and *New Stories from the South.* Though Bass is dead-serious about Montana's wilderness debate, only four of the stories are located in this region of the country; the rest come from the Deep South of his past. If there's a common thread, he explains, it has to do with hanging on to things worth hanging on to, deciding where to stand and fight.

All are told from the first-person, and like the novellas in *Platte River* (1994), they feel nearly mythological. Often his narrators find themselves chronicling the life and times of a small, good-hearted band of citizens. As the narrator of "The Valley" says, "I wake up smiling sometimes because I have all my days left to live in this place." Bass shares this sentiment, though for him it is tempered by a deep foreboding. "I'm scared to death that these woods and this valley will get trashed," he says.

For generations, Bass's family lived in Texas. Born in Fort Worth in 1958, raised in Houston, Bass trained as a scientist, studying wildlife biology and geology at Utah State, then worked several years as an oil and gas geologist in Mississippi. His passion for the mysteries of finding oil fills the pages of *Oil Notes* (1989). A sneaky book in some ways, amiable and journal-like at the surface, its bigger concerns pool abundantly below: how to act on the unseen, how to cope with plenty and scarcity, how to respect one's work, how to love.

But he had no formal education as a writer. He began to write on his lunch breaks while working as a geologist. "I didn't know there was a publishing world out there, I just wrote." These pieces eventually became *The Deer Pasture* (Texas A&M Univ. Press, 1985). Later, he wrote essays and travel pieces for the Sierra Club, that were collected in his second book, *Wild to the Heart* (Stackpole). And he began writing fiction. His early efforts were routinely rejected, but gradually editors offered more and more feedback. "It was like going to school through the mail. I'd focus for a week or two on one mysterious little line. *Lacks depth,* for instance. Then I'd address the problem in the next draft."

In the mid-1980s, Bass frequented the Lemuria bookstore in Jackson, Mississippi. Its staff kept urging him to read Jim Harrison's *Legends of the Fall,* and he kept shutting them out. The jacket called Harrison an outdoorsman. Bass says he thought, I don't want to read about deer hunting and that stuff, but finally relented. "It threw a mental switch, a big door just swung open." The next story he wrote was published in the *Paris Review.*

Readers will find echoes of Barry Hannah's zaniness in Bass's plots, and he credits Eudora Welty's writing for teaching him how elegant orthodox storytelling could be (a photo of Bass and Welty conversing graces a table in his living room). He's indebted as well, he feels, to Thomas McGuane and fellow Texan John Graves. And not only as craftsmen. "It's who they are as people. I need to learn to live with being a writer as much as learning *how* to write. When times get tough artistically, those models, those forebears give you support and confidence."

These days, Bass writes in a cabin some distance from the new house. No electricity, no distractions. He attends to his fiction first thing, before the day intrudes, writing in longhand in notebooks, perhaps for five pages on a good morning. "I used to get my work done in a couple of hours," he says. "Now it takes four or more, same amount of work." He expects the novel will take a year to finish drafting, another to edit. It's a massive manuscript, over 1300 pages at present, his most complex and structured work of fiction to date.

"When you're really in love with something you're working on," he says, "90% of the time you think: Man, this is it, this is the only thing in the world. It takes on its own light and magic. The other 10% you have this huge despair—you saw the way you wanted it, but you just missed it. You're the only one who sees it; it's invisible, it's vaporous."

Later in his typical work day, he turns to the environmental work that has increasingly commanded his time—newspaper editorials, letter writing campaigns, essays. He used to write two or three magazine pieces a year, which felt about right to him. Lately, taking on environmental degradation in the West, he's producing 15 or 20. "It's like a war effort," he says. "It feels enormous trying to still do fiction with this—it's not sustainable, but then neither is what's being done to land up here. It's going berserk, just lobbing these essays, trying to publicize what's going on." A piece on deforestation he did for *Scholastic Scope* brought him some 2000 responses from schoolkids. "Such beautiful letters," he says. He handwrote each one an answer.

His work day typically ends in physical labor. Lately he's been hauling slabs of rock for a wall along the road and building a slew of wire cages to keep the deer out of his aspen saplings. And at least once a week, he drives 45 miles to the gym in Libby for a session of powerlifting, which he views as another form of meditation.

He and Elizabeth passed their first winters in the Yaak caretaking the Fix Ranch—not far, as it turns out, from their new property. He wrote about this period of acclimation in a memoir called *Winter.*

Norton had already published his first collection of stories, *The Watch* (1989), and he was under contract for two more works of fiction, but they declined his nonfiction projects. Bass's agent at the time, Tim Schaffner, sold *Winter* and *Oil Notes* to Seymour Lawrence at Dutton, who shortly thereafter took those manuscripts with him to Houghton Mifflin. For a time, it appeared that Bass would continue to split his fiction and nonfiction between the two houses, but he was eventually released from the contract with Norton. Houghton Mifflin is now his sole hardback publisher. His present agent is Bob Datilla of the Phoenix Literary Agency.

Bass is lavish in his praise for his editors. His magazine editors, among them Gordon Lish and Rust Hills; Carol Houck Smith at Norton; and his editors at Houghton Mifflin—the legendary Sam Lawrence, along with Leslie Wells, Camille Hykes, Larry Cooper and Hilary Liftin. "I was *very lucky.* I needed a lot of editing and still do. It's not just lip service, I mean they're literally life savers. It's a triangle, me doing the grunt work, and them refining it, and then the resting time out in the woods. Those three anchor points."

The only recent project Houghton Mifflin did not release is *The Ninemile Wolves* (1992), which Bass decided to publish with Clark City, a Montana press. In it, he tracks the largely unhappy fate of each wolf in one small Montana pack, making a passionate defense of wolf reintroduction in the Northern Rockies. It's a deeply heartbreaking story, one of dueling bureaucracies and incompatible myths. (And a footnote Bass finds sadly ironic: Clark City has since had to shut its doors.)

In *The Ninemile Wolves,* and in a manuscript of environmental pieces called *The Book of Yaak,* Bass's anger becomes palpable. "Traditionally," he says, "the literature of protest, if it's going to be called literature, has been gentlemanly, restrained. But when you turn the flame up, the water's going to boil, and the West is on fire, environmentally. Corporate industry has taken and taken until there's this last fragment of wildness left and now they're coming after that. They'll come and take the last owl, they'll come and take the last owl's habitat, the last bear, by rifle or bulldozer. I mean, if you don't yell now you're going to miss your chance."

For all that, Bass is determined not to mix his activism and his art. Political agendas corrupt a fiction writer's choices, he's convinced. Even so, questions of ownership and land stewardship *do* surface in his new stories. "Days of Heaven" begins bluntly: "Their plans were to develop the valley, and my plans were to stop them." The narrator, caretaker of a ranch, holds emotional title to the place but is ultimately at the owner's mercy and hates to jeopardize his tenancy. The story ends in a profoundly elegiac mood, the narrator wondering whether, if he keeps still, the would-be developers will simply go away. He knows they won't. A metaphor for the Yaak, Bass readily admits.

Bass's characters are at their best—generous, tolerant of one another's foibles—when residing in the smallest communities. In this, too, there's slippage between his fiction and nonfiction. "Well, it's a kind of crisis for me as a writer," he says, "because I'm trying hard to keep those themes separate, but they really want to merge—the social history of the stories, and the natural or biological history I'm writing about in my nonfiction. Basically, a community of people that has a large respect for each other's differences is just an expression of the beauty of the natural world—what they call species diversity."

As it happens, our interview takes place the week after the bombing of the federal building in Oklahoma City. The newspapers are full of reports about paramilitary cabals in Montana's backwoods. But there's none of this in the Yaak, Bass says with a note of optimism. "People wouldn't tolerate it here. The hate groups establish themselves where they can drown out everybody else, and they couldn't do that here. They couldn't drown out the communal acceptance. There are no loose seams; we've woven our lives together here and they can't disrupt that social fabric."

DAVID LONG
June 26, 1995

CARL BERNSTEIN

As HALF OF the most famous reporting team in history, Carl Bernstein has made a career of taking readers to the other side of closed doors. In *All the President's Men,* Bernstein and partner Bob Woodward told the story of how two little-known *Washington Post* writers broke the biggest story of their time by pounding the pavement and literally knocking on hundreds of doors. In *The Final Days,* their feverishly anticipated follow-up, the pair seemed to have floated through the keyholes—and often into the thoughts—of their subjects, giving an incredulous America a God's-eye view of the imploding Nixon White House.

Now, in *His Holiness,* Bernstein has set his sights on an even more heavily guarded seat of power, the Vatican, at an even more pivotal moment, the final decade of the Cold War. Instead of Nixon and Kissinger on their knees in the Oval Office, praying for the country, the book reveals John Paul II and CIA director William Casey (a devout Catholic) literally praying for the world in the course of a remarkable long-running geo-spiritual dialogue on Poland, Central America and other fronts in the holy war against communism. Documents dug up in Moscow show an anxious politburo, just after the founding of the Solidarity movement, worrying about losing all the achievements of the revolution to the followers of history's first Polish pope. While the book is written as a biography of the former Karol Wojtyla, the strand that holds it together is Poland. As Bernstein writes: "For a decade, his Poland was the crucible of the cold war, and he was the hinge on which history swung."

On a sticky August afternoon, Bernstein meets an interviewer in the spacious prewar apartment on Manhattan's Upper East Side he shares with a querulous tabby cat and some of the Italianate furniture and American folk art that has earned him admiring attention in *Architec-*

tural Digest. The furniture may be vaguely papal, but Bernstein himself is all streetsmart American. At 52, this self-confessed "design maven" bears faint traces of the boyhood freckles that once won him a Howdy Doody lookalike contest at a D.C.-area amusement park, and more than a shadow of the cocky charm Dustin Hoffman made famous in the movie version of *All the President's Men.* "If you had told me 25 years ago that one of the great figures of our time would be the pope of Rome, and that I'd be writing about him," Bernstein says, "I would've said you're smoking something."

It was an offhand remark by a Vatican-based priest at a party in Rome shortly after the Berlin Wall fell that first put Bernstein on the trail of the famously peripatetic pontiff. Bernstein recalls saying to the priest that the real beneficiaries would be the Vatican and the U.S. government. "You don't know the half of it," the priest said. "He wouldn't say anything else," Bernstein recalls. "And I said to myself, this makes a lot of sense—there were parallel interests. So I started checking around."

The result was "The Secret Alliance", a 1992 cover story in *Time,* where Bernstein was a special correspondent. Soon after the article appeared, Steve Rubin, then Doubleday's president and publisher, approached Bernstein about expanding the piece into a book. He declined. But three weeks later, Gorbachev published an article in the Italian newspaper *La Stampa* saying that events in Eastern Europe would have been impossible without the pope's "enormous" political role, which suggested to Bernstein that there was even more to the story. "Like the Nixon White House," he says, "here was this amazingly powerful institution sitting under our noses that no one had really looked at. To me that was a great story. It's about power. All my books are about power."

But writing about a spiritual power—and a highly secretive one, at that—had its special requirements, so Bernstein, after a lengthy search for a collaborator, enlisted the help of coauthor Marco Politi, a well-respected member of the *Vaticanisti* (the Vatican press corps) who had also spent five years reporting on the Soviet Union. John Paul II did not grant them an interview, though some of his closest confidants did. Back in New York, editor Eric Major took on the project.

Bernstein is optimistic that *His Holiness*—the product of more than 300 interviews and extensive document-sifting—will definitely establish the theory of a "holy alliance" between John Paul and the equally millennial-minded Reagan. "I think what will happen is the same thing that happened with *The Final Days*. From here on in, everything has to be written against the record that is established in this book. We finally got a dollar amount [$50 million] for CIA aid to Solidarity, finally found out when the CIA's role took over from the American labor movement."

The book also shows Casey giving John Paul the broad outlines of the U.S.'s secret Central American strategy—and Oliver North giving money to the pope's priests in Nicaragua (without his knowledge, Bernstein is careful to point out). And Bernstein was amazed to find that John Paul was crucial to the introduction of new U.S. missiles in Western Europe beginning in 1983.

Bernstein doesn't expect the largely admiring portrait to raise many hackles in the Vatican. "As Cardinal O'Connor said to me, he found the Vatican's reaction to the *Time* piece a 'nondenial denial,'" Bernstein says, relishing the Nixonian undertone. "The pope said it was 'an after-the-fact-assessment,' or something like that. The interest of the Vatican is to show the pope acting always in a spiritual dimension, never in a temporal one. But they don't deny it; they just minimize it."

But will they like being portrayed as not-so-strange bedfellows with the CIA? "I think on many things the Vatican is an unbelievably sophisticated intelligence agency, particularly in Catholic countries. It has an office in every parish, and the priests are close to the people—they know what's going on. But intelligence doesn't necessarily mean something nefarious; neither does an alliance. And that's what makes the Vatican gun-shy—we used each other."

Bernstein himself is no stranger to the underside of intelligence. *Loyalties*, the memoir he started after resigning from the *Post* in 1977 and published only after a decade of famously fitful work, chronicles the 35 years of FBI scrutiny to which Bernstein's family was subjected under Truman's 1947 Loyalty Order, which established investigative boards to root out subversives within government ranks. As a lawyer for a federal employees' union in Washington D.C., Bernstein's father, Al, defended some 500 members accused of disloyalty until the aftermath of his own hearing forced him out of professional life and into the laundry business.

Of the countless writers who have attempted to climb back through the windows into their own childhoods, few have had the help of 2500 pages of reports filed by FBI agents who were literally peering in.

Bernstein may be the only American journalist to have had federal agents working his bar mitzvah. Both Al Bernstein and his wife, Sylvia, refused to answer questions about their previous membership in the Communist Party; their fearful reluctance to cooperate with their son's own investigation decades later gives *Loyalties* much of its poignance.

The book was met with mixed reviews and disappointing sales. Still, Bernstein says he's perhaps more proud of *Loyalties* than of his Watergate blockbusters (all three were edited by Alice Mayhew at Simon & Schuster). "I thought it was an important piece of history," he says, noting that David McCullough cited some of his research in his 1992 biography of Truman.

But *Loyalties* is not just about the tortured politics of the gathering McCarthyite storm. It's also about a peculiarly complicated childhood—and about Bernstein's entry into the hard drinking, brawling world of old-style newspapering at the underripe age of 16. "I was spending more time at the pool hall than at school, getting terrible grades," he remembers. So his father took him to meet a friend at the now defunct *Washington Star.* "They didn't want to hire me—I was too short, I looked like I was about 12. But I kept banging on the door. And the minute this guy showed me the newsroom, I thought: This is the most exciting thing I ever saw. When I think of the newspaper business, I really think of my experience at the *Star* rather than at the *Post.* Watergate kind of transcends the newspaper business. But the real fun of the business was at the *Star.*"

Bernstein is scathing about the sins of "post-Watergate journalism"— creeping obsession with celebrity, a scandal-of-the-month mentality, a national press corps unwilling to venture beyond Washington—though he hesitates to characterize his and Woodward's reporting as either the last gasp of one era or the birth of another. "Great reporting has always been anomalous. With Watergate, a sort of mythology was born of some golden age of journalism that never existed. The Watergate reporting involved a lot of luck, skill, incredible perseverance, some intelligence. We had great editors. Everything came together. To me, the terrible thing that has happened in post-Watergate journalism is the eclipse of context. The dominant values of sensationalism, gossip and celebrity have totally disfigured real journalism."

It's hard to hear Bernstein talk about the advance of "Page Six" on the front page without thinking of his own famously rocky relationship with journalism's wagging tongues. In 1980, Bernstein's four-year marriage to Nora Ephron had a spectacular public collapse after

Ephron, seven months pregnant with their second son, discovered he was having an affair. Gossip columnist Liz Smith announced the fact in the *New York Daily News,* touching off a tabloid feeding frenzy. Then, in 1983, Ephron published *Heartburn,* a roman à clef which only enhanced Bernstein's long-standing wolfish reputation. In 1984, he ended a tempestuous four-year stint at ABC News to work full-time on *Loyalties.* In the five long years before the publication of that book, accounts of his squiring a string of famous and not-so-famous women around town appeared in print more often than his byline.

Bernstein talks about those days with an equanimity that quickly turns into high-minded generalization. "I'll be up front about it. I think there's a lot of envy involved," he says, shrugging. "But the breakup of my marriage wouldn't be a blip on the screen today. This thing had a life on its own—it was the scandal of its time, to my utter amazement even today. Some of what was written bears some relation to the facts, some bears no relation to the facts. The real thing is that it became part of the celebrity culture that looks at the world as a black-and-white soap opera—which is the opposite of what journalism is."

Again, for Bernstein, it comes back to *The Final Days.* "The reason I love it so much is because it's empathetic to Nixon in some ways. While the Watergate reporting was truly good reporting, only in a book can you really get a little distance, get more and more context. Reporting is about context. The accounts of my life had little to do with any context."

It might seem a bit grandiose for Bernstein to link his own fall from grace to the tragic fate of a president he played some role in bringing down. But interestingly, it was the backstairs gossip about the Nixons' private life—most famously, Pat Nixon's confession to her doctor that she and her husband "hadn't been intimate for years"—that earned *The Final Days* some of its harshest criticism.

In a 1989 joint interview, Woodward said he thought an older Woodward and Bernstein would not have included Pat Nixon's confession. Would a still older Bernstein agree? "Probably. I don't know. It would be the only thing I'd leave out now. The theory was that it was relevant because Nixon made his family life so much a part of his defense. But I don't think it's a question of great importance."

Bernstein doesn't seem much exercised about past indiscretions, whether his own or those of the press. He's resolutely middle-aged, comfortable with himself, confident that his work has nailed down parts of the history of his time—and that it has secured his own place in it. "I've had a helluva life," he says. "I might as well own it."

JENNIFER SCHUESSLER
September 23, 1996

DORIS BETTS

Doris Betts knows that, contrary to popular belief, it's something of a curse to be born Southern and a writer. When her first novel, *Tall Houses in Winter*, was published in Italy, the cover featured every cliché she hates: a gowned Scarlett wannabe in front of a decaying mansion covered with Spanish moss. Yet Betts's themes are far from conventionally Southern. Idiot cousins and run-down plantations don't darken the pages of her new novel, *Souls Raised from the Dead*, (Knopf); nor do the long shadows of race relations and white guilt.

Throughout the New South, Betts believes—including Chapel Hill, N.C., where she teaches creative writing at UNC—a renaissance has been taking place, a reclamation and redefinition of the Southern literary tradition. And Betts, lifelong North Carolinian, short-story writer, novelist and teacher, is one of the quiet and under-appreciated forces behind it.

"I dislike the typecasting that the word *Southern* suggests," says Betts. She is a small, energetic woman of 61 with the lively drawl that bespeaks a small-town North Carolina upbringing. "I'm not carrying that patrician, aristocratic guilt. I come out of yeoman farmers and Piedmont red clay country. There weren't many slaves there, and there wasn't an aristocratic tradition at all." Her parents worked in cotton mills, and when they read, they read the King James Bible. "They're wonderful stories, and the language of the King James Bible is not a bad place to start."

Though the new novel, like its predecessor, *Heading West* (Knopf, 1981), explores the lives of the North Carolinians Betts knows so well, its themes would certainly not be congenial to the "professional Southerners" of whom its author is so suspicious. "I get tired of that cramped quality of being a Southern writer," complains Betts. "Knopf very much wants to bill this as a Southern book. It must be good for sales, but all my life I've been bored with that."

True, *Souls Raised from the Dead* is filled with the echoes of Betts's rural childhood, with Bible stories and lessons, and with the sense of generations moving off the land and into the city, wondering how to keep hold of family traditions in the process. But the book's focus is resolutely contemporary, and urban; its drama—the death of a beloved child—could take place anywhere, anytime.

Set in Carrsboro, the working-class town across the tracks from up-scale Chapel Hill, the book follows N.C. Highway Patrol sergeant Frank Thompson, a hardworking, well-meaning, unexceptional man, as he struggles to do his job and raise his 13-year-old daughter, Mary Grace. Mary's pretty, frivolous mother, Christine, abandoned the family three years before the story begins, leaving Mary and Frank to look after themselves—which they're doing pretty well until Mary, poised on the brink of adolescence, is diagnosed with progressive kidney disease. Frank can't donate a kidney, having lost one to a bullet a few years back; that leaves an anonymous donor as Mary's only hope, unless the feckless Christine can be convinced to overcome her squeamishness and give Mary a kidney and a second chance. Revolving around Frank and Mary during the crisis are two sets of loving, helpless, warring grandparents. All of them must learn to cope with the tragedy.

It's how that philosophical drama plays itself out in ordinary lives that fascinates Betts. *Souls Raised from the Dead* begins with Frank directing traffic at the site of the wreck of a chicken truck. Pittsboro, the small town where Betts and her husband, Lowry, live, happens to be in the heart of North Carolina chicken country; driving the 20 miles to Chapel Hill, Betts has had any number of chickens splattered on her windshield after they've fallen off poultry trucks.

One drive home took her past the scene of a chicken-truck wreck. "It's very much as described [in the book]," she says, "with the same mixture of funny and awful." The memory of the policeman directing traffic around the wreck stayed with her. "The look on his face—I thought, 'Well, now, that's existentialist despair,'" she says. "If Jean-Paul Sartre had lived in Chatham County, he would have said, 'That's mine.'"

She realized she had found the metaphor for her next book. "If you become absorbed in abstruse philosophy, you forget that all of those questions [also] exist in perfectly ordinary people," she says. "What has interested me are ways to tell those stories through ordinary people who wouldn't articulate them, who wouldn't read Sartre, but who nonetheless are troubled by exactly the same questions."

Although it's understated in *Souls Raised from the Dead*, a strong feminist current also runs through Betts's work. That, too, explains some of her ambivalence towards the old South, which has tended to exclude women. "We weren't part of that tradition," she says. "We weren't sitting around there listening to [stories about Civil War exploits]—we were cooking." As for slavery, Betts says "most of the women of that age, if they were not very well off, were equally enslaved. The poor redneck farm wife was every bit as exhausted as the field hand, and not much more appreciated, and often not much better treated."

In her previous novel, *Heading West,* Betts took up the theme of emancipation and how it seizes a librarian in a small North Carolina town. But *Heading West* has a fitfulness about it, as if Betts weren't always quite sure what to do with the material. She still winces in recalling Jonathan Yardley's review: he called the last section of the book "women's fiction." Betts says, "It both enraged me and also gave me pause. But I did see what he meant."

The new novel has been a long time in the writing; nearly a decade has passed since Yardley's snub. *Souls* has taken an "outrageously long" time, Betts says, partly because of her extensive teaching and administrative obligations, partly because of family events (the death of her father, the arrival of grandchildren) and partly because she found she'd gotten too fond of Mary Grace to let her die. Ultimately Betts put the time to good advantage, refining her novelistic style and learning how to sidestep the perils of "women's fiction": *Souls* has a tautness and control to it that you don't feel in its predecessor.

Part of the novelistic process, for Betts, involves going against her natural inclination. "I feel I'm by nature a short-story writer and that I've been trying to learn to write novels. People are by temperament inclined to one form or the other. The short-story writer has a fast metabolism, never returns library books on time, doesn't carry umbrellas in case it might rain, whereas the novelist writes longer sentences and has a different breathing rate." She has increasingly turned to novels because, she says, "the older you get, the more it seems that the rhythm is much slower, that change is rare. One begins to take an interest in the changeless."

Betts established herself early with short stories, winning the *Mademoiselle* College Fiction Contest in 1953. The intervening years have been liberally sprinkled with awards and critical acclaim, including a

Guggenheim Fellowship (1958–1959) and a National Book Award nomination in 1973 for *Beasts of the Southern Wild and Other Stories,* one of three collections she has published. Her short fiction tends to find its way into anthologies, from *Best American* to *The Signet Classic Book of Southern Short Stories.* She has also worked as a journalist on various North Carolina papers, an experience that she says made her hungry for the subtleties that fiction affords.

Nowadays Betts devotes most of her non-writing time to the University of North Carolina at Chapel Hill and its undergraduate creative writing program. UNC has no MFA program, but many of its undergraduate writing students have gone on to be working writers. Betts follows their progress eagerly: Randall Keenan, Charlene Baker, Garrett Wyer, Tim McLaren, Jill McCorkle, David Payne.

She also worries about them. "I think young writers have a real problem," she says. "They're not sure if they write about the bluebird that it'll be around in 30 years. On the other hand, if you write about a Hershey bar, it's probably not going to be there, either." She speaks of the writers she knows who are burdened by "a sense of everything disintegrating under you."

Between having three children and pursuing a writing career, Betts never finished a B.A., but that didn't stop the UNC English Department from making her a chaired professor. She was also the first woman to hold the position of faculty chairman. "That has made me less of an angry feminist than I might have been," she says.

She stresses the importance of cultivating a female support network. "When I was beginning to write, I thought, 'Well, I'll just work harder, be superwoman,' " she recalls. "It's a great relief to be able to say, 'Listen, kid, you're going to be tired, and as soon as you've gotten to the best sentence you've ever written, the baby will cry or vomit. Women have begun to tell one another much more honestly that it is hard, and to support one another. Certainly the liveliest writing in North Carolina is by women, and they're nearly all good friends. There's not that competitiveness that I see among American male poets, for example."

Betts has developed good working relationships with her longtime agent, Tim Seldes of Russell and Volkening, and with Ann Close, her current editor at Knopf. Of Close she says, "She's been wonderful. She calls a lot—maybe it's true about women editors. The suggestions she makes for editing or changing are intelligent and useful. One doesn't mind being challenged or corrected, as long as it's done by someone you respect." Of Robert Gottlieb, the editor for *Heading West,* she says, "We never really got to know each other. He was very preoccupied."

Betts published her first two books with Putnam, before being handed over to editor Walter Mitten, "to whom I took a violent dislike," she says, "though I've never met him. He's probably a lovely man. He kept sending me things to read that made it very clear that he thought I ought to be writing pop fiction." She next found a more congenial home at Harper & Row, where she worked with M. S. "Buzz" Wyeth on her next several books. But Harper passed on *Heading West,* and Betts secured a contract at Knopf.

She'll be working with Close on her new novel, tentatively titled *The Sharp Teeth of Love.* Inspired by a recent trip to Sierra Nevada territory, where she spoke to the Western Literature Association, the book revisits some of the themes of *Heading West;* in it, an artist from Chapel Hill goes west to escape her creative and romantic troubles and rescues a child prostitute.

The book will be "haunted by the ghost of Tamsen Donner of the Donner party," says Betts, referring to the wife of the leader of the infamous 19th-century settlers who were trapped by snowstorms in the Sierra Nevada and turned cannibal to survive. "I didn't know until I began doing research that Tamsen Donner came from North Carolina, taught school here, married a man from Salisbury, N.C., wrote poetry all the way across the country, all of it lost. And it seemed a wonderful metaphor for contemporary women and feminists—the metaphor of being devoured by men, which is probably what did happen to her."

Since she and her husband, a retired lawyer and judge, built a house on their Pittsboro farm in 1989, Betts has for the first time had her own writing space. "The odd thing is now that at last I have Virginia Woolf's 'room of my own,' I've found that I still do a great deal of work sitting down in the den with the TV blaring, because you get used to these things."

She and Lowry keep Arabian horses, 18 of them, once designed to be breeding stock but now mostly pets. And then, there's also a canine menagerie, including an "ugly little redneck dog" name Clovis. And the old-fashioned roses she grows, many of them imported from Europe. "If I live long enough," Betts declares, her roses "will cover all of the horse fences, and they will bloom in a brief but beautiful riot."

This may be the same impulse that sustains her characters through the worst that life throws at them: the hope that something lovely might grow, now and then, from chaos.

JENNIFER HOWARD
April 25, 1994

LARRY BOND

"I DON'T KNOW if I have any deep thoughts in me. I would be happy if somebody could pick up my books 10 years from now and have a good read, and maybe learn something about the way the political system was set up. I'm not Hemingway, let's be real."

No, he's Larry Bond, and the hundreds of thousands of fans who have propelled his epic military adventures *Red Phoenix, Vortex* and *Cauldron* onto bestseller lists don't seem to mind a bit. His newest work, *The Enemy Within* (Warner Books) seems destined to climb the charts with similar alacrity. Bond's modesty about his work scants his expertise at storytelling, but it's what you might expect from a writer whose novels reflect the bedrock American values of hard work, fair play, family and country. It's not false modesty, either, we learn during the afternoon, at his trim, suburban home outside of Washington, D.C., where he lives with his wife, Jeanne, and two small daughters.

He seems like an overgrown kid, bounding down the stairs to greet us. "Hi!" he says, pumping our hand. As he marches us upstairs to his office, we glimpse in the living room a Christmas tree ablaze with lights, though it's three weeks into January. Two Santa hats perch on the back of an armchair.

The converted second bedroom where Bond writes doesn't mute our sense that we've wandered onto the set of *Big*. It's a room full of toys and games and doodads—a boy's room. Posters of warships and a large red Soviet flag decorate the walls. Dozens of model planes and ships stand at attention on shelves along one wall. On the table in front of us sits the fossil of a large trilobite. "That's 350 million years old," Bond notes with pride.

On other shelves and around the floor stand stacks of military journals such as *Warship International* and *Jane's Intelligence Review*— serious reading for grown-ups. Bond's physical self, too, seems to bridge generations. His smooth face, though meaty with middle-age, belies his 44 years, as do his dark hair and surging energy. He's dressed like a studious prep-school kid in a blue shirt and off-white trousers, eyeglasses, neat leather shoes. But we realize that he's also dressed like a Navy man—which, in fact, he was.

Bond grew up outside St. Paul, Minn., where he attended St. Thomas College, gaining a degree in programming in 1973—"back when we had wood-burning computers," he jokes. He worked for two years as a programmer but "hated it." Coming from a line of military airmen, he pursued the obvious and joined the armed forces. Unlike his ancestors, however, Bond was forced by poor eyesight to join the Navy. Six months at Officer Candidate School landed him on a destroyer based in Seattle. Two years later, he switched to antisubmarine warfare.

"It's a lot of fun. You hunt subs! Oh, it's really cool, because when I actually find a sub, I take control. I'm steering the ship, as a lieutenant j.g., and that's a rush. That is a *real* rush. I mean the skipper and everyone just stands back and I'm driving, running the whole show."

In his excitement, Bond puts the pedal to his words, but then his delivery never slows to a cruise. His mind seems set in fourth gear, burning up ideas, puzzles, problems, challenges. It's no surprise to learn that his interest in gaming began young. "When I was eight, I had an uncle who sent me the game Afrika Corps. I've been war gaming ever since. I was still playing them in the Navy and was casting about for a modern naval game. There were a lot of games that looked at World War II, but nothing on the modern side. So I said: 'There is a need. I have the knowledge.'"

Need and knowledge added up to Harpoon, a general-purpose tactical naval board game that Bond designed while still in the Navy and that has gone on to sell about 150,000 copies as a computer game. After mustering out, Bond parlayed Harpoon into a position at the Center for Naval Analyses, a federally contracted think tank. While there, he encountered the man who would jump-start his life as an author.

"I met Tom Clancy for the first time while *The Hunt for Red October* was still in manuscript form," Bond recalls. "I reviewed it and made a couple of comments about Navy terms and standard usage and stuff like that."

Bond grew close enough to Clancy to act as godfather to one of his children—and to collaborate on a novel, begun after Clancy read

Bond's treatment for a computer game, Convoy, premised on the Soviet Union attacking Europe.

"We sat down and plotted it out together" ("it" being Clancy's *Red Storm Rising*, 1986). "Clancy went on to write about 95% of the text, because I just couldn't keep up with him. I was writing big operations orders, playing war games, doing research. Basically, I was his apprentice." The book carries only Clancy's name on the cover, but Bond's contribution is acknowledged in an author's note and in the joint copyright.

While working on *Red Storm Rising*, Bond hosted regular "gaming sessions" during which he and others would play out various combat scenarios. Grown men all, they would put miniature warships and planes on a board or field of green felt and push them around. "We were gaming-out one of the chapters in *Red Storm Rising*, 'Dance of the Vampires,' " Bond says. "I really called in the clans on that one, because it was a big scenario." One man invited to play was Patrick Larkin, a historian and Reagan administration speechwriter. The two hit it off and put together a proposal for *Red Phoenix*, a novel chronicling an invasion of South Korea by the North. Tracing scores of characters through numerous confrontations, laden with military technospeak, the book, published in 1989, owes much to Clancy.

"I inherited Tom's agent, Robert Gottlieb [of William Morris], and enough of Tom's rep. We were going to auction the proposal, not expecting much. Then Warner editor Mel Parker, asked, 'How much to buy the rights outright and circumvent the auction?' Robert named a figure and Mel said 'Okay.' "

Each of Bond's novels has been conceived and gestated with Larkin, and midwifed by Gottlieb and Parker—a remarkable record of consistency that testifies to Bond's loyalty toward, and ability to work with, others. "I think I'm a creative person," comments Bond, "but I know I don't have a monopoly on creative ideas." He honors Larkin's contribution just as Clancy did Bond's in *Red Storm Rising*: by sharing copyright, and through author's notes. Still, if Larkin and Bond each, as Bond puts it, "do 60% of the work" on every book, why isn't Larkin's name on the covers?

"That's a marketing thing," Bond explains. "In an ideal world, it would be 'Larry Bond and Pat Larkin.' I am senior partner, okay? Because I was there first. Pat and I have discussed this with Warner several times. But buyers have come back very negative on the idea of two authors on the front. And when the buyers say 'no,' that's it."

Calculation pervades Bond's novels. Plot-heavy, they often seem the result of more perspiration than inspiration. Like *Red Phoenix,* Bond's subsequent novels, *Vortex* (1991, about an American invasion of racist South Africa) and *Cauldron* (1993, pitting the U.S. against France and Germany), read more like finely tuned machines than organic creations; in their precision of interlocking parts, they can resemble computer games. But Bond contends that writing a novel and creating a computer game are "very different processes. You don't have to debug a novel."

In fact, Bond's approach to writing is methodical. For each novel, he and Larkin block out in exacting detail a plot synopsis, chronology and characters. Only then do they lay down words, modeming chapters back and forth. Bond's writing habits are just as regular. Each morning at about 8 a.m., he sits at his computer, working at a 21" monitor that gives him maximum control over the shape of his prose by projecting a full page of text at once. He reviews the previous day's output, then generates about 1500 words of finished prose, wrapping up by lunchtime.

The Enemy Within, which details federal response to Iranian-sponsored terrorist attacks on U.S. soil, charts a new course for Bond. The story emphasizes suspense rather than military fireworks. It is his first novel set primarily in the States and the first to feature a female lead, Helen Gray, head of an FBI Hostage Rescue Team. It's also shorter than his previous novels (496 pages in hardcover compared, for example, to *Cauldron*'s 592 pages).

"At Warner's level, I'm sure cost was a factor," explains Bond. "A less expensive book is obviously more appealing to readers. Also, Mel thought we should be working on a tighter, more personal story. The other three books were about armies in conflict. You can only do so many of those before they all start to sound alike. And fewer characters allowed us to develop them more fully."

This is important to Bond. The critical acclaim accorded his novels has been tempered by a pervasive knocking of his characters as wooden. "Well, it's obviously something I want to work on," he acknowledges, but he is pleased, and rightfully so, with Helen Gray and her Delta Force counterpart, Peter Thorn; so much so that he plans to bring them back in his next novel.

By contrast, critics have praised the realism of Bond's books, which is the result of prodigious research. "This is something I learned from Clancy. If you're going to do a book about something, talk to the people who do it for real. When we did *Red Storm Rising*, we went down to SACLAN, Supreme Allied Commander Atlantic Fleet, in Norfolk. I've ridden on an F16, I've driven an M1 tank, landed on a carrier."

When we ask Bond what in his books will endure, he hesitates, then suggests the realism and "valid observations" about how the world works. Certainly, his books display a deep understanding of geopolitical power; it's amusing, then, to watch him reach out with his foot and idly spin the globe by his desk as he speaks. He fails to mention, however, the brilliant plotting, juggernaut suspense and dearth of sentiment that make his novels so exciting. He also passes over his promotion of the middle-class values that he himself lives by.

"I don't believe in messages, you know," he demurs. But, he adds, "I had a very straightforward upbringing. Very nuclear family, very conventional. I've never done drugs, never gotten in trouble with the law. I always have liked to read books where there was a strong hero who does the right thing—and manages to stay within the system. It always disturbed me when the hero broke the rules to get a job done, because then why do we have the rules?"

As *PW* departs at the end of the afternoon, Bond waves from his doorway, looking as clean-cut as a prom date. We're reminded of something he said earlier: "I've been very fortunate. I started at the top. And you know, I have no beefs. No beefs at all." There's nothing wrong with that. But it's worth wondering if Bond's writing, though mightily entertaining, might not be a bit more artful if a little control were given up for some of the whimsy, the rebellion against adulthood, that has this middleaged dad putting together models of battleships. Perhaps Bond realizes this, by altering his tried-and-true formula with *The Enemy Within.* Perhaps he senses that the American heart, which his work embodies in so many ways, embraces change as well as constancy, defiance as well as allegiance; that this nation of laws—of rules—was created by breaking them.

JEFF ZALESKI
March 4, 1996

JIMMY BRESLIN

To the rest of the country, he is the quintessential New Yorker—opinionated, brassy; a man who can throw a zinger or a wisecrack with the best of them. To a generation of New Yorkers, who have read him daily in a number of papers, he has personified his city in a way that only a native son can, for he sees it not as a landscape of steel and metal but as a place that is tough and funny, with a big heart that holds promise for everybody, regardless of skin color.

Jimmy Breslin's mop of curly hair is gray now. Clad in a rumpled sweatsuit, he seems shorter than he appeared the last time he was on TV. It's as if the Pulitzer Prize-winning, chronicler of life in the Big Apple and the author of 10 books has gone from tough barroom philosopher to gentle Irish gnome. But the eyes that have covered every important event in this country over the last 40 years are still the same: peering over half-moon reading glasses, they are alive with laughter one minute, recalling a rogue acquaintance in a saloon long ago, or aflame with anger as he discusses the ways that racial bigotry has harmed this country. In a time when it is fashionable to be conservative, Breslin is more liberal, more outspoken than ever.

Now 65 and with a new memoir, *I Want to Thank My Brain for Remembering Me,* out from Little, Brown, Breslin welcomes an interviewer into his Upper West Side Manhattan apartment. *Thank My Brain* chronicles the events that led up to the successful removal of a brain aneurysm in Phoenix, Ariz., in November 1994. Structured as a drive through old New York neighborhoods on the way to the airport, it is interspersed with recollections of his newspaper career. Asked why he didn't write a more formal autobiography, Breslin replies: "Oh, forget that. I wanted to do the brain thing because I thought the medical stuff was wonderful. And you just can't sustain a brain operation for 80,000 words because you're not around for it. It made sense in that I left this house in the morning and drove through a lot of the streets where I spent my life and got on the plane and went to Phoenix. So it all fit, I thought."

In *Thank My Brain*, Breslin confesses that his biggest fear is that he'll be left a vegetable, unable to write. "If you wind up in some nursing home in the desert in Arizona with some nun wiping drool off you, then you're a dead man," he says.

With his life in the hands of his neurosurgeon, Breslin introduces the reader to a side of himself rarely glimpsed—the old-fashioned Irish Catholic who proudly proclaims: "There is no such thing as an ex-Catholic." He fills his book with Catholic images and pre-Vatican II phrases ("sins of omission," "examination of conscience" and "state of grace") that would bring a smile to the face of Pope John XXIII. Before leaving the city, Breslin goes to confession at St. Francis of Assisi on West 31st Street in Manhattan. St. Francis is special, Breslin says, because "they get all the murderers going there" to confess their sins.

Breslin was born in Queens in 1930 and says that his father "left the arena early." He was brought up by his mother, a high-school teacher and social worker, and began working on newspapers at the age of 16. Breslin became a columnist for the old *New York Herald Tribune* because of the worst baseball team in the history of the game, the 1962 New York Mets, managed by the legendary Casey Stengel. Editor Cork Smith at Viking encouraged Breslin to write a book about the Mets. More than 30 years later, he still refers to *Can't Anybody Here Play This Game?*, which Viking published in 1963, as "the book that got me out of hock." Jock Whitney, who ran the *Trib*—and was the brother of Mets owner Joan Payson—took notice and made Breslin a columnist.

His first big story—now famously known as his "gravedigger's" column—dealt with the assassination of John F. Kennedy. "I went to the White House in the morning," Breslin recalls. "I walked into the lobby and that was packed and I said, this is not for me. So I saw Art Buchwald and we talked for a second and I said, 'I can't do any good here. I'm going to go over and get the guy who dug Kennedy's grave.' 'Yeah, that's a good idea,' he told me, instantly. And I left there right away. I just turned and walked right out of the place and over to Arlington Cemetery, and they got me the guy."

When reminded that his gravedigger column is now taught in journalism school, Breslin, with some pride, chimes in: "Yes! They should, too. It's the gravedigger's theory [of journalism]."

From the JFK assassination, Breslin went on to cover the Vietnam War, and he still remembers seeing his first casualties at the Fairfax,

Calif., air base. He was in the kitchen of the Ambassador Hotel in L.A. in 1968 when his friend Bobby Kennedy was assassinated. Asked how he could cover a story about the death of a friend, he shrugs. "You have to do it to make a living. That's your business. Two or three days later, you get sick to your stomach, then it's over. No, you can't let the emotion of the moment affect you. Maybe show it in the writing, but just don't let it get in the way of what you're doing."

He married "the former Rosemary Dattolico" (as he always referred to her in his columns) in 1954, had six kids and settled in the New York working-class borough of Queens. With the turmoil of the 1960s still ringing in his ears, Breslin took his family to Ireland for a time. It was there that he started *World Without End, Amen,* a novel about a New York cop of Irish descent. When told that a lot of readers feel that the first hundred pages of this novel are dynamite, but that the book suffers when Breslin sends his protagonist, Dermot Davey, from New York to Ireland, Breslin shakes his head. "I know, I know. It didn't bother the reviewers, but it bothered me and I shouldn't have done it. The character's still around and I owe him a conclusion."

Back in the U.S. as Watergate was heating up, Breslin began covering the impeachment proceedings. "[Agent] Sterling Lord suggested I just try a magazine piece," Breslin recalls. What began as a short article soon evolved into a full-blown handbook on the inner workings of American politics: *How the Good Guys Finally Won* (Viking, 1975) was a major bestseller.

After Watergate, the next big story he covered was that of New York City serial killer David Berkowitz, known as "the Son of Sam" because of his claim to have taken his orders from a dog named Sam. "When he killed a couple of people within four or five blocks from my house [in Queens], a detective I knew was handling the case. I wrote about it and then after one column I got a letter from Berkowitz. And it was an evil freakin' thing. I had to assume he knew where I lived when he wrote me." Breslin later learned that apparently Berkowitz had stalked him one evening as he and his wife ate at a diner in the Hamptons, but "it was raining and the dog told him to go home." Breslin later collaborated with Dick Schaap to produce a novel based on the case, called *.44* (Viking, 1978).

After Cork Smith left Viking, Michael Korda published *Forsaking All Others* at S&S in 1982. Breslin says the novel "was regarded as just another book about narcotics . . . nobody cared," but he enjoyed working with Korda. "I think he's one of the last keepers of the language in the city of New York. Away from the glitter, Michael is a patient editor with an enormous respect for the language."

When Cork Smith landed at Ticknor & Fields, however, Breslin followed. "Cork's terrific; the main guy," says Breslin. With *Table Money* (T&F, 1984), a book about "sandhogs," the men who dig New York's water tunnels, he decided to change agents. "I had *Table Money* out to monstrous reviews and nothing happened. I should have been a billionaire and I wasn't." ICM's Esther Newburg became his agent in 1986, the same year Breslin won the Pulitzer Prize and the George Polk Award, both for his collected newspaper columns.

Breslin stayed with Cork Smith and Ticknor & Fields until Houghton eliminated the imprint. He ended up with editor John Herman at Houghton Mifflin for the biography *Damon Runyon* (1991), which was his biggest bestseller since *How the Good Guys Finally Won*. Although he's often been compared to Runyon, he insists that that's not the reason he wrote the book. "I wrote about him for the classic reason you write about anybody—cash money!"

Breslin has always had problems with his "own people"—Irish Catholics. "I used to write columns and make fun of them. They've got big schools but they don't produce anybody who writes. They produce a lot of insurance agents and corporation lawyers and police. They write tickets instead of stories. They've taken a great heritage and not done anything with it over here." Breslin pauses. "They also associate me with the blacks. They just see me and say, 'those are his friends.' "

Breslin's "friends" over the years have been underdogs, regardless of race or creed. The old saying that the purpose of a newspaper is to "comfort the afflicted and afflict the comfortable" describes Breslin perfectly, because while others have sold out (check the talking heads on the Sunday morning political shows), he has always been there, writing about the disenfranchised and about those without hope. More frequently than not, they have been African Americans. He sees race tensions as the most important issue in the nation. "Nothing has changed at all," he says, raising his voice. "It's measurably worse than when it started."

Breslin's writing den is cozy. There's a panoramic view looking south to Lincoln Center, and a Macintosh computer sits against one wall under a painting of an old El station in the Bronx. "I usually write in the mornings," he says. "Two, three, you can't do more than four hours on fiction. But I've never been able, as much as I've strived, to keep that Kurt Vonnegut schedule. He told me it's all over by noon—that's been the story of his life. I'm up before five in the morning I'm so nervous about things that I'm going to write about, but I can never get to the point of being through by noon. Anybody that sits down and does it straight out has spent a lot of time in bed looking at the ceiling, putting it together before it started. I do it in the morning and it's the only sensible way. That's the horrible thing starting out, you get distracted a lot because anything is easier than writing. It's just the same enemy—blank paper."

At this point, Breslin's wife, New York City Councilwoman Ronnie Eldredge, enters the room. *Thank My Brain* is also a love story, for it tells the tale of how Breslin and Eldredge, both widowed, came to get married. Breslin's first wife, Rosemary, died in 1981, shortly after Eldredge's husband passed away.

It's strange that Breslin's wife is a politician because the more you talk to Breslin the more you come to realize how much he despises politicians. He refers to them as "cowardly" on the Vietnam War and has recently had a running battle in print with New York City Mayor Rudy Giuliani.

Eldredge has come to know the meaning of "Irish Alzheimer's"—which afflicts those, like Breslin, who forget everything except for grudges. "I can't discuss my work because then he has a lifelong grudge," say Eldredge.

What is ironic about Breslin's dislike of politicians is that he's an ex-pol himself. In 1969, he ran for city council president on a ticket that had Norman Mailer running for mayor. The campaign buttons said, "Vote the Rascals In" and "No More Bullshit," and the platform included a petition to make New York City the 51st state.

Over the years, Breslin has managed to antagonize almost everyone in his columns, from presidents to writers trying to copy his style. When asked if he's ever regretted anything he's written, he remains defiant and steadfast: "Never apologize," he says. "I don't care who takes offense." It's heartening to know that he has no intention of abandoning his lonely job of tormenting the prominent and championing the underdog.

DERMOT McEVOY
September 2, 1996

ANDRÉ BRINK

ANDRÉ BRINK finds himself in an almost unbelievable position for a writer: one where he can see a profound kinship between his own work and the aspirations of his country—a newly minted South Africa free of the intolerable burden of apartheid under which it had labored for most of the author's life.

"There's just such an overwhelming amount of material to be used that sometimes you want, as an author, simply to take a breather from it," says Brink, whose latest novel, *Imaginings of Sand*, begins, very notably, to make use of such new material. It has just been published here by Harcourt after winning stellar reviews in its Secker & Warburg London edition. "What was it the poet said?" asks Brink, echoing Wordsworth. " 'What bliss was it in that dawn to be alive!' "

A degree of comfort with his native land has been a long time coming to Brink, who, as an Afrikaner born into a conservative South African household 60 years ago, has improbably (for most of the vociferous opponents to apartheid came from the English-speaking side) spent most of his mature years at war with it.

Brink arrives for an interview at a chic Chelsea Italian restaurant during one of his occasional visits to this country just before returning to his work as Professor of English at Cape Town University. With his open-neck black shirt and leather jacket, dark, curly hair tinged with gray, brooding eyes behind his glasses and rugged features, he looks not unlike what James Dean might have looked like had he lived to see 60.

And in fact, Brink has cut a rather romantic figure in his homeland, a rebel ever since he first began to write for publication. "I knew that I would be a writer, whatever else I might be, since I was nine years old," he says in his distinctive South African twang that is a strange cross between Australian and Merseyside. "That's when I published my first atrocious little poem. I wrote my first novel at 12, sent the first one to a publisher at 14. They turned it down as too erotic. I didn't even know what the word meant!" When he did start to publish, as a student at an Afrikaans university in the late 1950s, it was "very unimpressive stuff. The Afrikaner tradition then was all naturalistic." It was when he went to the Sorbonne in Paris for postgraduate studies in 1959 that Brink's life turned around.

"I saw this huge Picasso retrospective exhibition, and I was amazed; I thought if he could turn everything upside down like that, so could I as a writer." When he went home, it was to join with a handful of other young writers who became known as "The Sixtiers," and whose very experimental work aimed to question every kind of authority—political, religious and moral. The only work from that time that achieved any overseas circulation was *The Ambassador,* translated by Brink (who at that time wrote only in Afrikaans) as *File on a Diplomat* (1965).

But although the 1960s were an exciting decade, Brink also became increasingly uncomfortable in his rigidly conservative—and increasingly brutal—surroundings. "The massacre at Sharpeville [where, in 1960, dozens of demonstrating blacks were gunned down] really shook me up," he remembers. He went abroad again, back to Paris, in 1967. "I was sick and tired of South Africa and thought I'd settle abroad permanently." Then, the next year, came the French student revolt and the whole "Year of Revolutions," which turned out to be a watershed for Brink. "It made me realize I couldn't just be a solitary agent as a writer. I had to be involved in society. So I went back, knowing it would be difficult but knowing too that I had to explore where I'd come from, where the whole country had come from and what was really happening there."

Brink's next book, *Looking on Darkness* (1973), was his first overtly political work, the story of a "Cape Colored" man (one of the many endless gradations of nonwhite in South Africa) who has a suicide pact with his white lover but is jailed for her murder and becomes aware of the torture of political prisoners in South African jails. It was promptly banned, the first book written in Afrikaans ever to suffer this fate and which, Brink asserts, "was devastating to me. It meant I'd lost my readership." From then on, he realized he would have to look for English-speaking readers overseas, because he could expect little circulation at home. *Looking on Darkness* was published a year later, in Brink's own English translation, by W.H. Allen in London and, another year later, in the U.S. by William Morrow, whose Larry Hughes became an admirer—a pattern that was to last for most of the next decade.

Because much of his audience was now in the U.K. and the U.S., Brink began writing not only in his native tongue but also in English.

For 1977's *Instant in the Wind,* he says, "I started making notes in both languages, which is something I've done ever since as necessary. It was intended to establish in my own mind different attitudes towards the material."

The banning of *Looking on Darkness* immediately drew the attention of the omnipresent South African state security apparatus, and from then until the 1994 triumph of the ANC, Brink was a watched man, at home and abroad. "My phone was tapped, my mail was opened in very obvious ways—they *wanted* you to know they were doing it. Then of course there were the anonymous phone calls, at all hours of the day and night, threatening to kill you and your family. Once a fire bomb was thrown at my house. There was an attempt to sabotage my car. I would be called in for interrogation, they would search my house, turning everything upside down. They even confiscated my typewriter, but I borrowed one from a friend, and it inspired me to work harder than ever."

Brink's *A Dry White Season* (1980), which studies the consequences of a white man's investigation into the prison death of a black acquaintance, became the best-known of his early books, partly as a result of an admirable movie version—incidentally, one of the earliest movies made by a black woman director, Euzhan Palcy. While acknowledging its virtues, Brink notes wryly that "It was vastly overshadowed by the big-budget *Cry Freedom,* which covered some of the same sort of ground."

Meanwhile, one of the indirect effects of the ban on his work in South Africa was to make him a sort of guiding figure for many unhappy Africans. "Since it was obvious I was dead against apartheid, they assumed I could help them, and I had an endless stream of people coming to me with their problems, asking for help. Some of them I was able to help, some not." But it all took its toll on his time, and for some years in the 1980s Brink found he had little time for writing.

When he came back, in 1988, it was with a peculiarly personal novel—one embracing the difficulties faced by a writer in his circumstances who wants to create work that is not essentially political: *States of Emergency,* he says, was set down in a rush. "Day after day, I worked at it, fitting together the pieces of a mosaic." Its publication also marked the end of a chapter in his American publishing life: Hughes retired at Morrow, and Brink (who, like most foreign writers with things worth saying, is represented here by agent Georges Borchardt) was taken up by Jim Silberman, then at Summit. There, and later at

Little, Brown, Silberman remained Brink's publisher until the most recent book. "Jim was a splendid man to work with, and I don't think he has been well treated," notes Brink, who enjoys working with his new Harcourt editor, Drenka Willan, and hopes this too can be a long relationship.

After such recent books as *An Act of Terror* (Summit, 1991), an intense and disturbing examination of the lives and motives of anti-apartheid terrorists, and *On the Contrary* (Little, Brown, 1994), a quirky retelling of South African history as a series of picaresque legends done in the style of an 18th-century English novel, *Imaginings of Sand* is a bold departure in many ways. At once a starkly realistic picture of a country in the midst of major upheaval and a lyric relating of its past in a series of tales strongly laced with elements of magic, the book is infused with an intensely feminine perspective.

Brink thought long and hard before taking such a chance (in fact, one London reviewer lambasted him for trespassing on feminist concerns). "For a long time, I couldn't be involved in anything but apartheid, it was all-pervasive," he muses. "Now I felt the silences of the past could be revisited. And one of the things I discovered was that the real enemy wasn't apartheid, it was the abuse and misuse of power, which is the enemy, in different forms, everywhere in the world. Previously I concentrated on racial aggression, but there are many other kinds—sexual, for instance—which went hand in hand with it. I felt it inevitable that I should explore the female side, and to do this I had to adopt a woman's voice."

The results are astonishingly successful. The story is told through the eyes of an attractively feisty, liberal white South African woman who returns home, after years of exile, to be at her ancient grandmother's deathbed. Issues of sisterhood, motherhood and crude male predation are in the contemporary forefront, and the history of grandmother Ouma's amazing ancestry is laid out in a series of dazzlingly vivid parables centered on the essentially female ethos of procreation.

If the current turnaround in South Africa (one of the great scenes in *Imaginings of Sand* is a joyful pageant of the election day that brought Nelson Mandela to the presidency), has freed Brink to concentrate on concerns other than the political, it is not without its poignancies. "In the old days, we [meaning also anti-establishment writers like Nadine Gordimer, Athol Fugard and the late Alan Paton] had the opportunity to establish regular, active contacts with writers in like circumstances in Central Europe and Latin America. We got used to being seen as beacons in the struggle against demonic systems, and that gave us as writers a sense of importance we lack now. We tend to be absurdly nostalgic from time to time."

For the past five years, Brink, formerly at the secluded Rhodes University in Grahamstown, has taught half the year at Cape Town, which has meant a much broader literary life. "I got to know J.M. Coetzee, the best writer South Africa has ever produced—if anyone can be said to really know him." And he tells the story of how the highly reclusive Coetzee, who had once unprecendentedly agreed to give a speech at the university, did so by getting up from his seat, turning on a tape recorder and sitting down again while the machine played his pre-recorded speech.

Brink is still hard at work, even if fiction at present, despite a multitude of ideas and themes, is on the back burner. He has just completed a book on the narrative language of the novel, and currently making the rounds ("Georges is peddling it, and I hope Drenka will take it") is *Reinventing a Continent: Essays on South African Writing & Politics,* for which, Brink is delighted to report, President Mandela has written a foreword. There are fine South African writers he would like to see better known overseas, and he mentions Njabulo Ndebele and Joel Matlou, both short story writers ("Black South Africans excel in shorter forms, for a good reason; they never had time or opportunity for anything longer") and a playwright, Zakes Mda.

And, surprisingly, Brink himself has theatrical ambitions. "I wrote some plays back in the '60s, but unless you had your own theater group, like Fugard, you had no chance of getting them mounted. But two months ago, at a conference in Salzburg with Ariel Dorfman and Arthur Miller, I found all my old passion being rekindled. I've written a new play, and it will be staged in South Africa. After that, who knows?"

He breathes the happy sigh of a writer for whom new material is no problem. "It's as if the whole nation is going to the shrink, and you're sitting there with your notebook," he exults. No 50-minute hour for Dr. Brink.

JOHN F. BAKER
November 25, 1996

A.S. BYATT

To MEET Antonia (A.S.) Byatt at home, you must travel, unless you want a very hefty taxi fare, by underground to a station a couple of stops across the Thames in Putney, a not particularly fashionable district in southwest London. A brisk 10-minute walk brings you to a substantial Edwardian semi-detached villa which, on an early March evening, dank and gloomy, seems to embody the essence of British middle-class complacency.

Inside, improbably, lives a polymath who is not only a bestselling novelist on both sides of the Atlantic but an admired critic, a highly productive reviewer, a radio dramatist, an editor, a university lecturer, a screenwriter, an authority on writers ranging from Proust to Grace Paley, somewhat of a pillar in the English intellectual establishment and a concerned mother to three grown daughters.

It was Byatt's *Possession,* a bittersweet romance that was also a tour de force of literary scholarship, affectionate parody and epistolary legerdemain, that, much to everyone's surprise, catapulted her onto American bestseller lists for a dazzling five months in the first half of 1991. Before that, she had won admiring reviews rather than readers and had enjoyed nothing like the presence on the American scene of her younger sister, Margaret Drabble. (It is generally understood in London literary circles, incidentally, that one does not discuss one sister with the other; but in terms of their respective careers, it seems that, after a much slower start, Byatt's is now clearly on the ascendant.)

She is an attractive woman in her upper 50s with sharply intelligent eyes and a softly humorous mouth. She settles herself into a chair beneath a wall of bookcases in the front parlor and proceeds to regale us for two hours, like someone well practiced in being interviewed, with the contents of a formidably well-stocked mind. Subjects touched on in passing included, but were by no means limited to, the Joan Collins lawsuit, 19th-century costume design, the work of

Anthony Burgess, the psychology of Salman Rushdie (a close friend), Hollywood and the writer, the state of writing in Britain today, the role of women in the American ethos, the relationship of psychiatry to literature and the need for publishers to understand better what many of their readers want.

The occasion for the interview is the publication by Random House of a new novel that is epic in both size and scope, called *Babel Tower.* Although the fact has not been much noted here (largely because its predecessors had made comparatively little impact in the States), it is the third in a series of novels chronicling the life and times of Frederica Potter, a brilliant, sensitive Cambridge graduate (like Byatt herself) as she comes to terms with the world of the mid-1950s to mid-1960s. The earlier volumes were *The Virgin in the Garden,* published by Knopf in 1979, and *Still Life,* published by Scribner eight years later.

Still to come is a fourth book, to be called *A Whistling Woman,* which will bring the Frederica saga to an end and, Byatt hopes, will conclude in 1968, the year of student revolutions that also saw the beginning of the rise of contemporary feminism. "I'm planning to write about a big conference on the mind, to be held in Yorkshire, that is invaded by all the forces of unreason abroad at that time—pop groups, the way-out variants of religion. I also want to write about a woman scientist, and I don't know quite how I can work her in at the moment, but I'll be working that out this summer."

Byatt, who has spoken of "intellectual passions being as vibrant and consuming as emotional ones," and whose best work balances both varieties, is the kind of writer whose mind is so compendious that deciding what to leave out of her books is more of a problem than an author's usual frantic search for ideas. Throughout her career, her fictional ventures have been interspersed with critical studies (of Iris Murdoch, George Eliot, Wordsworth); collections of essays (the revealingly titled *Passions of the Mind* was one); and even a recent book in which she collaborated with Argentine psychiatrist Ignês Sodrè to discuss the inner workings of a number of significant women writers (including Willa Cather, another favorite, and Toni Morrison, "a major writer by any standard").

And though her fictional works are much livelier than anything suggested by that dread phrase "novels of ideas," that is what, at heart, they are. She sees *Babel Tower,* for instance, as partly a study of how people behave in groups. There are long, delectable passages describing the deliberations of a learned committee studying the British school system. The book is also about "how language can be used to exclude people." Two of the novel's high points are engrossing trials: one of Frederica's petition for divorce from her husband, a smugly brutal country gentleman; the other of a sprawling, challenging novel (which gives Byatt's book its own title) for obscenity. And in both cases, language is being used by some to preserve entrenched positions and by others to win liberation from them.

Both versions of *Babel Tower* are also what Byatt sees as "a sort of pattern in the '60s—a longing for freedom leading to excess and ultimately to cruelty." Even those who embarked on a spiritual quest, as many did, found that it ran alongside "a damage-doing thing." Byatt is hard on cruelty. As one of the judges for the latest series of *Granta* awards to young British writers (seen in some quarters in England as a falling off from an earlier one), she asserts that "the books we didn't list were full of nasty, sadistic things. It's not hard to be shocking, but it's best if it's done quietly and neatly; don't just beat people over the head."

Discussions of contemporary British writing today, she says, tend to focus on how members of minority cultures are reinvigorating a lifeless tradition. "In Salman [Rushdie]'s wonderful phrase, 'The Empire strikes back,' but I think there's more to it than that. A tradition that can embrace writers like Murdoch, Doris Lessing, Anthony Burgess, William Golding, is not at all moribund. And look at Penelope Fitzgerald, a wonderful writer whose little books are as good as Salman's big books."

Byatt is so intent on discussing the present state of writing, and some of her favorite theories ("People don't seem to understand that one of the things that drives Salman is his English public schoolboy sense of mischief, a love of pranks—hence *The Satanic Verses*") that it is quite hard to get her to focus on herself as the subject of the interview. "I always wonder if I shall survive a publicity tour; most people always ask the same things, and after a while you find yourself looking on amazed at the strange things you say. You find yourself being *observed* all the time, whereas I like it to be the other way round, with me doing the observing, sitting in a corner, quietly watching."

But the details emerge. Byatt was born into a North Country family (in the steel town of Sheffield); her father was a judge who had risen to that eminence, incredibly, from working-class origins. The bright Drabble daughters went off to Cambridge and shining careers. A first marriage to an economist, Charles Byatt, saw the birth of a daughter, also Antonia, and a son, Charles. There followed the beginning, in the late 1960s, of a series of books, published as Byatt taught and lectured, in English and also, for a time, at an art school (her knowledge of art is extensive, and everywhere apparent in her work). Then, in 1972, tragedy struck when her son was killed by a drunk driver; and for years, Byatt was unable to write a word. A second marriage, to Peter Duffy, saw the births of two daughters, Isabel and Miranda. "I wanted things better after my son died," says Byatt. "And Miranda was the right name for the daughter who makes things better."

Miranda has just gotten her degree ("she doesn't know what she wants to do, but it's not literature"); Antonia runs the literary festival at London's South Bank Centre; and Isabel was "somewhere up in the mountains of Peru, on the trail of the Incas—and I hope she'll come down soon."

Byatt is still somewhat bemused by her strangely checkered publishing history in the U.S. "Somehow, editors didn't seem to know about me for a long time, but others did. I was taught in colleges, and people studied my books." Her American career began when Harcourt published *Shadow of a Sun,* her first novel, in 1964; it got good reviews but small readership. "Then they thought my next book, *The Game,* was too intellectual, so I went to Scribner's, and again good reviews, but. . . . " Her agent at the time, Norah Smallwood, got her a deal with Bob Gottlieb at Knopf, who brought out the first Frederica book, *The Virgin in the Garden,* in 1979. He didn't want *Still Life,* however, so it was back to Scribner—at which point Byatt encountered, in the person of Laurie Schieffelin, "a lovely editor, the best I had in America, who asked great questions. Most American editors, you know, do far too much editing, and you have to spend your time trying to stop them."

That was certainly the case with *Possession,* which had a most curious history here. "No one wanted it. Peter Matson [representing her current London agent, Michael Sissons] kept sending me glowing letters of rejection saying how everyone loved it, but they just couldn't visualize who would possibly want to read it. Then Susan Kamil, to her great credit, decided she wanted it for Turtle Bay. But she wanted lots of changes—to take out most of the poetry and many of the letters, for a start. She came over and we had tea at the Ritz. I wasn't feeling well, and when she started talking about what would have to go, I fainted dead away. It was very dramatic. She took me up to her room, and when I came round I said I couldn't agree to any of it."

Then the book came out in England, albeit initially in a printing of only 7000 copies, caused an immediate stir and ultimately won the Booker in 1990, "and after that they told me I could have it just as I wanted it. It was real luck that Random took it over; there seems to have been a lot of luck in my life lately." This included the publication of her novella *Angels and Insects* (1993), which had been all set to come out as a Turtle Bay book just as that imprint folded: "There were no ads, no promotion, nothing." Then word of the forthcoming movie saved it. Byatt was closely involved in the movie, which got glowing notices, and worked on the screenplay with director Philip Haas and wife Belinda. "I wanted it to be over the top, and they gave me a real say in how it went." She was particularly interested in the costume design for the movie, and the fact that the Victorian period in question favored bright, gaudy colors rather than the pastels so often seen in period movies: "That comes from an overdependence on old photographs."

Possession, as befits a big bestseller, has been bought outright (by Warner) for a movie, but Byatt is anxious about how it will be handled. "The real romance in the book is in the letters, and I think the partners in the contemporary romance are a bit foolish. You've got to have someone who sees that, and mocks them just a little." She goes on: "Hollywood people think writers know nothing about films, but at least we know enough to make sure the original quality that persuaded them to buy the book isn't lost."

Byatt was on tour in the U.S. in 1995 for her most recent work, an elegant short-story collection called *The Matisse Stories*. According to Byatt, you could tell where she'd been because in those cities the book showed up on local bestseller lists. As she went, she found herself talking, at readings and signings, about her experience with *Possession*, and the cuts originally asked for, and finding a strong response. "People in the bookshops actually began to yell: 'Listen to us! Publishers should listen to us!' There are enough passionate readers out there, and publishers could keep them going if only they would try to look after them. Real readers buy 20 to 30 books to every one bought by people who look for big gold letters on the cover. If you sell only 2000 or 3000 copies of a good book you're not doing too badly; just don't print two million and make a muddle."

Dusk is enfolding Putney now, and Byatt suddenly seems to realize how long, and with what concentrated energy, she has been holding forth. "I must stop talking now and let you go," she says, in a judicious mix of compassion and self-preservation. Later that night, an admired literary and until recently (as part of Harper Collins) somewhat embattled London publisher, Harvill, is throwing a late-night party to celebrate both an anniversary and its recently won independence in a remote and distant corner of North London. Byatt is tired and wonders aloud whether she should go all that way: "But I really should. I want to show my support."

She goes.

JOHN F. BAKER
May 20, 1996

JAMES CARROLL

For the better part of two hours one morning midway through Holy Week, the Boston writer James Carroll talks about the uncommon circumstances that transformed him from a politically concerned Catholic priest during the 1960s into a husband, father of two children and bestselling author of nine novels and the memoir *An American Requiem: God, My Father, and the War That Came Between Us* (Houghton Mifflin).

During a lull in the discussion, Carroll leaves the sitting room of his brick townhouse in Beacon Hill to fetch a book from his upstairs study. A few minutes later, he returns with a copy of the poet Allen Tate's collected verse and opens it to the prescient inscription which changed his life 30 years earlier:

"To James Carroll, with all good wishes for his two vocations, Allen Tate, July 12, 1966."

One of the vocations Tate had referred to, of course, was writing. The other vocation was the sacred calling Carroll had already embarked upon when his Paulist superiors recommended him for a summer writing course with Tate at the University of Minnesota.

"Allen Tate was a wonderful teacher and a demanding critic, so when he handed me the book, I was very moved by what he had written," Carroll explains. "What really touched me was that he was affirming that I had the vocation to be a poet, and my heart just leaped. But when I looked up at him, he was sort of sadly shaking his head. And then he spoke the unwritten addendum: 'But you can't have both, you know,' as if I did know. I didn't think he was right. But he was."

Within eight years, Tate's frank assessment of the young man's future proved prophetic. Carroll would no longer be a priest, and he would be pursuing the life of a writer whose output to date now numbers nine highly regarded novels, beginning with *Madonna Red* in 1976, and including *Mortal Friends* (1978), *Fault Lines* (1980), *Family Trade* (1982) and *Prince of Peace* (1984), all with Little, Brown.

With Dutton, he then published *Supply of Heroes* (1986) and *Firebird* (1988). *Memorial Bridge* (1991) and *The City Below* (1994) were published with Houghton Mifflin.

Though decidedly different in subject matter, there are similarities among all the novels in structure, execution and moral preoccupations. "There is nothing understated about James Carroll," Renee Loth wrote five years ago in the *Boston Globe*. "He writes with sweep—his heroes all are handsome and principled, his themes grand—about faith, redemption, truth, and honor."

Faith, redemption, truth and honor, it turns out, are among the forces that persuaded Carroll to write *An American Requiem*, a book he undertook partly as an act of closure.

"I call this book a 'requiem' because there is for me very much the end of something here," he says. "It embraces this idea of laying to rest, laying to rest *someone*—my father, literally. The story quite pointedly begins and ends with a Mass; it begins with my first Mass as a priest, and ends with my father's funeral Mass."

Between those two solemn milestones is the honest recollection of an American family caught up in the events of the 1950s, 1960s and '70s, the story of a young man torn between love and respect for his parents and their wishes and his own deep moral sense of right and wrong. As an accomplished novelist, Carroll recognized this as the grist for an extraordinary narrative.

"I knew years ago that my family was embarked on a fantastic story. The story of my father's early life in Chicago and his romance with my mother, his career with the FBI, the Air Force and the Defense Intelligence Agency—I certainly knew that was something. Then there is my brother Joe's polio and the curse of that, and everything coming to a terrible climax in Vietnam. And then I have another brother who is a draft fugitive; and a third brother who is an FBI agent out looking for him; and here I am, a priest who is secretly opposed to the war; and there is my father in the Pentagon helping to pick targets that will be bombed the next day in Vietnam. So there are these moments running through my life that I, as a fiction writer, would never be able to invent."

James Carroll was born in Chicago in 1943, three years after his father, Joseph Carroll, had joined the FBI—fresh out of a night law school course that took him six years to complete while he worked days in the stockyards. The young special agent's high-profile arrest of Roger "Tough" Touhy earned the admiration of J. Edgar Hoover and a promotion to Washington, where he moved his wife, Mary, and their young family. In 1947, Joseph Carroll was assigned to the newly formed U.S. Air Force to establish an office of special investigations, a temporary post that quickly became permanent, and brought with it an entry rank of brigadier general.

The Carrolls were devoted Irish Catholics—Joseph Carroll himself had briefly aspired to be a priest in the 1930s—and the children grew up firmly schooled in the ways of the faith. As an undergraduate at Georgetown University in 1960, Carroll had every intention of following in the footsteps of his father, who by then was a three-star general. "I enrolled in ROTC, and I was named outstanding Air Force cadet of the year," he says. But with a growing sympathy for the civil rights movement and with the looming specter of Vietnam, Carroll admits to being "a divided young fellow" at the time. His decision to enroll in a Paulist seminary was made in what, he recalls, was a moment of weakness.

Usually reserved with his sons, Joseph Carroll, on one occasion and one occasion only, had confided in James his fear of a coming war with the Soviet Union in which nuclear weapons would be used. 'My father was a reserved man. But I remember that moment as a moment of tremendous closeness and warmth." Deeply touched, James announced, in response, that he wanted to become a priest.

"There was this piece of me which was, and which still is, for want of a better word, 'religious,' and the felt presence of God is a very powerful experience. That's what enabled me to do what I did. But there also was this other piece of me that wanted a girlfriend, wanted the world, wanted worldly success, wanted to fly airplanes, all of that. But once having committed myself to my father, I was stuck with having said it."

The Mass that opens *An American Requiem* takes place on February 23, 1969, in the Catholic chapel at Bolling Air Force Base on the east bank of the Potomac River in Washington, D.C. There, with his parents and assorted military dignitaries present, the newly ordained Father Carroll gives his first sermon. To emphasize a biblical metaphor, he uses the word "napalm," a catchword for antiwar activists which he knows will upset the congregation. "There was a sick silence in the chapel," Carroll writes, and an irreparable breach had been made with his father.

Carroll worked in Senator Eugene McCarthy's campaign for the Democratic presidential nomination in 1968, and he supported the antiwar activities of the priests Philip and Daniel Berrigan. He also found himself differing with the church on numerous fundamental matters. In 1974, he took a year's leave of absence and was granted a full release by the Paulist Fathers in 1975. "I didn't leave the church, I left the priesthood," he says pointedly. "It was the culture of hierarchy that was destroyed for me. It wasn't poverty, chastity or obedience, exactly. It was the way in which the whole culture presumes superiors and inferiors, and I couldn't be part of that anymore. But I am still a Catholic who cares very much about the church. I argue with the church, and I argue against this hierarchical, authoritarian form that it has embraced."

Once he was on his own, Carroll plunged forward with his dreams. "I was free as a bird when I left the priesthood. I was cut loose on the world. I had optimism, I had freedom, I had no money, and I had no need for it. It was a wonderful period in my life. The Paulists had encouraged me to write, and I sort of fell into it. I loved writing sermons, I loved telling the stories of the Gospel, and I had written a few nonfiction things that were published while I was a priest." Among Carroll's theological books are *A Terrible Beauty: Conversations in Prayer, Politics, and Imagination* (Newman Press, 1973) and *The Winter Name of God* (Sheed & Ward, 1975).

Carroll's tenure as playwright in residence at the Berkshire Theater Festival in Massachusetts, where his play "O'Farrell, Oh Family" was staged, brought him in contact with the literary agent Donald Cutler. Cutler not only placed his first novel, *Madonna Red* with editor William D. Phillips at Little, Brown but also introduced him to another client, the novelist Alexandra Marshall, whom he married in 1977, and whose next novel, *Wedding Pictures,* will also be published next year by Houghton Mifflin. An ordained Episcopalian minister, Cutler also officiated at their ecumenical wedding service; Jim Carroll and Lexa Marshall have two children, Lizzy, 16, and Patrick, 14.

Madonna Red is a suspense novel involving a priest and an Irish terrorist campaign that makes no apologies for being a work of genre fiction. "It is the most deliberately commercial novel I've ever written," Carroll readily admits. "I didn't have any literary pretensions about my work. I still don't. I think of myself as a storyteller, and I set out to tell a story. I wanted to tell a story about the priesthood, since I had just left it, but I did it indirectly. It was as direct as I could do it at that point in my life. So in a sense, I took refuge in the form of a political thriller. What I also found was the form of the novel. I feel very much a novelist. The spaciousness is important to me."

A "military brat" who spent his childhood living on "generals' row" at various air force facilities, Carroll has found permanence in Boston, where he served as Catholic Chaplain at Boston University from 1969 to 1974. Since leaving the priesthood, he has remained politically active, helping to organize such programs as the Walk for Hunger, AIDS Action Committee and an annual "Read-a-thon for Peace." He also writes a weekly op-ed column for the *Boston Globe,* teaches at the Ploughshares International Fiction Writing Seminar and is chairman of PEN/New England.

"What I loved doing most on my days off when I was a priest was walking, and by walking I discovered the stories of the city. The solid, rooted culture of Irish Boston swept me away. So after I had written *Madonna Red,* I realized that I really wanted to write here. Boston's busing crisis was under way, and the Irish conflict with blacks was very powerful. I was obsessed with what was behind this, how did the Boston Irish get to be who they are. I told a story, and that turned out to be *Mortal Friends,* which is the book that gave me my career."

A full selection of the BOMC, *Mortal Friends* was a bestseller and is still in print, having sold more than a million copies. He published his next three novels with Phillips at Little, Brown before moving to Dutton, and editor Joseph A. Kanon. He followed Kanon to Houghton Mifflin, where his editor is now Wendy Strothman.

It was Strothman, after hearing Carroll give a talk in Boston, who suggested he write a book about the first half-century of his life. In fact, Strothman acquired the book while she was the director of Beacon Press in Boston and brought it with her when she became editor-in-chief of Houghton.

"The single most powerful motive I have in telling this story is so that my children can have it," says Carroll. "One day, when I watched my children shrink back in fear and mystification from my father, who by that time was in the grip of Alzheimer's, I was overwhelmed with sadness because I knew they would never have a memory of him when he was great. I want them to understand who he was, who my mother was, and what we've been through together. So I quite deliberately dedicate this memoir to Lexa, Lizzy and Pat."

With the memoir now behind him Carroll has embarked on a new novel, which he finds refreshing after working through the prism of so many painful memories. "I had this fantasy when I was writing *An American Requiem* that by the end of it I was going to feel fine," he says. "I kept thinking that at the end I would have worked through all of this stuff, and there would be a knot that I'd tie, and I'd be able to put my pen down and say, 'Thanks be to God, this has been a great experience.' But it has shocked me to get to the end and just feel completely, to use my father's word, 'heartbroken,' by it. It's confusing to me, really, because it's a very sad story."

Though his hairline has receded somewhat over the years, Carroll, 53, remains trim, ruggedly handsome and committed to his work. A practicing Catholic, he attends church every Sunday, often at the Paulist Center where he lived as a priest, not far from the gold dome of the Massachusetts State House.

"For me, prayer is handing over to God the things we can't carry by ourselves," he concludes softly. "In this case, I feel like I'm handing over to whoever reads the book what I couldn't carry by myself."

NICHOLAS A. BASBANES
May 27, 1996

ANA CASTILLO

THE ROAD FROM the nearest el stop to Ana Castillo's North Side Chicago home curves for several blocks alongside the solemn, deserted expanse of historic Graceland Cemetery and then enters an offbeat shopping district that features a fortune-teller's storefront, a shuttered nightclub and a Mexican restaurant incongruously named Lolita's. Far from seeming out of place, these picturesque locations mesh perfectly with the bustling everyday Chicago life that surrounds them. Such harmonies between the romantic and the mundane, manifest in Castillo's neighborhood, also resonate in the adventurous chords of her art—as heard most recently in the story collection *Loverboys* (Norton).

Castillo lives halfway down a side street full of lush lawns and profuse sprinklers, in the ground-floor apartment of a tidy brick two-flat. Her son, Marcel, just out of seventh grade, ushers her interviewer into a modest combination living room and study. Decorated in a subtle Southwestern style, the room is dominated by a series of striking paintings of Castillo—self-portraits, it turns out. Literary quarterlies share space on the coffee table with an issue of *USA Weekend* that features a Castillo story, "Juan in a Million."

The day has been a scorcher. When Castillo herself enters the room, however, her bold features set off by her long black hair and simple white sun dress, she appears totally imbued with cool. As she begins to hold forth, a wry sense of humor catalyzes energy together with reserve; she couches passion for life and work in gentle ironies. One of the most prominent Latina writers in the U.S., Castillo is already the author of three novels, several volumes of poetry and an essay collection. Today, however, our conversation starts with the latest events in her fast-moving career: the publication of her story in *USA Weekend,* with its circulation of nearly 40 million, and her appearances at the just-concluded 1996 Chicago ABA, where she did an autograph session and served on the Booksellers for Social Responsibility panel.

Talk of the ABA sparks an account of Castillo's interest in the independent bookstore scene. In the title story in *Loverboys*, Castillo draws on her experience with, and affinity for, booksellers, to create a narrator who "runs the only bookstore in town that deals with the question of the soul." This protagonist handsells a volume of Camus to a philosophically inclined customer, who subsequently emerges as the main "loverboy" of the piece.

No particular store served as her model, but Castillo has long depended on independent bookstores to nurture her public. When she wrote "Loverboys" she was living in Albuquerque, writing her novel *So Far from God* (Norton, 1993) and organizing occasional events at the Salt of the Earth bookstore. Castillo extols Salt of the Earth for its support of the writers' community in Albuquerque and across the country and laments its demise this past year. Owner John Randall originally coordinated the Booksellers for Social Responsibility panels at the ABA.

"As a writer whose books were published with small presses," Castillo says, "it was a natural for me to talk about the importance of bookstores." She speaks in rapid cadences of full sentences, given a musical lilt by her warm voice. "The kind of literature I write is not directed for the mainstream, although *So Far from God* did very well, and I'm hoping that we're entering a new era now where it will be more and more the case that writers from the fringes occupy the mainstream."

If *Loverboys* bids to occupy the mainstream of contemporary fiction, it nonetheless retains strong connections to Castillo's tremendously varied, and often quite radical, previous body of work. Born and raised in Chicago, Castillo began publishing poetry in the mid-1970s, when she was a college student. Norton's recent edition of her poetry, *My Father Was a Toltec and Selected Poems*, 1973–1988 (1995), collects work from the period when writing was her calling, but not yet a career. It includes selections from two self-published chapbooks, *Otro Canto* (1977) and *The Invitation* (1979), together with many poems from *Women Are not Roses* (Arte Publico, 1984) and all of *My Father Was a Toltec* (West End Press, 1988). Castillo's verse moves freely between English and Spanish, interlacing unvarnished accounts of her life, her family and her friends with boldly erotic passages and matter-of-fact political statements.

Castillo links her impulse to write to idealism. "In the mid-'70s, the idea was to work towards social change. The call of the day for young people everywhere of all colors and backgrounds was to contribute in some way to a more just society. Being of Mexican background, being Indian-looking, being a female, coming from a working-class background, and then becoming politicized in high school, that was my direction. I was going to be an artist, a poet. Never once did I think of it as a career. I certainly never thought I could possibly earn a dime writing protest poetry. So all those years I went around like a lot of young poets—and a lot of old poets—going anywhere I could find an audience, getting on a soapbox and reading. I was a Chicana protest poet, a complete renegade—and I continue to write that way."

Even as Castillo continues to write as a renegade, however, her work—in particular, her fiction—has found a home with the reading public. Her first novel, *The Mixquiahuala Letters,* was published by Bilingual Review Press in 1986. It brought Castillo critical acclaim, an American Book Award from the Before Columbus Foundation and steady sales. Without consulting Castillo, Bilingual Review sold the rights to that novel and to Castillo's subsequent effort, *Sapogonia,* to Doubleday/Anchor, which brought them out in paperback in 1992 and 1994, respectively. This annoyed Castillo, who would have liked to have had more involvement in the publication (she eventually was able to make some revisions to *Sapogonia*). Her chief comment on the matter now is to urge young writers to have their contracts vetted, no matter how small and friendly the press.

In the wake of the success of her first fiction efforts, Castillo signed up with agent Susan Bergholz, of whom she speaks warmly. Bergholz, Castillo says, played a key role in the genesis of what would become Castillo's debut publication with Norton, the novel *So Far from God.* In an emotionally bleak period during her sojourn in New Mexico, Castillo had happened upon an edition of *The Lives of the Saints.* Reading its spiritual biographies inspired her to write a story about a modern-day miracle that happens to a little girl known as La Loca. After dying, La Loca does not only rise from the dead: she ascends to the roof of the church that had been about to house her funeral and reproves the Padre for attributing her resurrection to the devil. Upon reading this story, Bergholz suggested that Castillo develop it into a novel.

"So," recalls Castillo, "I wrote two more chapters, Susan sent it out, and eventually Gerald Howard took it at Norton." The story grew to encompass the lives of four sisters, martyrs in different ways to the modern Southwest, and of their mother, Sofia, who turns her bereavements to positive account by organizing the community politically and by

67

working to reconfigure the Catholic religion. Castillo speaks very highly of Howard's editing.

"When *So Far from God* came out," Castillo declares, "I started looking at writing as a career, because indeed, after 22 years, I began to earn my living from it." Having settled back into the very same apartment where, more than a decade ago, she wrote *The Mixquiahuala Letters,* she now plans to write full-time in Chicago, forgoing the itinerant writer-in-residence life that took her in recent years to colleges from Chico State in California to Mount Holyoke in Massachusetts.

Castillo has made forays into writing cultural criticism, collected in *Massacre of the Dreamers: Essays in Xicanisma* (Univ. of New Mexico Press, 1994), which earned her a Ph.D. from the University of Bremen. While she speaks positively of the resident-writer experience, she is disdainful of fiction-writing workshops. This sentiment has its roots in her own formation. "By no means had I, as many young writers do these days, gone for an M.F.A. and said 'well, I want to be a writer,' " Castillo says. "I had wanted to be a painter, but I was discouraged in college. And so I thought, I'm not going to go through that with my writing." For Castillo, a more idiosyncratic, personal path is best.

Castillo does have a strong investment in pedagogy, however, a commitment currently finding its most direct expression in a children's book project, *My Daughter, My Son, My Eagle, My Dove.* This manuscript consists of two long poems based on Aztec and Nahuatal instructions to youths facing rites of passage. "These poems are teachings from my ancestry," she says, "hundreds of years old, from the time of the conquest of the Americas, and yet applicable today—we're going to package them with contemporary illustrations."

Also underway is a new novel, *Peel My Love Like an Onion.* In this project, Castillo focuses on the Chicago gypsy community, for which a good friend serves her as native informant. Uncomfortable with the idea of fully assuming gypsy character in relating this work, Castillo currently has the novel narrated by a Chicana woman involved with a gypsy duo.

Clearly, Castillo's social conscience continues to inform the choice and development of her projects. Forthcoming from Riverhead is *Goddess of the Americas,* an essay collection which she has edited on the Virgin of Guadalupe, beloved patron of the oppressed peoples of Latin America. Castillo's good friend Sandra Cisneros is one contributor; others include Elena Poniatowska and Luis Rodríguez. The idea for the book originated with its editor at Riverhead, Julie Grau. When

Grau asked if she were interested, says Castillo, "I couldn't say no to the Virgin of Guadalupe—I saw that as a discreet message to me." While Castillo herself is not a practicing Catholic, she feels that celebrating the Virgin can help redress the sad fact that "what we could call the feminine principle is too absent from—is too denigrated by— Western society.

"I don't particularly care if people want to worship the Virgin of Guadalupe," she continues, "if they get the message that we need to respect the things that we call female, which we don't. You know, we put so much pressure on mothering, and as a single mother I understand that, but how much support and respect do we really give mothers in our society?" Castillo is not afraid to provoke controversy. "One of my goals in life is to get an encyclical from the church—if not from the pope, then from the bishops—to ban the book. I think that would be the best advertisement for the book, if a cardinal or someone would say that it definitely should not be read by any good Catholic in the world."

It might seem that Castillo's new offerings, *Loverboys* and *Goddess of the Americas,* separate sexuality and spirituality into distinct packages. But this is not the case. For Castillo, "spirituality is a manifestation of one's energy, and that energy includes who you are as a total being"—including your sexuality. She sees the propinquity of the two publications as a clear message that "these are not two separate issues for me, but one issue for us to consider."

The spiritual epiphanies that sexual desires and experiences bring in *Loverboys* occur not as religious visions but rather as aesthetic fulfillment. Sometimes characters recognize such fulfillment themselves. More often, they remain confused, even lost, even while Castillo's rendering of their lives into stories lends them grace. Thus does Castillo employ the graceful touch of the master storyteller: to fuse together the mundane and the magical for characters and readers in Chicago, the Americas, and the world.

SAMUEL BAKER
August 12, 1996

MICHAEL CHABON

MICHAEL CHABON, once pegged as a wonder boy for his first novel, *The Mysteries of Pittsburgh*, languidly lounges in an overstuffed, slip-covered chair in his old-fashioned Spanish duplex in Los Angeles. With lanky hair, loose-fitting clothes and a modest demeanor, he looks like a sweet boy that any mother would be happy to see her daughter bring home. He's self-deprecating, soft-spoken, and he has the endearing habit of paying more attention to the squeals of delight or the occasional cranky whimpers issuing from his four-month-old daughter in the back bedroom than to the discussion of his long-anticipated new novel, *Wonder Boys,* out from Villard.

The novel has wonderfully wry connotations. Narrator Grady Tripp, once deemed a "wonder boy" on the strength of his first novel, remains mired in his second attempt, a hopelessly long work-in-progress called *Wonder Boys.* His editor, Terry Crabtree, also once a rising star, is on the skids. And the next generation is coming up fast: at the college where Grady teaches, a talented but incurably mendacious student seems poised to begin a stellar writing career.

Chabon knows whereof he speaks. His own career took off like a rocket, and then slumped into a waiting game.

Born in 1963 in Washington, D.C., and raised in Columbia, Md., Chabon recalls that he had a love of words from early childhood. "I liked word etymologies," he says. "I was always a good speller. I guess that my love of language is chiefly a function of having a good memory for words, like having an ear for music. My parents were big readers and my grandmother used to read poetry to me. Books were respected and valued in our family." The city Pittsburgh has also been a major influence in his life. After a year at Carnegie Mellon, he transferred to the University of Pittsburgh, where he graduated with a B.A. in English in 1984. Then he crossed the country to the University of California at Irvine, where he entered the M.F.A. program run by

Oakley Hall and Donald Heiney, who wrote under the name Mac-Donald Harris.

There are many pundits who say that you can't learn how to write; that you either have the talent or you don't. Chabon agrees with this, to a point. "You certainly can't learn how to write a good novel," he says. "But you can learn what *not* to do. You can learn about structure, point of view, and not biting off more than you can chew."

Heartened when he won a *Mademoiselle* short-story contest in 1987, Chabon wrote *The Mysteries of Pittsburgh* for his master's thesis. He turned in the final draft on a Friday. The following Monday, Chabon found a note in his box from Heiney/Harris saying that he had sent the manuscript to agent Mary Evans at the Virginia Barber Agency in New York. Two months later, Evans sold the book to editor Doug Stumpf at Morrow.

Published in 1988, *The Mysteries of Pittsburgh* made a major splash, garnering a spot on the *PW* bestseller list for seven weeks. Chabon was instantly lumped with other brat packers of the day—Jay McInerney, Tama Janowitz and Bret Easton Ellis. The Gap asked him to model jeans; he turned down the offer. *People* magazine wanted to include him in its "50 Most Beautiful People" issue; he turned that down, too.

Looking back, Chabon says he wishes he'd appreciated that time more for the "amazing ride" that it was. "But I was married at that point to a would-be writer. The fact that nothing like this was happening to her made it difficult for me to enjoy what was happening. All the good things were a mixed blessing." Nor did he particularly care for being identified with the brat pack. "I never thought I had anything in common with 'the usual suspects,' but I suppose that 'youth' was the main handle, an inevitable handle. I just didn't pay much attention to it. I was 23. I thought in terms of what did I have in common with Cheever, Nabokov or Flaubert when they were 23? I had high aims."

Chabon says he strived very hard not to be the flavor-of-the-month or a cool member of the New York literati scene, but instead to refine his craft. He worked on short stories, many of which were published in the *New Yorker* and *GQ*. He also wrote travel articles—on Key West, Prague, Las Vegas and Tuscany—for *Vogue* and the *New York Times*. By 1991, when his collection of short stories, *A Model World,* was released, Chabon was already two years into his second novel, a sprawling saga called *Fountain City,* that was gradually becoming his albatross.

Coming up with a second novel is hard for any writer. For Chabon, there was the intense pressure of having to produce something that would meet and surpass the promise of *Mysteries*. The plot of *Fountain City* involved Paris and Florida, utopian dreamers and ecological activists, architecture and baseball, an Israeli spy and a man dying from AIDS, a love affair between a young American and a woman 10 years his senior. He had bitten off more than he could chew.

As he struggled for five years to make the Paris half of the book mesh with the Florida half, his personal life was in constant flux. He moved six times. He got divorced from his first wife, took up with another woman, split up, met Ayelet Waldman and married her. All the while, the unfinished book was almost a palpable burden. "You know that scene at the Seder in *Wonder Boys* when someone asks Grady how his book is going? I can't tell you how many times I was asked that. I always felt like an incompetent handyman. I always thought that I was *just about done.*" Instead, it was never done. "Doug Stumpf kept saying that it was full of amazing stuff. I'd try to fix it, cut it, restructure it." Chabon estimates that he wrote 1500 pages of what he tried to turn into a 700-page—and still unpublishable—manuscript.

At the beginning of 1993, Chabon and Waldman, who was clerking for a federal judge, lived in San Francisco. She was due to take the bar exam in July. Instead, she decided to tackle it earlier, in February, which meant that she would be studying nonstop for the following six weeks. After her announcement, Chabon went downstairs to his basement office, turned on the computer and fantasized longingly—as he had done every day for years—about the book he would rather be writing.

He imagined a scene: a troubled young man standing in a backyard, holding a derringer to his temple, while, on a nearby porch, a shaggy, pot-smoking, older man tries to decide if what he's seeing is real or not. Chabon elected to pursue the idea. He wrote 15 pages in the first four hours, producing what eventually became a pivotal scene in *Wonder Boys*. "It was flowing out in a way that I remembered from *Mysteries of Pittsburgh*," he recalls. By the end of the first day, he also knew that the story would take place in Pittsburgh.

"After *Mysteries*, I never intended to use that city again in my writing," he says. "I don't really have an explanation for my fascination with the place, except perhaps that my father moved there when I was 12. I spent my summers and holidays there. And, of course, I attended college there. Pittsburgh is where I became who I am now. College formed my ideas on art, literature, friends, sex. It's where I started to write in earnest." Just as in *Mysteries,* the new project—which Chabon stored in his computer simply as *X*—was written in the first person. "I like to read books that are in the first person. I like the intimate confessional tone, as though the person has pulled up a chair and is telling you about his life."

Chabon kept X a secret. Within a matter of days, he'd written 50 pages of what became an intricate plot. In addition to his endlessly revised manuscript, Grady Tripp is—in ways that he cannot control—revising his life. He loves his wife and everyone in her family, but he's having an affair with the wife of the chairman of the English department. His dissolute editor (based on an unnamed New York editor whom Chabon met at a Pittsburgh writers' conference), is trying to wrest the manuscript from Tripp to salvage his own career. But what drives this wacky, almost slapstick, tale are the subplots. They involve a tuba, a dead dog, a dead boa constrictor, the fur-trimmed satin jacket worn by Marilyn Monroe at her wedding to Joe DiMaggio and that hefty manuscript.

Six weeks later, after his wife took the bar exam, he gave her the first 117 pages to read and was amazed at her reaction. Incredibly, he hadn't thought of the book as humorous. "I'm not at all an intentional writer," Chabon concedes. "I don't plan. I don't think about how my writing will strike the reader. To me, Grady was a wry tone, but I felt sad writing about him. In a lot of ways, he is a projection of my worst fears of what I was going to become if I kept working on *Fountain City.* So it wasn't until Ayelet read the manuscript that I realized it was funny."

Having completed the first draft in seven months, he called Mary Evans with a variation on a cliché: "I have some good news and some weird news." The good news was that he'd finally finished his second novel; the weird news was that it wasn't *Fountain City.* Fortunately, his contract with Villard was simply for a novel.

Nevertheless, the road to publication was bumpy. Over an eight-month span, Chabon's agent and editor played musical chairs. Mary Evans left the Virginia Barber agency and went out on her own. Doug Stumpf, exited Villard for *Vanity Fair,* leaving publisher David Rosenthal to shepherd the novel. At the same time, Villard's publicity department was undergoing an upheaval. Mary Evans persuaded Villard to hire independent publicist Susan Ostrov to give the book the special attention it deserved. On a personal level, Chabon moved once again when Waldman took a job in Los Angeles as a federal public defender. And Sophie was born.

A letter from Stumpf accompanies the galleys of *Wonder Boys*. Stumpf writes that the theme of the book is "the terrible emotional and spiritual cost of not growing up." Chabon, who does not know about the letter until we mention it, is somewhat bemused. He says that he's never really understood the idea of themes in novels. He considers for a few moments, then continues: "To me, the book is about the disappointment of getting older and growing up and not measuring up to what you thought, and the world and the people in it not being what you expected. It's about disillusionment and acceptance."

Chabon has drawn two lessons from his failure to complete *Fountain City* and the ease and joy of writing *Wonder Boys*. "Don't take advances on books, because they put too much pressure on you," he advises. "And don't be afraid to abandon something you don't like." Another lesson might be that when the words start to sing, follow them.

So far, *Wonder Boys* seems to be singing a happy tune. Villard is sending Chabon on a nine-city tour; audio rights have been sold to Brilliance; and Avon has a substantial floor for the paperback. Meanwhile, reviews have been outstanding. Steve Rubin (producer of *The Firm, The Addams Family* and *Little Man Tate*) has optioned the book for Paramount. Rubin also optioned *The Gentleman Host*, an original screenplay that Chabon wrote for fast cash when Waldman announced she was pregnant. The story concerns the so-called gentlemen hosts who, in exchange for free trips, agree to dance and play cards with women on cruise ships. "In retrospect, it wasn't the most commercial idea," says Chabon. "But I feel close to the older generation of Jews, people in their 70s and 80s. I was very close to my grandfather, who died about six years ago. I have felt his absence and have looked for ways to fill the gap." Chabon may be the only successful writer who also does volunteer work in an old-age home.

The publishing world is littered with former wonder boys, but every once in a while a young writer comes along who goes on to fulfill his early promise. *Wonder Boys* may indeed be the means by which Chabon becomes one of the few wunderkinds of his generation who makes the transition to a mature writer with a solid future. Maybe now he'll be able to enjoy his amazing ride.

LISA SEE
March 31, 1995

BERNARD CORNWELL

 Tʜɪs ɪs ᴛʜᴇ ʜᴏᴜsᴇ that Sharpe built," says Bernard Cornwell as he smokes a Honduran cigar on the deck of his comfortable Cape Cod home. The Cape is also where he sails the 24-foot gaff-rigged cutter he calls *Royalist*—the boat that Sharpe bought. The prolific British writer and former journalist is barefoot, tanned and relaxed after two months in Florida with his American wife, Judy, whom he met 15 years ago in Northern Ireland when he was head of current affairs in Belfast for BBC-TV and she was a visiting travel agent.

Since 1980, when he married, moved to the States and started to write fiction after being denied a green card, Cornwell has produced 29 books, including five sailing thrillers and four books in the Starbuck Chronicles, a U.S. Civil War series published by HarperCollins. But he remains best known for the adventures of British army captain Richard Sharpe as related in a popular series of military history novels set during the Peninsular War against Napoleon, dramatized on *Masterpiece Theatre* and published by Viking in the U.S.

His latest book, *The Winter King*, (St. Martin's Press), is the first installment in an entirely new trilogy called the Warlord Chronicles. With this series, Cornwell turns his attention from the 19th century to the fifth century and the story of King Arthur.

The Winter King is Cornwell's attempt to remove Arthur from all the legends of chivalry and romance and tell a tale of the Dark Ages set against the more certain historical background of a country fast succumbing to civil strife and invasion. Cornwell's Arthur is a heroic warlord who repelled the enemy, yet whose enemies still love him 1500 years later.

Cornwell compares his effort to an earlier Arthur trilogy, The Kingmaker, written by Helen Hollick and published in England. "She did what I originally thought I would do," he says, "tell the story and leave out everything that came after the 12th century and Chrétien de

Troyes," the romantic French poet who was responsible for introducing the character of Lancelot and the idea of Camelot. Cornwell took a purist's approach, at first, and decided to eliminate Lancelot and even Merlin, "because it's almost certain that Merlin had nothing to do with Arthur whatsoever. But if you do that, there's nothing left. Arthur suddenly doesn't have any meaning. So, of course, I put it all in again."

Searching for the meaning of Arthur led Cornwell back to the earliest histories, folktales and epic poems, which he describes in an author's note. His Arthur is what he says the eighth-century historian Nennius called a "dux bellorum," a great warlord. He is also "a Celt fighting the English—something no one ever says about Arthur," Cornwell notes. "Everyone thinks that England is the home of King Arthur, and that he is a great English hero. He's not. He is the great enemy of the English, and yet the English revere him, which means he must have been something quite special."

Arthur doesn't appear in the first pages of *The Winter King,* and Cornwell says he uses those pages "to establish a world. You've got to convince the reader that this grim and beautiful fifth-century world existed.

"I simply try to tell as compelling a story as I possibly can," he says. "I don't know if there is any moral. I'm not clever enough to point out morals in my tales. The most important thing you do is the plot," he explains. "If you are telling a story and elements in the plot are unlikely, you are failing your audience."

When T.H. White wrote *The Once and Future King,* he claimed that the central theme of his Arthur stories was "to find the antidote to war." Asked about the long shadow White casts over any attempt to rewrite the Arthur legends, Cornwell observes: "I had him in mind to avoid. In some ways, I think of the Arthur stories as the Becher's Brook of English historical fiction—that dreadful fence in the Grand National where horses used to die in droves. It's this big, high fence, and you cannot forget the giants who have been over it before you. I'm not competing with T.H. White. He was much wittier and more learned than I am—and a very strange man. He was doing a quite different thing."

Cornwell's background is, in fact, neither academic nor literary. He was born in 1944 in Wessex in South-End-on-Sea and adopted as an infant. His father was a Canadian Air Force officer, but the family that adopted him belonged to a Protestant sect known as the Peculiar People. He served briefly in the British army before becoming a TV producer for the BBC. "In fact, I grew up in a family of conscientious objectors and great pacifists," he says. "I'm a soldier manqué, and I think [writing military fiction] is my rebellion against them." Hence the interest he displays in *The Winter King* in Arthur's Britain as, he writes, "a place as racked by religious dissent as it was by invasion and politics."

Cornwell says he doesn't miss being a journalist, but he does admit that "for a time I missed the company of journalists. They are very beguiling and amusing, very cynical and wicked and witty." By the time he married Judy, he had really done everything he wanted to do at the BBC other than a desk job, and he didn't want that. Nor was he drawn to American television when he moved here; he knew what he knew—British television—and he knew what he didn't know—the culture and audience of American television.

Cornwell nevertheless attributes the speed with which he writes to his training and experience as a journalist. He's a fast reader, as well, according to his wife. "He reads three books on a trans-Atlantic flight," she says. At the BBC, she recalls, he'd often be writing copy while the nightly news program was already on camera and feeding it to the anchor, because no one else could do it. He likes that sort of fast-pace pressure and deadline, and it's carried over to his novel-writing, she says.

Cornwell's longtime British editor, first at Collins and now at Michael Joseph, is Susan Watt. His editor at St. Martin's is Hope Dellon. At HarperCollins he's edited by Buzz Wyeth. His longstanding literary agent is fellow Englishman Toby Eady. They met in 1980 at a party in New York City just after Cornwell had written his first book, *Sharpe's Eagle* (Viking, 1981) and received a small offer from Heinemann. "I told him I had written a novel, so he turned and walked away," Cornwell recalls with amusement. "I followed him and told him that I had an offer on it. He asked how much," and when Cornwell revealed the paltry sum, Eady told him it must be an awful book and walked away again. ("He absolutely hates it when I tell this story," says Cornwell.) "So I found him a third time, said 'please read my novel' and met him in Grand Central Station to give it to him. He phoned me up that night and said, 'Don't you dare sign that contract. How much money do you want?'"

Cornwell has said that his Sharpe novels are shamelessly based on C.S. Forester's Hornblower series and his own research on the Duke of Wellington's army. They are also his response to having gone into too many bookshops and found only books on Britain's military defeats. "It seemed to be a very obvious gap on the shelf," he explains, "and so it has proved. It also seemed to me that people didn't particularly want to read long books about Dunkirk. They would much rather read books where we won and the ending is happy." With that in mind, he plans eventually to write a book about one of Britain's greatest victories, Henry V's defeat of the French at Agincourt in 1415.

Maps of Roman Britain are pinned to all the walls of Cornwell's windowless, subterranean writing room in one end of the house ("maps are a great resource for writing") and also a panoramic photograph he took on a hill at South Cadbury in Somerset, an area where he lived for a few years and where he has set Camelot in his own mind's eye. The influence of three years spent in Ireland has also found its way into his new book. "I fell madly in love with Ireland," Cornwell confesses. "I noticed a complete difference between Celts and Saxons. Celts think in circles, and Saxons in boring straight lines."

In the U.S., Cornwell admits he has become a very happy expatriate, though "the longer I live here the more British I feel. I miss the small, everyday things about Britain, like cricket and decent beer and Radio 4, that wonderfully intelligent channel, and British newspapers, which are very different from American ones." But he recently filled out citizenship papers since "it's quite plain that I'm going to live and die here."

Instead of an author tour for *The Winter King,* Cornwell will spend a few days in early June back in England watching Somerset play cricket. "I always go back once a year to see a first-class game of cricket," he says. He set out only once in his career on an author tour. It was against his better judgment, he recalls ruefully, and he vowed he would never do it again. His aversion to book tours stems from the simple belief that they don't work if you're not a well-known author or a celebrity. But he has accompanied a tour group to visit Sharpe's battle sites in Spain and Portugal, and he plans to make the same trip again. Far from abandoning the Sharpe books, he is also at work on a new one set in India, where he recently scouted battle locations.

"I tried once to get away from writing about battles," says Cornwell. "I am slightly bored with it." He switched to sailing thrillers, including *Sea Lord* and *Storm Child,* both of which were published here as Harper Paperbacks. They sold well in England but not in the U.S., he recalls. "It was plain that what people wanted was more battles. Arthur is an attempt to escape from it. I don't see this as a book about warfare. It is about Arthur's attempt to make a blessed land, and the failure of that attempt.

"The story is about striving after perfection," he adds. "That's a very American thought, isn't it? Americans actually believe you can legislate perfection into existence. It's one of the most endearing things about you."

But Cornwell can't get away completely from the well-written battle scene. *The Winter King* concludes with a glorious, albeit brutal, battle, the consequence of Arthur's taking Guinevere instead of the intended Ceinwyn (a glossary of names and places provides a guide to the original Welsh names Cornwell uses). It's followed by a brief teaser extracted from the first chapter of book two in the trilogy, *The Enemy of God*, which Cornwell has already completed. Book three will begin with Arthur's most famous battle at Mount Badon.

To tell his tale of Arthur, Cornwell has invented the narrator Derfel Cadarn, an orphan raised by Merlin, a warrior against the Saxons and eventually a Christian monk who answers the questions of his patroness, Queen Igraine, about Arthur. Their relationship, Cornwell discloses, is "my joke. Igraine asks all the questions that I know Susan [Watt], my editor, is going to ask after each section. Susan's a great one for wanting to know more details about people's childhoods, and I hate writing about childhood. I do see Igraine absolutely as a sort of editor inside the book."

In the end, Cornwell believes *The Winter King* is not just another blood-and-guts battle book but "a novel about extraordinary high ambition that failed. Arthur is a disgustingly classic liberal," he concludes. But according to Cornwell, T.H. White got it right, too, when he said that the whole Arthurian story is "a regular Greek doom." Says Cornwell: "It has got to end rather unhappily. That's the moral, isn't it? Hard as we try—and here is a man trying desperately hard to do something good—it's all going to end in tears."

But does it end? In Cornwell's trilogy, at least, Arthur—this time not as a wise king or great lover, but as a soldier—has returned to us yet again from Avalon.

MISSY DANIEL
June 10, 1996

79

BRAM DIJKSTRA

I T'S A LITTLE too easy to make vampire jokes about Bram Dijkstra's name. Resist the urge. The author of *Idols of Perversity* (1986) and *Evil Sisters* (Knopf)—a study of early–20th century popular culture in which vampires figure prominently—writes big, serious books that bleed nothing redder than vast erudition, showcasing a genuinely broad mind having a really good time.

When *PW* rings the bell at his house in the hills above Del Mar, Calif., we're not sure that an intellectual of his stripe could exist in this well-heeled community overlooking the disarmingly blue Pacific. We're quickly disabused of that reservation. Perched on the ottoman of a leather Eames lounger, amid dozens of large figural oil paintings (a trove he and his wife, literary agent Sandra Dijkstra, gathered during the 1970s, when museums were ridding themselves of anything that didn't scream "modernism"), Dijkstra looks a lot more like an impish former hippie than the father of *Dracula*. His longish gray-blond hair seems recently tamed. His purple—yes, purple—striped shirt (worn open-necked) and cotton vest, along with the socks *and* sandals, suggest a portrait of Southern California ease. Add a pair of round-rimmed spectacles and delicate, expressive fingers, and one almost forgets how tall the guy is.

Or, for that matter, how serious and ambitious his books are. Dijkstra's genial manner masks an intellectual sophistication that manages to combine courtly European admiration for his readers with a generous American breadth of vision. After nearly two solid hours of conversation, about everything from his undergraduate days at Ohio State to *Origin of Species* and Reid Miles's designs for classic Blue Note jazz album covers, it becomes clear that Dijkstra could keep talking for weeks. His enthusiasm for ideas is infectious, but his manner is light and free of pretense. A professor of comparative literature at the University of California, San Diego, since 1967, Dijkstra is a genuine eclectic who can get down with the big ideas yet still giddily discuss the distinctions between mono and stereo versions of John Coltrane's *Ascension.*

"If I were to go into academia now, I'd probably not last," he says, vestiges of his native Dutch accent clinging to his words. "The focus of most humanities has become so narrow and specialized, and I've never been much of a specialist."

But he did go into academia, and his record of scholarly publication is commonly salivated over by students and professors alike, in a variety of disciplines. Everybody from hardcore feminists to bowtied art historians think Dijkstra is great, and with good reason. His groundbreaking doctoral dissertation, *Cubism, Stieglitz and the Early Poetry of William Carlos Williams,* has been in print with Princeton University Press since 1969, and his signature work, *Idols of Perversity: Fantasies of Feminine Evil in Fin-de-Siecle Culture* (Oxford Univ.) is an ambitious interdisciplinary study, reviewed favorably in newspapers from the *New York Times* to the *Baltimore Sun* which called it "a monumental labor of profound importance."

Idols of Perversity is one of those watershed books that make academics uncomfortable and changes the rules forever, engaging the full sweep of fin de siècle European painting right alongside the aggressively political feminism that stormed campuses in the wake of the women's movement of the 1970s. The book also takes a healthy swipe at an uncritical faith in science.

"There used to be an interesting interchange between older scientists and the humanities," argues Dijkstra as he settles into one of his elegant fusillades against Enlightenment arrogance. "But what happened then was that scientists who focused much more narrowly took control and the older generation died out. The consequence of that has been that younger scientists who are intellectually not that far removed from the large populace are about to determine the limits of social reality. Rather than leading us toward a more enlightened future, they're rediscovering the broken wheel discarded by their parents, through their return to the glorification of that same genetics that created such a mess at the turn of the century.

"Scientists these days," he continues, "have no larger sense of the ideological prehistory of the concepts they use. At the end of the 19th century, science was king—and science is now king again, with blinders on."

Dijkstra doesn't hate science. What he detests is the regimentation that he believes characterizes the way science is often practiced, an ossification of thinking that comes with an embrace of ingenuity over humanism. "I never finished high school in Holland because it was so regimented," he says. "That's why, among other reasons, I came to the United States."

Evil Sisters could almost be subtitled "Against Regimentation" rather than "The Threat of Female Sexuality and the Cult of Manhood," so thorough is its critique of pseudo-scientific views of race and gender. The book's hinge figure, of course, is the vampire, which Dijkstra views as a pop-culture construct expressive of conventional early-20th century beliefs about the differences of race and gender. "I don't think we need vampires," he claims, "but as long as our society is structured according to principles glorifying the deprivation of the 'other,' vampires will be present in the popular culture. Metaphorically, this kind of aggression still proceeds according to a sort of nutrition theory of power—you control those whom you devour."

Attacking the "natural laws of the entertainment industry," as he calls them in his introduction, Dijkstra demonstrates how popular culture and post-World War I science formed an ugly creative partnership that churned out cautionary morality tales aimed at worried white men in an age of accelerated social change. The effeminate, non-Aryan "inferiors" who populated these fictions fit perfectly into both evolutionary hierarchies and popular culture, perpetuating a swirling discourse of hate, in which science and entertainment viciously cross-pollinated. The movie business, Dijkstra claims, was infatuated with social Darwinism from the beginning.

"What's powerful about the Darwinian theory of evolution," Dijkstra says, "is that it's so *visual:* there's a ladder to perfection, and you're on this rung and I'm on this rung. This works very effectively to create a notion that there's an inherent inequality among races and genders. In the beginning, it wasn't the word, it was the image. The word is a corrective to the image. We destroy the logic of the word by privileging the image."

Dijkstra's interest in gender inequality might have something to do with his upbringing. Born in 1938, the son of a Dutch engineer, he spent his formative years not in Holland but in Indonesia, where he was surrounded by women: his mother and three sisters, Yoka, Adri and Marijke (*Evil Sisters* is dedicated to them). Sexism, when he first began to encounter it in Holland during his high-school years, baffled him because he had no frame of reference for "dangerous" females—the women in his immediate family were "so talented" that they defied such a simplistic characterization. World War II brought tragedy: he and his mother and sisters were in Holland, but his father, still in Indonesia, was put in a concentration camp by the Japanese. The Japanese concentration camps were just as bad as the Nazi ones," Dijkstra says. His father survived but was destroyed by the experience and died soon after. He left Dijkstra some money, which he used to attend Ohio State University in the late 1950s and early '60s, to study journalism.

While at OSU, he moved from one controversy to another, consistently running afoul of OSU's iron-fisted president, Novice Fawcett. Fawcett took exception to a cultural magazine that Dijkstra started for the school paper and reportedly called the head of the journalism department to have Dijkstra ousted from the program. Dijkstra's department head refused, but it wasn't the last time Fawcett would affect Dijkstra's life.

After earning his B.A. at OSU in two years, Dijkstra headed west to Berkeley for graduate work and was soon immersed in the Free Speech movement. There, while his wife-to-be, Sandra, marched in demonstrations, Dijkstra completed his doctorate and worked as Gary Snyder's teaching assistant. "Stones were bouncing off the windows while I was taking my qualifying exams," he recalls with a chuckle.

It was during the Berkeley years that Dijkstra published his first book, a collection of poetry he titled *Faces in Skin* (now out of print), with Oyez. The startup small press wanted Snyder's work, but when the celebrated Beat poet realized he was short of material, he steered Oyez toward Dijkstra. Famous artists dog the man: following the appearance of his dissertation monograph on Stieglitz and William Carlos Williams, Georgia O'Keeffe invited him to her home in New Mexico and later to Los Angeles (O'Keeffe "never liked Bill Williams" but asked to meet the young scholar anyway). The eventual result was *America and Georgia O'Keeffe: The New York Years*, brought out by Knopf/Callaway in 1991.

In the mid-1960s, the University of California, San Diego, was just getting started—with a humanities faculty substantially plundered from Ohio State (they had had it with Novice Fawcett, who had bussed in agricultural extension agents to put down a free-speech vote). Dijkstra agreed to join the fledgling institution as an assistant professor and has been there ever since.

Dijkstra's mercurial intelligence is distinguished by a tentativeness refreshing among an academic crowd captivated by jargon and obscurantism. "I'm scared of coherence. Wherever you find coherence, you also find repression," he declares. His books are free of postmodern cant, but "dated" or "nostalgic" are not words that one would use to describe their method. A supremely confident writer, Dijkstra compares his style to moviemaking and jazz improvisation.

"It's the combination in jazz between knowledge—that is, extraordinary control over the instrument," he says, "and a willingness to explore that allows the musician to defy dualism and create a more dialectical kind of music. I structured each chapter in *Evil Sisters* like a jazz number: there was an introduction, a theme, an improvisation and a return to the theme at the end."

It shows. At nearly 500 pages, *Evil Sisters* is one of those books that skirts contradiction and collapse with every paragraph, every so often threatening to propose a Unified Field Theory of Culture before pulling back and indulging a fanciful digression that somehow reconnects to the main argument before developing a life of its own.

"Victoria Wilson, my editor at Knopf," he says, "had a wonderful attitude toward my range of interests. She more or less left me alone. *Evil Sisters* was something like six years overdue. She never once said 'When is this thing going to happen?' She said 'When you're ready.' She's let me do my own thing and interfered where necessary. The first *Evil Sisters* manuscript was 900 pages long, and she said that it 'could be shorter.' I had planned to call the book *Vamps, Virgins, and Material Girls,* but Vicki's advice that I stress the link between race and gender dictated that the book be restructured."

Perhaps the most prominent example of Dijkstra's range of interests is his vast collection of jazz albums which fills an entire wall in his tidy, modern house. There are thousands of snugly shelved examples of the best vinyl any jazz junkie could ask for in Dijkstra's floor-to-ceiling collection, along with hundreds of CDs and several turntables. Like any good audiophile, he knows exactly where everything is, apologizing demurely for showing off as he flips on a light switch to reveal the hard evidence of his passion but diving right in to produce an insanely rare Coltrane recording, *Cosmic Music,* pressed on the legendary saxophonist's own label. "I love jazz," he enthuses. "I loved it from the first moment I heard it. I had a naïve notion that all I needed to do was go to the United States and I would hear jazz on every corner."

In this extreme southwestern corner of the United States, a nation whose convoluted culture Dijkstra had adopted with reverence and glee, the smiling, cerebral, but perfectly accessible Dutchman can hear all the jazz he wants. He plays his own tune.

MATTHEW DEBORD
October 14, 1996

MARK DOTY

SOME WEEKS after the death of Wally Roberts, his partner of 12 years, the poet Mark Doty found himself wandering ruefully through Beacon Hill, the Boston neighborhood where he and Wally first lived together more than a decade earlier. Revisiting his old, moldering, rent-controlled brownstone, once home to numerous friends, Doty found it empty of all but two of the original tenants. "Where had they all gone?" he mused. "Disappeared, moved away, and mostly, of course, died; this was a house full of gay men, in 1981, and now it's a house full of no one."

That encounter forms one of several eerie set pieces from Doty's new memoir, *Heaven's Coast,* marking the poet's slow passage from sorrow to a kind of catharsis in the wake of his lover's diagnosis of HIV in 1989. (Doty tested negative simultaneously.) That diagnosis, Doty writes, "blasted the world apart," imbuing much of his subsequent poetry with imagery of impermanence, mortality and loss. For a time, it robbed him of his ability to write. *Heaven's Coast* (HarperCollins) is the story of his love affair with Wally and the unraveling of the world they shared, tracing Wally's gradual decline and Doty's own spells of despair, self-doubt, rage and fleeting hints of transcendence.

His white, clapboard house in Provincetown, Mass., is walking distance from the crashing surf, sand dunes and salt marshes, whose stark presence frames much of *Heaven's Coast.* But for three days a week, Doty lives in New York, teaching writing at Columbia and Sarah Lawrence College. It is there, in an apartment off Gramercy Park, a cozy nest of antiques, books and overlapping carpets, that *PW* catches up with him one blistering cold February morning.

Having published four books of poetry in less than a decade and received a slew of honors, including a Whiting Writer's Award and a T.S. Eliot Prize (of which he is the first Stateside recipient), Doty has risen among the ranks of the most acclaimed young, American poets. "Over the last two years," he says, "I've realized I can easily spend a lot of time being a poet, not writing poetry, but being a poet. And that can sort of be a job in itself."

At 42, his handsome, boyish angularity has softened. Dressed entirely in charcoal and black wool, one slender black boot resting on his knee, his thinning hair impishly balanced by long sideburns, and a goatee, Doty's 6'2" frame is draped on a couch beneath a portrait of James Joyce. As he walks us through his "long, checkered background," the veins on his wide forehead bunch up and his long fingers take flight from his lap, gesturing in the air or teasing the fabric of his wool trousers.

In *Heaven's Coast,* Doty traces his WASPy ancestry to the "archetypal American scoundrel" Edward Dotey, who arrived in Provincetown on the Mayflower in 1620, fought the first duel on American soil and filed the nation's first lawsuit. His more immediate forebears, he says, were "a ragtag batch of poor Southerners." Doty's father, an army engineer, dragged his family from suburban Tennessee to Florida, Southern California and Arizona. His boyhood feelings of deracination and difference, he says, may engender a subsequent book of prose. "I've been playing a little bit with some short pieces that have to do with having been a sissy," he says. "I remember very distinctly hiding during kickball to work on my embroidery."

Doty was married at 18, "in flight from both my family and a sexual orientation that scared me half to death," he writes. Moving to Des Moines, Iowa, he finished his B.A. at Drake, divorced his wife and arrived in Manhattan "in my little yellow Chevette" in 1981, with $600 to his name. Temping in New York, he took an M.F.A. in part time stints at Goddard College in Vermont, where he met Wally, a department store window dresser with "tobacco-leaf brown eyes."

As Doty tells it, his first volume of poetry, *Turtle, Swan,* was initially turned down by David R. Godine despite a plug from fellow Godine author Andre Dubus. "He said, 'Well, it's very nice, but publishing a book of poems is like dropping a rose petal in the Grand Canyon,' which is apparently something he says to everybody." A year later, however, Doty's friend Roger Weingarten, also a Godine author, convinced the publisher to reconsider that manuscript. Godine released the book in 1987; a second collection, *Bethlehem in Broad Daylight,* followed in 1991.

Pursuing an option in his contract to enter competitions, Doty submitted his next book of poetry, an early draft of *My Alexandria* (1993), to the National Poetry Series, which honors five poetry manuscripts annually with publication by a small press. It was chosen from roughly 1200 submissions by Philip Levine and published by Richard Wentworth, editor-in-chief of the University of Illinois Press.

Now the recipient of many more laurels, Doty, who judged the National Poetry Series in 1995, concedes that poetry contests don't matter a great deal to the commercial mainstream. "They can feel incestuous—it's of course a temptation for a judge to choose a favorite student or someone whose work he or she already knows." But in his view, poetry prizes are invaluable engines for launching new talents in a poetry scene that's grown increasingly decentered and heterogeneous. "We're in an age where there's an explosion of poetry readings, creative writing programs and opportunities to publish relative to, say, 20 years ago. This is a good healthy fecundity. What prizes do is point to interesting books. A first book of poems which appears without some kind of push behind it is fairly likely to disappear these days."

Doty nevertheless views with some ambivalence the hoopla surrounding National Poetry Month. "Anything which holds up the reading of poetry as a worthwhile activity is good for us," he says. "But one can't help but feel it's like having a poetry unit in school, which makes that topic seem like something that can be compartmentalized, when it should remain a part of life, a part of every month."

My Alexandria (1993) was a watershed for Doty. A series of luminous studies of urban and natural flux, it highlighted the influence on Doty of the poet C.P. Cavafy (to whose eroticized, native cityscape the title pays homage) and pondered, in tender, orderly stanzas, the metaphysical meaning of such evanescent things as a building being demolished; a jellyfish; a drag performance; a dog left to die by the side of the highway; an HIV-positive blood test.

"I felt *My Alexandria* was a real change," says Doty. After two poetry collections that focused primarily on his suburban upbringing, "I was casting around for what would come next. And what came next for me was looking around at the present and adult life, in a different way. It wasn't long after that change that Wally's HIV diagnosis underlined the need to pay attention to now."

My Alexandria, which received the NBCC poetry prize, also caught the attention of HarperCollins editor Robert Jones, whom Doty met in 1994 at a dinner in New York with James Merrill, following an Academy of American Poets reading. "I was thinking very seriously about the prose book at that time," Doty recalls. "And I wanted someone to work with me who would not be just a receptive editor, but who would actively help me give shape to the book because I was very uncertain about its final form." Jones bought Doty's prose work in progress, as well as his next poetry collection, *Atlantis* (1995), which earned the *Boston Book Review* Poetry Prize. "My only trepidation," says Doty of signing with a commercial house, "was that I was moving from a small press where poetry was a staple and a center of their activity to a large corporate publisher where poetry was a sort of lovely ornament." Those anxieties were quickly allayed, he notes. "Everybody that I've dealt with at HarperCollins has been enormously responsive and serious and really cared about the work. And Robert was willing to take the sprawling manuscript of *Heaven's Coast* and both respect it and help push it into shape."

Emotionally adrift after Wally's death in January of 1994, Doty stopped writing for a month. Eventually, sparked by a friend's solicitation of an essay for an anthology on gay men and religion, the memoir began to percolate. "I went to the computer and found that one sentence followed another. And this was at a time when I couldn't even read. That kind of focus hadn't returned to me. So it was a real gift to be able to write it."

Never having felt much of a facility for prose, Doty discovered that the inclusiveness and open-endedness of nonfiction allowed him "to meditate, to describe the experiences of everyday and investigate them for what kind of meaning or metaphor they might yield." He pauses, his hands grasping the air, as if molding a ball of putty. "I think that it would have felt in some way dishonest to the gravity and intensity of this time of grief to attempt to order it, to shape it in that very controlled way that poems are shaped. Potentially, it was an infinite book."

What finally emerged was a patchwork of essays spanning the year that followed Wally's death—a period of great turmoil, during which Doty was immobilized by a long-neglected back injury and lost another friend to a car accident. Framing his reminiscences of Wally, the homes they shared and the onset of AIDS are images drawn from the beach near his home—including encounters with seals and a coyote, in whose otherworldly gazes he imagines Wally's presence. While lacking the assurance and unity of Doty's verse, the memoir unveils the experimental process from which the language and tropes of his poetry spring. Full of references to Job and Dante, Doty's prose follows the same encircling, inquisitive rhythms that distinguish his poetry, putting the ailing Wally at the center of a kind of pietà.

"I felt that if I just used one voice, my own explanatory voice, the book would be too thin," says Doty. "So I wanted to let in the less refined voice that shows up in my journals and some of the more refined voices from letters from my friends or from other poets.

"My working method is to wander about in the world, looking for what strikes me. The object which is going to contain for me or represent or convey a question or an emotional state is a *given*," says Doty, dropping his voice in a kind of hushed reverence. "And writing a poem becomes a process of trying to understand what it is about that image that is compelling to me, because it's always more than beauty or novelty. If I'm moved to write about those jellyfish in the water or the mackerel in the supermarket, it's because something that I need to understand is coming to light through that vehicle. I think of it myself as leaning against the given. I'm given an image, and my job is to push against what I'm given until I understand it."

In Provincetown, with his two Labradors, Beau and Arden ("one golden and one beautiful, black, curly-coated creature") behind the confines of a white picket fence and a "lush tangle of climbing antique roses." he spends most mornings at his desk. "I need to work while I'm fresh and before my head has been stuffed with other language and business," he says.

Doty confesses to "an *absolute need* for the work. It's what I have to find some sense of order in the flux and wash of things. If I'm not writing, I don't feel good. I feel as if I'm going through the motions of living but not really engaging with things fully, not living deeply enough."

JONATHAN BING
April 15, 1991

Roddy Doyle

Given Ireland's pride in its artists, it's an alarming and bizarrely incongruous vision: Roddy Doyle, author of the 1993 Booker Prize winner, *Paddy Clarke Ha Ha Ha,* successful screenwriter and one of the country's most popular contemporary novelists, slips furtively through the streets of his native Dublin, anxious to avoid the remote but worrying prospect of physical attack from a seriously aggrieved public.

The first episode of *Family,* a harrowing, four-part television drama scripted by Doyle that graphically probes domestic violence and spousal abuse in a working-class Irish household, aired on national television in the summer of 1994, causing an immediate uproar. RTE, Ireland's state-operated broadcasting authority, was inundated with calls, most challenging the veracity of the material and castigating Doyle, author of a hugely popular clutch of comedic, family-centered novels, for daring to perpetrate a calculated slight upon the character of the Irish family. The series was addressed in the Dail (roughly the Irish equivalent of Congress), occupied inches of newspaper and magazine columns and was debated at length on every radio and television chat show in the country. In delineating the brutal vocabulary of marital violence in a representative Irish setting, Doyle had exposed a tender national nerve, and much of his audience was displeased.

"I had won the Booker Prize with a rather charming little book, I'd been given a sort of knighthood in Ireland and was something of a little hero," explains Doyle, whose new novel, *The Woman Who Walked into Doors,* out from Viking, revisits *Family*'s bleak social landscape and develops the story of Paula Spencer, the series' battered, 39-year-old mother of two. "Then comes *Family,* which is grim and sordid and violent, and it really shocked people because domestic violence is one of the great secrets of Irish society, and we'd much rather not have to admit it occurs.

"Going down to the shops to get the milk the day after the first episode was a bit of a struggle," he adds, smiling, but only half-joking.

"I was waiting for a car to skid to a halt behind me and to be hit by a hammer or something!"

Eighteen months later, the dust, both accusatory and sympathetic, has settled. But is Doyle about to aggravate his audience again? *The Woman Who Walked into Doors*—the title alludes to a common euphemism used by victims of domestic violence—traces narrator Paula's coming-to-terms with a 17-year marriage of violence, abuse and alcoholism. It represents a significant departure from the relative optimism and edgy, frequently scatological raillery of Doyle's previous urban narratives. Undaunted by the *Family* affair, however, the author contends the book is a natural progression from *The Commitments* (Random, 1989), *The Snapper* (Penguin, 1992), *The Van* (Viking, 1991) and *Paddy Clarke Ha Ha Ha* (Viking, 1993). The shattered beings of the new novel are "the flip side of the Rabbittes," Doyle says, referring to the disorderly but endearing family of his first three books.

"I didn't set out to write about domestic violence but I felt there was a whole lot more to Paula Spencer than what was on the screen in *Family*," he says. "I could imagine her, once she's gotten control of her life, joining a literary group or something and writing her own story. I thought it would be great for her to try and get back and 'account for' her life, to try to answer that question that must infuriate victims of domestic violence: Why did she get involved with such a brutal man in the first place?"

Now 38, Doyle is the very antithesis of the fanatical, anti-family subversive many critics declared him after *Family*. A soft-spoken, amicable father of two, he relaxes into a chair at the Dublin offices of his manager, John Sutton, and maintains the emphatic demeanor of an individual accustomed to an attentive audience—the fruits, perhaps, of 14 years spent teaching English and geography at a Dublin school. Sporting a single gold earring and marine-tight buzz cut that suggest less an ex-educator than a streetsmart urbanite from one of his own novels, Doyle is quick to smile and displays an open and disarming sense of humor. He ignores the dramatic posters trumpeting his Booker victory from the office walls and entertains us with the dispassionate air of a veteran interviewee.

The third of four children, Doyle grew up in Kilbarrack, a solidly working-class district north of Dublin's city center that would later serve as a prototype for Barrytown, the fictional locale of his first three novels. Qualifying as a teacher, Doyle began work in the same school he had attended as a youth, a stone's throw from his family home. He was, he says, "a fair, but strict teacher," and enjoyed the work. But, inspired by fellow teacher and playwright Paul Mercier, he made use of the generous vacation time afforded Irish educators to begin writing.

Commentators later cited his teaching career—which he quit the day *Paddy Clarke* was published—as the major source of his work, but while acknowledging its incidental influence, Doyle dismisses the suggestion that his writing taps directly into his classroom experience.

"I think it's true to say that without teaching, I would never have written *The Commitments*," he says. "I was confronted day to day by these kids and I tried to imagine them a few years on, without parental or teacher supervision. But after that, teaching became less important. *Paddy Clarke*, for example, had absolutely nothing whatsoever to do with my being a teacher, despite what everyone says." The literary inspiration, says Doyle, was the Richard Ford novel *Wildlife,* in which "a 40-year-old looks back to when he was 16 and his parents' marriage was falling apart. Also, my first child was born and, in anticipating his future, I began to think about my own childhood in a way I hadn't done for years, and all these wonderful images and memories came back to me. If you have to simplify things, they're the two reasons I wrote that book. Not because I was a teacher."

Doyle completed *The Commitments*, a rags-to-riches comedy about a Dublin soul band, in 1985. In 1987, smarting from rejections for a previous, still unpublished book, Doyle formed King Farouk Publishing with Sutton, a friend since university, for the sole purpose of publishing *The Commitments*. Three thousand copies of the novel were issued. It sold well in Dublin and beyond, thanks to strong word of mouth and enthusiastic reviews in local papers. Doyle forwarded copies and reviews to all the British publishers he knew, and the do-it-yourself approach paid off: Dan Franklin at Heinemann signed him and published *The Commitments* in the U.K. The novel became the first in a sequence familiarly known, and eventually published, as *The Barrytown Trilogy* (Penguin, 1995).

"One book grew out of the other really," says Doyle. "Sharon Rabbitte [sister of the protagonist in Doyle's debut], has only one line in the first book—'go and shite!'—but I thought, 'here's a good woman!' and it struck me as a good idea to write about her becoming pregnant in *The Snapper.* Then, as I was writing, her father became a more important character and began to take over the book in many ways, so I decided there was a book in him too. *The Van* came out of that and it just happened to be three books. I fought the idea of calling it a trilogy at first, but the books are actually at home together."

By the time *The Van* was completed, Doyle had gathered a significant following, particularly among young, urban readers—he groans audibly when reminded he was hailed by some critics as a spokesman for a whole generation of Irish youth. "I'm a spokesman for nobody except myself—and even then I'd get a third party to speak on my behalf!" He had also begun a career as a screenwriter, receiving a co-writer's credit on Alan Parker's 1991 film version of *The Commitments* and completing the screenplay for Stephen Frears's 1993 screen version of *The Snapper. The Van,* also directed by Frears from Doyle's script, will be released later this year. But filmwriting remains a secondary career, and Doyle considers himself a novelist who happens also to write screenplays.

"Ideally, I like working on two things at the same time," he says. "I was working on the screenplay for *The Van* while I was writing the new book, and it was a good antidote because with a screenplay, the work is not as intense at all. Often it's just a question of fleshing out the treatment and putting in the dialog."

Paddy Clarke Ha Ha Ha marked Doyle's first move away from Barrytown and the Rabbittes and, behind its charming, nostalgic veneer, hinted directly at some of the darker themes his newest work displays. The novel, also his first foray into first-person point of view, examined a 10-year-old narrator's growing understanding of his parents' marital difficulties. Characteristically, Doyle downplays the importance of the Booker Prize to his career.

"I don't want to be dismissive, but on one level, it didn't mean a hell of a lot. For example, *Paddy Clarke* will be translated into 21 different languages, but the bulk of the contracts had been signed before the Booker. Foreign translations haven't made an enormous impact financially anyway, but where the Booker has made a difference is that the first time I went to the States there were very few newspapers interested in talking to me. Afterwards, I was talking to all of them, so the books were more prominent in the shops." (The recent excerpt from the new novel in the *New Yorker* may be further evidence that Doyle has achieved greater recognition in this country.)

Doyle is equally dismissive of suggestions that the Booker brings pressure to repeat the successes of *Paddy Clarke Ha Ha Ha.* His British editor, Dan Franklin, whose faith in *The Commitments* Doyle rewarded by following him from Heinemann to Secker & Warburg and finally to Jonathan Cape, is a stabilizing factor: a book-by-book contract grants Doyle complete freedom to write without interference and at his own pace. The arrangement works both ways, however, Doyle says—his publishers receive thoroughly edited manuscripts that need little further polishing. He claims, in fact, that the editing work with Franklin on *The Woman Who Walked into Doors* lasted only two hours. Doyle's editor in the U.S. is Caroline White. Doyle notes that John Sutton also acts as his "manager" here, dispensing with a need for a Stateside agent.

As for the new novel, Doyle says, not without a degree of relief, that he is certain it won't prompt controversy on the scale of *Family*. His confidence is such that he is already considering another Paula Spencer book.

"I think Paula is a wonderful person, and although the subject matter insists hers is a dark book, she is actually a very funny woman with a great sense of sarcasm," he says. "I'll probably let her be for another five years or so and then come back and see how she's coping with the rest of her life. I've always wanted to write a love story, and that might be the opportunity."

Then again, Doyle's idea of a love story is certain to have a disturbing, rough-and-tumble side. And one suspects that he'll only be content if it ruffles a few feathers along the way.

COLIN LACEY
March 25, 1996

95

RIKKI DUCORNET

WE CAUGHT UP with Rikki Ducornet while on a visit this past May from her home in Denver to Bard College in Annandale-on-Hudson, N.Y. What started as a convenience of timing and geography turns out to be more fortuitous. Ducornet was born in nearby Canton, N.Y., in 1943. Her father taught at Bard. She lived on campus all her young life. It is her alma mater.

Over the past three decades, Ducornet has written and illustrated some two dozen books, but it's only recently that her name has won wider attention in this country. This year has been particularly fruitful. She was a 1993 NBCC fiction finalist and also was awarded a Lannan Literary Fellowship, which aside from the prestige it brings, allowed her to take a sabbatical from teaching English and creative writing at the University of Denver to finish *Phosphor in Dreamland* (Dalkey Archive Press). It is the story of a 17th-century Caribbean island and its resident photographer/poet which, like all of Ducornet's work, mingles the radiantly fantastical and the grotesque into a richly metaphorical novel encompassing good, evil, time and life.

Enveloped by patchouli and dressed in brown and black that match both her hair and huge eyes, Ducornet makes for an earthy, elemental contrast to the pastel chintz of "The Pink House," the on-campus bed-and-breakfast where she is staying. Snuggling into the overstuffed couch, with her legs folded under her, she starts to talk excitedly. Her voice is very high and airy and becomes slightly higher when any one of a number of enthusiasms overtakes her.

And she has *many* enthusiasms, the result of a peripatetic life and perpetual curiosity. Ducornet, who majored in fine arts with a minor in medieval studies while at Bard, has wide-ranging interests in philosophy, religion (the more esoteric, the better), art, literature and politics. Her early interest in writing, however, waned after an "extraordinarily destructive" college writing class. "I was working on a novel at the time and I stopped writing for 10 years . . . The teacher was very vicious in his criticism. He would say things like 'painters think this way, writers don't think this way.' I thought, 'Oh well, that's the proof. I'm really not a writer, I'm a painter.'"

As a precocious teenager, Ducornet had become interested in surrealism because of a connection with the work of Max Ernst, Paul Eluard, and Salvador Dali—"early Dali," she's quick to add, "before he became marketed and proFranco and was quite rightly kicked out of the surrealist movement." She began corresponding with a surrealist group in Belgium, then with a group called Phases, a successor to CoBrA. For several years following college, Ducornet devoted herself to art, showing with Phases in surrealist exhibitions around the world and illustrating books.

Although she continued illustrating books—recent examples include Robert Coover's *Spanking the Maid* (Bruccoli Clark, 1981) and Borge's *Tlön, Uqbar, Orbis Tertius* (Porcupine's Quill, 1983)—she hasn't been as involved with surrealism recently. While she says she doesn't "much like labels because I think they're so easily misunderstood," her connection to surrealism's tenets remains strong. "I have a visceral belief in the power of the imagination for aesthetic, political and psychological change," she says, adding that she is addicted to the "exquisite corpse" games that surrealists use to tap the imaginative power of the unconscious. And she is also committed to radical leftist politics—"people forget that surrealism was very rooted in politics."

It was politics that inspired Ducornet to write her first book of poetry. She had grown up in a politically aware family: her father, Gerard De Gré, was a social philosopher who worked with Heinrich Bluecher (Hannah Arendt's husband) at Bard; her mother, Muriel, was the host of what Ducornet describes as "an enlightened women's program" first on local radio, then on television. She was, says Ducornet, "very interested in politics, in fact she worked for Gore Vidal's first political campaign when he ran for the House."

That book of poetry, *From the Star Chamber* (Fiddlehead, 1974) was "rooted in politics . . . it was precipitated by reading about a woman who had been tortured in a Greek prison at the time of the *coup d'etat* in Greece . . . The story was so shocking I found myself writing all night long." She included a few short stories (also politically inspired) that would later appear in *The Complete Butcher's Tales* (Dalkey, 1994), but at the time she was taken with poetry. "Poetry is a curious process; it seems to me to get down to the darkest spaces very quickly, down to the bones of things. It's a baptism of fire in a way for a beginning writer—it was very much that experience for me."

It was also politics that kept Ducornet on the move. Her (now ex-) husband, Guy Ducornet, a French Fulbright scholar she met at Bard, had protested French involvement in Algeria, postponing his military service until the war was over. The couple then moved to Algeria for what Ducornet describes as "the French equivalent of the Peace Corps." After two years, they moved briefly back to the U.S., but in 1968, prompted by the escalating war in Vietnam and the murder of Martin Luther King, they decided to leave for Canada. "In some ways I feel now it was a very naïve thing to do but I felt a desire to leave the U.S. for a cleaner climate politically," she says.

In 1970, the couple departed Canada for France, and the tiny town in the Angevin department of Maine-et-Loire, which Ducornet would call home for the next 15 years. At the time, says Ducornet, "it was like living in the 19th century—there weren't cars, nobody had washing machines." But the village's 19th-century character extended beyond the absence of cars and household appliances. "It was very evident when I first arrived that the church was all-powerful the way it had been for centuries." Combined with her experiences as a woman in Algeria's stifling Muslim culture, the encounter instilled in Ducornet a fascination with—and strong distrust of—orthodoxy. "I became very anti-clerical in a kind of French way," she says. No surprise, then, that her upcoming projects include a book of short stories about "imperialism and the activity of missionaries which is part of imperialism."

While running the family pottery studio, Ducornet began work on *The Stain,* her first novel and the first part of what would become the Tetralogy of Elements. Set in France in the late 19th century, *The Stain* was lauded by Robert Nye in the *Guardian* as "the most brilliant first novel that I have read in years. . . Imagine *Cold Comfort Farm* revamped by Ronald Firbank, or [Gabriel Chevallier's Rabelaisian farce] *Clochemerle* sent up rotten by Angela Carter after a night on the sloe gin, and you may have some small notion of its outrageous flavour."

While the characters and situations can be macabre and chimerical, the Tetralogy is charged with political reality. In a 1994 review in the *Nation,* Charlotte Innes called the Tetralogy "linguistically explosive and socially relevant." The books address very real historical horrors—Nazism; vicious, exploitative colonialism; environmental degradation; subjugating orthodoxies—but they also tackle a more cosmic evil. "I think that's what I'm always muddling over: the problem of evil and problem of control," she says. Which is true. At one point, she muses that evil proceeds from "terror of the uncontrollable chaotic universe. It's the incapacity to accept space and time and accept that everything is in constant mutation, wanting to freeze it once and for all." Later she says that she believes "evil comes out of terror of the other . . . a desire to control the other, whether it's a child, or another group, or a country, or another tribe, or the natural world."

About half-way through *The Stain,* Ducornet began to think of it as "a book of earth, a book of sin, involved in gardening. It's also about the earth in a gnostical sense of the world as a cage and place of perdition. As I came to the end I thought, the next one will be fire." *Entering Fire* was followed a few years later by water (*The Fountains of Neptune*) and in 1993 by air (*The Jade Cabinet*). In retrospect, Ducornet thinks the idea of doing the Tetralogy of Elements came from reading French philosopher Gaston Bachelard, whose "law of four elements" claimed that all images could be tied to one of the four elements. But as behooves an artist with a penchant for surrealism, each book was inspired by a single waking or dream image: a huge leaping hare she saw in France and a dream of childbirth inspired *The Stain*; a dream of drowning led to *Fountains of Neptune;* and a visit to an enormous orchid greenhouse on the outskirts of Paris influenced *Entering Fire.*

What informed her NBCC fiction finalist, *The Jade Cabinet,* was a person—Lewis Carroll. "I love the Alice books and read them obsessively." When the University of Denver first invited her to teach, she immediately suggested a course of Borges, Nabokov, Angela Carter, Kafka and others that she called "Looking Glass Fiction." "In a way *The Jade Cabinet* came out of previous research I had done for the course. I felt intimately enough engaged with Lewis Carroll to dare present him as a character, which is very risky business."

Phosphor in Dreamland arose from research on Jonathan Swift for a lecture she gave at the University of Trento in Italy. "I realized the lecture's themes were similar to the themes that I was developing in *Phosphor in Dreamland,* the body as a corrupt sphere: Phosphor's terror of the body, terror of women, his inability to love. And, of course, that was very much Swift's personal story."

Ducornet's publishing career has been as unsettled as her life. Her poetry and short stories were originally issued by very small presses. *The Stain* and *Entering Fire* were both published by Chatto & Windus in the U.K., which sold the rights to the former to Grove; the latter to

City Lights. *The Fountains of Neptune* was published by McClelland and Stewart in Canada, which then sold rights to the book to Dalkey in the United States, where she's been since. "I feel I have a home."

Larger presses are once again expressing an interest in Ducornet but it's an interest she says she doesn't return. Her experiences with big publishers haven't been entirely happy. An editor at Harper & Row solicited her first novel, liked it, but had no support from his colleagues. When Chatto & Windus was acquired by Random House UK, she recalls, "they dropped me because I wasn't making enough money."

She feels comfortable at Dalkey, and Steven Moore, her editor there, has allowed her to illustrate her books (as she did with *Phosphor*), and to submit not disk or typescript but handwritten manuscript. "Not only does Dalkey type up the books, but they really love them. The books are beautiful, they keep them in print. I don't feel I have to write a bestseller in order to live. It seems ideal to me."

After the interview, Ducornet wants to take a walk around the campus to see if she can find her childhood home. While she doesn't remember exactly where it is, she does recall that it was a low-lying building from the first half of the century and that it had a porch. After a few false starts she finds it—squat, yellow and with a porch. Outside is a sign, obviously added in the past few years, that says "Lewis Cottage." For a moment, anyway, it seems the "uncontrollable, chaotic universe" has ordered itself for her.

MARIA SIMSON
October 9, 1995

ANNIE ERNAUX

ALL WRITERS DRAW ON their lives in their work, but few subject their pasts to the kind of unflinching examination that Annie Ernaux does. Whether she is describing her adolescent transgressions or her mature, infatuated affair with a married man, she never heroizes or editorializes, never tells readers what they should be feeling.

"Displaying one's feelings in a book," she says, "is immodest. It's like crying on the shoulder of the reader." Ernaux leaves much up to the reader, even what exactly her books are: "It doesn't matter to me if something I've written is called a novel or autobiography," she says. "It's readers who decide if what they're reading is one or the other."

Which is all well and good, but it does make it hard to predict what she will be like as a person. From the outside, Ernaux is easy enough to characterize—tall, slim and extremely beautiful. After spending six hours on a plane, on her first day of a series of lectures, readings and signings promoting her new book *Exteriors,* (Seven Stories), she arrives dressed simply in slim gray pants and a black turtleneck. Her gray-streaked brown hair falls straight down her back, and she wears a minimum of makeup; her high cheekbones and large, sad eyes don't require further enhancement. She is, in short, elegant without being coiffed. Gracious and soft-spoken, she punctuates her lilting French conversation with easy laughter.

Ernaux was born in 1940 in the little Norman town of Yvetot, where her parents owned a small store. Her parents tried to give their only child the advantages they never had, sending her to parochial school and eventually to Rouen University in Normandy's capital.

Ernaux's mother, although not, she points out, a cultured woman, "had a profound desire to learn things and a taste for words. She really encouraged me in my studies and in my reading." But she also speculates that her mother was not solely motivated by love of learning. "For her, being a writer was a great thing—there was nothing better. So in some ways, I became a writer to please my mother."

Becoming a writer didn't happen right away. There were several abortive attempts at fiction: a few short stories ("rather tragic." she says), and a complicated novel, influenced by the nouveau roman, that she finished when she was 22 but never published. Aside from a journal she kept when she was 16, there was nothing autobiographical.

For the time being, it seemed she was destined to be a "wife/mother/teacher" as she once described it in her novel, *A Frozen Woman*. She married Patrick Ernaux in 1964, and shortly thereafter had a son, Eric, and four years later another son, David. She followed her husband, getting teaching jobs in Annecy, in the Haute-Savoie near Switzerland, and in 1974 moved to Cergy-Pontoise, a town some 27 miles outside of Paris.

"I always thought about writing," she says, "but my first real work, *Cleaned Out,* wasn't finished until I was 32." In fact, she had mulled it over for several years after her father died. Told from the perspective of a young woman who has just had an illegal abortion, *Cleaned Out,* published Stateside by Dalkey Archive in 1990, describes a childhood and youth in Normandy that parallel Ernaux's. The novel is a raw, often angry depiction of an adolescent girl's burgeoning sexuality; of her distance from, and her disdain for, her uncouth parents. Ernaux was now a professional, a teacher with a comfortable living doing a respected job, but the cost had been a rupture with her working-class past.

"When I was 15," she writes in the novel, "I was dying to open their eyes and tell them that the real world was polite, well-dressed and clean. I couldn't stand being the only one who hated [how we lived]. Let them see their customers through my eyes, and our home, if you could call it that, so awful, so humiliating." It's a painful revelation of teenaged nastiness combined with guilt: "I hated myself for not being nice to them, for not being gentle and affectionate." That social and cultural divide, which her parents enabled and from which they suffered, informed much of her subsequent work. Ernaux describes her 1977 novel, *Ce qu'ils disent ou rien* (her only work not yet translated in the U.S.), as concerning a young woman's sexual awakening and her growing recognition of social inequality. And her 1981 novel, *La Femme gelée* (published in 1995 as *A Frozen Woman*) went a step further into the narrator's marriage and early motherhood. (This and subsequent novels were published in the U.S. by Four Walls Eight Windows; but, with the recent parting of the ways between John

Oakes and Dan Simon, the Ernaux backlist and future titles are being published by Simon at his new house, Seven Stories.)

While she had been working on these two novels, however, Ernaux had had another project in mind. "Right after finishing *Cleaned Out*, I wanted to write about my father, but I was having trouble." She began a novel in which he was the main character but then abandoned it. "Halfway through the book, I became disgusted. I had started to write about my father in the same style in which I'd written my first two novels, and I began to see this as a form of betrayal. If I wanted to be true to my father's life, to a life that was dictated in indignities, a life that did not lend itself to novelistic transformation, then the narrative had to be spare and factual."

Starting with the 1983 publication of *La Place* (or *A Man's Place*, as the 1992 U.S. edition was called), Ernaux's books were indeed more streamlined. This recounting of her father's youth as a Norman peasant and his struggle to better himself as a factory worker and a small shop owner only to watch the daughter for whom he worked so hard drift away, is not so much a narrative as an accretion of descriptive scenes.

A Man's Place, like Ernaux's subsequent books, was also increasingly punctuated by her thoughts on writing. "Just before writing *La Place*," she explains, "I began asking myself about the relationship between writing and the reality I was describing. I began thinking that it would be good to include these thoughts in the text—even if it seemed a little intellectual." She wanted to show her readers that writing didn't just appear out of thin air and so began, as she says, "to include all the marks of its fabrication."

Le Monde called *La Place* " a fine literary success"; *Figaro* deemed it "Exceptional . . . intense and extraordinarily powerful." Later that year, *La Place* won the Prix Renaudot, probably the highest award for a French writer after the Prix Goncourt.

But the prize was in some ways too late. Her father was dead and her mother was deteriorating rapidly as a result of Alzheimer's. Ernaux and her mother had never really talked about her books. "She never said anything about *Cleaned Out*," recalls Ernaux. "I think it was too hard, too violent for her and she preferred to say nothing. It was a way of maintaining good relations between us. At the same time, I think she was truly divided because, while she certainly wasn't pleased by the book, her daughter was now a writer."

Even more than her father's death, her mother's decline spurred Ernaux to write. The first book to result was basically a distaff version of *La Place. Une Femme* was published in 1987; four years later, as *A Woman's Story*, it was both a *New York Times* Notable Book and an *L.A. Times* Fiction Prize finalist. But Ernaux had already started on another tack while her mother was still alive, one that eventually resulted in her most recent book, the 1993 *Journal du dehors,* published here as *Exteriors.*

"My mother was no longer really of the world: her connections had disappeared," recalls Ernaux. "Her illness had been a real ordeal for me and I found myself constantly wanting to get outside of myself." Ernaux began to keep a journal of events, scenes, people she saw on the train, in town, or in the news. In retrospect, she recognized that these distinct episodes were interconnected: frequently, they involved people who were—like her mother—somehow outside, on the fringe. Although she tried to write without imparting any particular emotional significance to the record, she admits that the *Journal du dehors* (journal of the outside) was also a *Journal du dedans* (journal of the inside).

Her mother's illness also inspired her to write another, yet unpublished, journal which more explicitly describes that decline, and Ernaux also has plans for another book on her adolescence, though one written in a different style. But she is now in her 50s, which raises the question of why—after 30 years of an adult life that has included a successful career, a marriage, the raising of two children and, in 1985, divorce—she continues to write about events of the 1940's and '50s. "I'm not trying to write a real autobiography," she explains. "I don't believe that the feelings, experiences, encounters that happen to me are interesting *because* they happen to me. Rather they are things that happen to a person, who happens to be me.

"I make use of the various parts of my life. My divorce, for example, is something I haven't dealt with, or at least not yet. I don't have the desire to write about it. I don't know why." It's clearly not because she is shy. After all, as Ernaux points out, "I did write about a *Passion simple.*"

Passion simple is the 1991 book (published in 1993 as *Simple Passion*) that chronicled a recent love affair Ernaux had with a married man. During the affair, she had written a journal which, with her customary honesty, she later used to create a painfully vivid account of a grown woman's obsessive, embarrassing and all-too recognizable preoccupation with every nuance of her lover's behavior. It was for her the most terrifying book to write. As she describes the trepidation with

104

which she looked over the manuscript, she occasionally groans and buries her face in her hands.

But however painful it may have been, the book sold well for her French publisher, Gallimard. The Renaudot-winning *La Place* had sold 150,000 copies; *A Woman's Story* sold 100,000; but then *Simple Passion* doubled that with 200,000. Ernaux had garnered sales and awards, and her books were being taught in classrooms.

By any measure, Ernaux is a successful writer. But she doesn't really play the part as it often manifests itself in France. She continues to live in Cergy, which isn't exactly chic. It is, she says, "a very functional town, a town whose design shakes up our conception of beauty. Above all, it is a place with no sign of the past, a town without memory."

She also continues to work preparing students for the literature portion of their teaching certificates through the Centre National d'Enseignement par Correspondance, where she has worked since 1977. She says that on some level she would like to stop, but it's not likely to happen. "Because I need to make money to live. As things are now, I am extremely fortunate: I can write books and not have to worry about whether they make money or not. I'm free," she says. *"Mon métier, c'est ma liberté."*

She is also largely independent from the often confined French literary scene. It is, she feels, a "little world" alien to the lives of most of her readers. "I believe that writing has nothing to do with these little ceremonies. In the final count, writing is an attempt to understand through words the things of this world. It is an attempt to create links between people."

In *A Woman's Story*, Ernaux recalls meeting her aunt weaving drunkenly and unable to speak a single word. In the book she says, "My writing would never have been what it is had I not met my aunt that day." Expanding on this she says, "once one has confronted reality that difficult, that disturbing, you can't write light things, novels or works divorced from what's real. Writing can't be a luxury or a game, or anything but a serious endeavor, that takes measure of, or tries to take measure of, the sadness of the real."

MARIA SIMSON
December 9, 1996

105

CONNIE MAY FOWLER

AFTER A HARD winter, the sea oats are returning to the shore outside Connie May Fowler's rambling beach-front house at Alligator Point, an hour's drive from Tallahassee, Fla. The writer eyes the grayish tufts, which look like tumbleweeds stuck in the sand. "Florida's topography is unique," she says. "People have a hard time appreciating subtle, quiet beauty."

With long blonde hair, pale skin and catlike, celadon eyes, Fowler's own quiet appearance suggests a china-doll fragility. But don't be fooled. At 37, she is a survivor who has overcome a destitute and difficult childhood, become a crusader for Florida's wetlands and is the author of three novels that reveal beauty and meaning beneath the obvious and discarded. Avocet "Bird" Jackson, the young narrator of her new novel, *Before Women Had Wings,* (Putnam), also wrests hope from an abusive and impoverished childhood. In the dilapidated trailer where she lives, Bird prays: "Dear Jesus, wipe Mama's memory clean. Don't let her come home and beat me."

Bird's mother does beat her. She also beats Bird's sister. After Bird's father, an alcoholic country singer, commits suicide, Bird's mother takes her daughters to Tampa for a new start, but it isn't a happy one. She drinks and terrorizes her daughters. It's rough stuff—and a lot like the author's past.

Like *Sugar Cage* (Putnam, 1992) and *River of Hidden Dreams* (Putnam, 1994), Fowler's new novel is born of real events. "Of course there's a lot of Bird in me. That was my childhood," says Fowler. Like Bird, Fowler lost her father as a child and lived with her sister and alcoholic, abusive mother in a trailer outside a Florida hotel. But in *Before Women Had Wings,* she has sought to transmute a personal and painful truth into something valuable. Setting down her coffee cup, Fowler explains: "You don't want a novel to be a recitation of facts, of reality. It's a lump of coal you hone into a diamond. Writing a novel turns it into art, not gossip."

Fowler has always written, though she found it easier to articulate her past after her mother died of liver cirrhosis 17 years ago. "It's a form of survival." she says. "As soon as I could put sentences together, I was making sense of what I knew. I write because I have to. My sister battles with anorexia, my brother with alcoholism. I battle with depression, but the writing helps me through that. The writing gives me balance."

Speaking has been the hard part. Already shy as a girl, Fowler suffered from a speech impediment. "I think that happened because I was so afraid of saying the wrong thing, of provoking another attack by my mother."

Though Fowler speaks without a trace of a stutter, she still finds speech to be a problem. "I couldn't talk about *Sugar Cage* at all, and with *Before Women Had Wings*, I'm walking on eggshells. There are sections I know I can't read in public." Fowler has perfected her public readings by practicing particular sections again and again until she feels comfortable with them. "I call it creating a callus. If I start to feel a break in the callus, I concentrate on the sound of the words, not their meaning. Usually it works. Sometimes it doesn't. I'm very private," she insists. "A lot of writers are. That's what's so ironic about what we do. On the page, we take off our clothes."

While *Sugar Cage* skirted some ugly family truths, *Before Women Had Wings* confronts them directly. The book is a culmination of writerly skill and personal strength. "It's taken me a while to get here, to tackle it, to open up a vein," she says. "I'm glad this wasn't my first book. It wouldn't be what it is." Fowler poured out the first draft in a six-month frenzy. When it was over, she says, smiling, "I was very relieved. I gained a lot of appreciation for Bird, for the fat, hopeful kid. I learned to love her."

A Florida native, Fowler maintains her privacy in a wooden blue-roofed house in Alligator Point. Filled with folk art, bright colors and warm wood, the former army barracks has a huge deck overlooking Alligator Bay. The author's husband, Mika, a photographer, has a darkroom there, and she has an office, an enclosed gazebo with a window on each of its eight sides. Three dogs and an enormous cat roam about, adding to the air of a cozy, nurturing life.

Despite her disciplined work schedule, Fowler believes that she is "having my childhood now. This house means a lot to me. I need more land than house, I need to be connected to things."

After growing up with so little, Fowler does seem bedazzled by her success, both literary and personal. At last, she has found faith and joy, so to speak: *Before Women Had Wings* is dedicated to Faith Sale, her editor at Putnam. Joy Harris is Sale's good friend and Fowler's agent. Fowler credits them both with going far beyond their official duties. They have been her friends and advocates. "They have opened the door for me. Faith has taught me so much about writing. Just because a writer gets published doesn't mean she's at the pinnacle."

As an undergraduate at the University of Tampa, Fowler began publishing poetry in literary journals and subsequently earned a graduate degree from the University of Kansas in 1990. In retrospect, however, she says she had little trust in her ability to write until Carolyn Doty, a writing teacher at Kansas, urged her to find an agent for *Sugar Cage*, her first novel and graduate thesis. In a storybook scenario, Fowler sent the manuscript to Joy Harris because she liked her name. Harris took the book and pitched it to Sale at Putnam. Fowler laughs, recalling how she and her husband took a meandering drive from Kansas back to Florida to find a frantic note from her agent saying Putnam wanted *Sugar Cage* but where the hell was the author?

Fowler, who is about to hit the road for a 15-city book tour promoting her new novel, cites several independent bookstores for having generated interest in her work. She believes that independent bookstores, and the word-of-mouth publicity they foster, are vital to the success of fledgling novelists like herself. Fowler worries about them being swallowed up by chains and superstores. "It has ramifications far beyond business. Without them, we're all reading the same 10 books."

While many authors get involved with the whole process of marketing, Fowler is glad to turn it over to Putnam. "What happens to a book is so separate from writing it, so separate from me." She doesn't need to be market-savvy. She has Faith. "Faith's a great businesswoman who goes to bat for her authors. She's proud of their books. That's the best way to sell them."

Fowler is at her desk by 7:30 or 8:00 a.m. every morning. "I keep going until I'm out of steam. Sometimes that's three hours, sometimes it's 10. The magic part is pulling it out of the back of the brain." While all her books are written in first person, *Sugar Cage* and *River of Hidden Dreams* employ multiple points of view. *Before Women Had Wings* is purely Bird's story.

Although it articulates a young woman's experience it isn't in Fowler's opinion, "a chick book. I know people need to categorize, to tape identifiers on to things, but the very term suggests this isn't quite up to par with that stuff written by dead white guys." Fowler eschews such labels as feminist, political and Southern and is just as uncomfortable with terms like poor, alcoholic and abusive. She has fought stereotypes all her life.

Fowler is much more interested in digging beneath the surface and finding the elusive part within people that "we can love." Her characters, like her own parents, "may commit despicable acts, but I don't want to hate them. I want to understand and forgive them."

The healing power of storytelling is something she knows well. "When my family gets together, we tell stories," she says. Often, they tell the same ones again and again. It is a way of mourning the past, of forgiving. "I write to reaffirm the past. All I have left are the memories, the stories, and sometimes that's not enough. I don't even know what my father's voice sounded like."

Telling stories is for Fowler a way of explaining the world by creating a personal mythology. "I'm captivated by the world of myth. How, in a technologically driven society, do we nurture any notion of spirituality?" asks the author who, in Bird, has created a character who feels "jilted by Jesus." "It's hard to do, and I'm impressed by people who pull it off. It dovetails with my fascination with folklore, with giving the world a greater meaning."

The most spiritual character in *Before Women Had Wings* is a loving black woman named Miss Zora, who becomes not only Bird's secret friend but her guardian angel as well. A healer and recluse, Miss Zora's yard is strewn with the bones of dead birds. "When winged creatures cross over to the other side, their bones need to be cared for, prayed over, so that as they journey through God's many skies, their wings will be sheathed in gold," she tells Bird.

Miss Zora is the author's tribute to the writer and folklorist Zora Neale Hurston, who has appeared in one guise or another in each of Fowler's novels. She is also modeled on a woman named Vivian, who cared for the author as a child. "She was my first experience with unconditional love," Fowler sighs. "Nights were still awful, the fighting and all, but my days were wonderful because of Vivian."

Sugar Cage and *River of Hidden Dreams* required a good deal of research. Her new novel needed very little. But it did require Fowler to revisit her past, some of it literally. She went back to the trailer parked outside Travelers Motel in Tampa. It's as bleak now as it was when Fowler was a girl, as bleak as she portrays it in the novel. "It was weird, sort of depressing. I was stunned by where we had lived," she says. "At the time, it didn't seem that bad. It's very small, not even a real trailer, just a travel trailer, awful, a tin can. And the hotel pool is all filled in and mucky." She manages a laugh. "Boy, when I was little, I just loved that pool."

While many would be inclined to flee a place with unhappy memories, Fowler knew she could never leave Florida for good. The landscape has always had an uncanny resonance for her. One of her first junior-high poems featured the line: "The voice of the trees spoke." "Florida has a grand, mythic sense," she says, peering out at the water.

Fowler participates in a Florida Arts Council project called Making Florida Home, where she seeks to make non-native residents feel as much a part of Florida as she does. She also speaks out on behalf of preserving Florida's natural resources. "It's something I got from my mother. She was an activist, very liberal, always taking up causes," she says. "Even though I never had anything as a child, I always had a connection to wild Florida."

While Fowler is wistful about her past, she is also forgiving. She hopes the forgiveness works both ways. "Sometimes, when I talk of my parents, of their negative nature, I feel guilty. The other part of me thinks if there is life after death, part of that process is gaining a divine enlightenment. They understand what I've done and they hail it." Fowler tears up for a moment, wiping at her cheeks with an impatient hand before regaining her composure.

"I want the reader to come away from my books with a sense of humanity renewed," she says. As she escorts an interviewer around the side of her house, the wind whipping back her hair, she stops suddenly and points to a cluster of plants all but hidden in shadow. "Look, my poppies are starting to bloom."

She bends down and displays their pinkish blossoms. As always, Fowler can find beauty underfoot. It's just a matter of knowing how to look for it.

ELLEN KANNER
May 13, 1996

MARSHALL FRADY

MARSHALL FRADY burst on the literary scene in 1968 with his campaign biography *Wallace,* a Faulknerian profile of the fevered, racebaiting populist George Wallace. Now, after several books (including a Billy Graham bio) and a long detour into television, this Southern clergyman's son returns to the bookshelves with *Jesse: The Life and Pilgrimage of Jesse Jackson,* an intimate look at the deeply contradictory preacher-politician, published by Random House.

"It's the biggest book I've written, not just in bulk," reflects Frady, 56, his drawl tempered by his years outside Dixie. "He's the largest-scale character. What made the book worth doing is how hugely mixed he is, and how richly mixed." In *Jesse,* Frady describes Jackson as "a combination of the prodigiously gifted, the naive, the splendidly aspiring, the rankly boorish."

Frady calls his eight-year venture into Jesse's world a "Moby Dick of an enterprise;" indeed, he describes tracking Jackson as "a kind of migratory, open-ended tournament of talking." (For the first time, he used a tape recorder.) Frady is no slouch at talking himself, his parenthetical excursions better suited, perhaps, to a breezy porch than the fancy New York hotel suite he occupies when meeting an interviewer. Tall, dark-browed and given to wide ties, Frady wears his bulk well; his profile, mixing flesh and crag, suggests a Southern Baptist version of a Roman centurion.

Jackson has long clashed with the press, often expecting partisan loyalty yet meeting dyspeptic scrutiny. Given that, Frady says his launch into *Jesse* was surprisingly simple. "It was just a matter of letting him know I wanted to do a fully dimensional piece," says Frady, who garnered a book contract and *New Yorker* assignment before getting Jackson's cooperation. "There was almost no negotiation. It was just talking," he says, adding with a grin: "We're just two South Carolina boys."

Frady had met Jackson briefly in the 1960s, when he was among those reporters who detected "that shimmer of portent" in the young Martin Luther King acolyte. Jackson didn't remember Frady, but he was, the author reports, "somewhat beguiled by the synchronicity," since Frady grew up just 26 miles away from Jackson's hometown of Greenville, S.C., and went to college there. Indeed, as Frady trailed him on his global peregrinations, Jackson got no small satisfaction from telling his audience that Frady, born more privileged in the Jim Crow South, was following *him* around.

Frady entered the scene in late 1988, watching Jackson stump for the doomed Dukakis campaign, so one might think he anticipated a 1992 Jackson bid. Frady says no: "I thought it might be a better book if he could be taken out of that strictly political analysis, and I could really write about him as an extraordinary character."

Moreover, adds Frady, had Jackson been campaigning, "he may have been a little less accessible." Jackson, in fact, may have welcomed such scrutiny. Frady reports that Jackson has long failed to deliver contracted autobiographies to several major publishers, as his initial efforts eschewed introspection to preach on the page.

Frady finds Jackson's drive deeply linked to his double dispossession—he was born not just black and poor but also illegitimate. Backtracking through Jackson's life, he records Jackson's uneasy tension between crusading outsider and system-seeking insider, his groundbreaking presidential campaigns in 1984 and 1988, and he delves into Jackson's questionable behavior bearing King's bloody shirt after the assassination and his widely rumored womanizing. With no campaign afoot, Frady found drama in spur-of-the-moment trips abroad, as Jackson pursued his role as freelance emissary to Armenia after the 1988 earthquake and to Iraq as the Gulf crisis broke.

"It's the Stanislavsky method," Frady says of his journalistic technique. "To the degree possible, you become the person. The trick then is, at one point, you somehow have to withdraw. That can be personally expensive, because inevitably you have feelings of double agentry.

"But I don't know any other way to do it, to move people about the really vital truths about a person or a conflict," he observes. "It's also great fun."

In *Jesse,* Frady argues that journalists, focusing on Jackson's notorious "Hymietown" remark or his dalliance with Louis Farrakhan, haven't done Jackson justice. Still, he hasn't heard Jackson's response to the book and admits to some trepidation. Some critics wouldn't predict offense. While the *New York Times Book Review* and *PW* praised the book, the *Washington Post Book World* called it a hagiography. Deeming Frady a romantic, the reviewer seized on episodes absent from *Jesse* in which Jackson's posturing suggested more racial reflex than the moral depth that Frady finds.

Frady bristles at such criticism. In the beginning of *Jesse*, he acknowledges—in one of several judicious personal interpolations—his own romanticism about the civil rights movement. And he argues to *PW* that his portrayal of Jackson in recent years, in a section titled "Adrift," encompasses much criticism. Still, Frady's ultimate judgment—that Jackson suffers most from "the absence of any distinct social front of crisis to engage that would match his King-scale aspirations"—should fuel long debate about his subject.

Frady's romantic streak developed long before the civil rights movement, as a young man facing small-town suffocation and the unsmiling rigor of religion. "I would put a Calvinist Southern mother up against Sophie Portnoy any day," he proposes.

Fired by reading *For Whom the Bell Tolls* and a short *Time* article about Castro's revels, the 15-year-old Frady decided to escape for Cuba. He took three bus rides to Florida; on his last effort, he went on to Havana, trying to trade his suit for a bicycle that would convey him to destiny in the Sierra Maestra mountains. He never made it, but the "not unwoozying carnival" of Havana, he once wrote, left him "transcendentally transformed."

But it was literature, not ideology, that fueled such drive. Frady describes his father as "one of the best talkers and orators and language men that I've ever heard." Even as he bridled at Southern provincialism, he imbibed his father's preaching thrice weekly. To the Biblical brew, he added Edgar Rice Burroughs, then Hawthorne, Dickens and Steinbeck. Frady moved on to Hemingway and then—"like turning into the full face of the sun"—Faulkner. For a quarter century, critics have termed Frady's lush and looping prose Faulknerian; Frady, not unseriously, now wonders whether his style now merits an eponymous term.

At Furman University, Frady majored in English and history, and helped edit the newspaper and literary magazine. After deferring a fellowship for a year of newspaper work in Atlanta, he found himself at the Iowa Writers Workshop. He left after a year, concluding that campus writers wound up writing only about similar types.

113

So he joined *Newsweek's* Atlanta bureau, from which he covered Wallace's 1966 gubernatorial campaign and felt a book blooming. *Wallace* began as a novel, but Frady decided the material was too good to fictionalize: "It struck me just uncannily like *All the King's Men* back into life." The critical praise astonished him, Frady recalls. "I was just so damn elated to be writing a book."

Frady moved to the *Saturday Evening Post* and then followed friend Willie Morris to *Harper's*. For *Harper's*, Frady reported from the Middle East, eventually compiling his work into *Across a Darkling Plain: An American's Passage through the Middle East*, published in 1971 by Harper's Magazine Press. Frady acknowledges today that the book suffers from "Mailerism". (In it, Frady refers to himself as "The American").

Frady went on to *Life* and freelance articles, then took four years to write *Billy Graham: A Parable of American Righteousness,* published by Little, Brown in 1979. The idea emerged from Frady's Watergate reportage, which led him to think that Graham had served as virtual chaplain to the White House during the Cold War. A year later, NAL, which had republished *Wallace,* published *Southerners: A Journalist's Odyssey*, a collection of Frady's magazine work.

In the wake of *Billy Graham,* Frady helped ABC do a *20/20* piece on Graham and promptly caught the TV bug, moving from Atlanta to New York to work as chief correspondent for *ABC News Closeup* from 1979-1986, and then for *Nightline* for the next two years. While Frady acknowledges the lure of the "manic energy and urgency of TV," he rues its impermanence: "It will steal your interior."

Then again, Frady reflects, it was that "electronic Babylonian captivity" that led Ransom's David Rosenthal (now publisher at Villard) to contact him for what would become *Jesse*. "So who can question these inscrutable choreographies?" Frady muses. Recalls Rosenthal, "I'd read a great deal of Marshall, and was rather in awe of him. I'd seen his work on *Nightline,* and it reminded me: Why isn't this man doing a book?"

Frady's TV career also led him to Los Angeles in 1988, as he began to work on a film about a televangelist, based on his *Nightline* reporting. While the film languished in development, Frady (who has three grown children) met his fourth wife, Barbara, a film and sound editor, and has remained in Lotusland. "It's a strange place," Frady allows, citing the distances he feels from compatriots local and national.

Though most of *Jesse's* long gestation can be attributed to Frady's reporting effort, he acknowledges that "it took some while to learn how to write again." He wrote the three-part *New Yorker* profile in six months, then spent another two years on the book. He also narrated the *Frontline* special on Jackson that recently aired on public television.

Frady's schedule was to write from 8:00 a.m. until 5:00 p.m. daily, with a break for lunch and reading, using pencil on a legal pad, then polishing on an electric typewriter. He praises Random senior editor Ruth Fecych as a "sorceress" who curbed his "tendency to over-oratin'," while he deems Rosenthal the "impresario." Rosenthal not only decided to reissue an updated *Wallace* but also recommended agent Frank Curtis to Frady, who had been represented previously by Robert Lesher and Sterling Lord.

Despite critical praise, his books have never earned him much money, Frady says. Easing this effort, the *New Yorker* paid for his trips, including the venture that had Frady pack quickly for Iraq, watch Jackson haggle with Saddam Hussein and his henchmen to release Western hostages. This drama became *Jesse's* extraordinary final chapter; Frady rewrote the final scene—his witness of the oft-posturing Jackson weeping privately—some 20 times.

Frady now has fiction back on his mind. He's long had several novels in progress, notably one about a group of Confederate refugees who, refusing to accept loss, follow their antebellum dreams to backwater Brazil. These days, fueled by reading the Gospels, Frady is writing about Jesus through the voice of his disciple Andrew. Not institutionally devout, Frady confesses to enjoying some Christian TV and gospel music.

Soon, Frady says, he and Barbara will move from L.A., probably to the Southeast. He's still unsettled. At age 30, in *Darkling Plain,* he wondered if he "would merely wind up as a writer in that limbo of success between mediocrity and glory." Today, he says, "I would strongly suspect that haunts every writer.

"I feel good about *Jesse,* that it was delivered in fullness," he muses. "But there's always the next one."

NORMAN ODER
July 1, 1996

MAVIS GALLANT

NOT EVERY expatriate writer in France likes to sit at La Coupole, the clean, well-lighted Boulevard Montparnasse brasserie. Some like to while away their off-writing hours across the wide thoroughfare at the smaller, darker Cafe Select. Mavis Gallant, a Montrealer who's lived permanently in Paris since 1960, is one of them. That's where she decides she'll be most comfortable talking about her fiction and particularly about *The Collected Stories* that she and Random House have put together.

A shortish woman, all rounded lines, with hair pushed back in a cropped russet wing on either side of her head, she's waiting at a small outside table. She has an umbrella, equipment anyone accustomed to local weather always has on hand, and she's watching a street person— a man dressed as if on a safari—obstreperously attempting to direct traffic from the middle of the boulevard. If you know anything about Gallant's work and the cast of keenly observed everyday people crowding it, you immediately wonder if this *type*, so serendipitously handy as a symbol of Gallic folly, will show up in a future story.

Of past yarns there's no small supply. And almost all of them have appeared in the *New Yorker*. "The *New Yorker* has published 119 of my short stories," Gallant reckons with a certain amount of visible pride. "Not counting seven excerpts from novels," she adds in a light, sweet voice, holding seven fingers in front of her face like a schoolgirl with important information. "I have never believed there was such a thing as a *New Yorker* story—I don't write like Nabokov or O'Hara or Updike," she insists. (There is no question, however, that she is a stellar member of the literary pantheon.)

In addition to those 119 stories, the *New Yorker* has published excerpts of two novels— *A Fairy Good Time* (Random House, 1970) and *Green Water, Green Sky* (Houghton Mifflin, 1959)—since 1951, when her first piece, "Madeline's Birthday," was accepted under Harold

Ross. When asked why that debut piece is not included in the new collection, Gallant replies, without further comment: "a fetish." There *are* 52 in her compilation, however, the basic criterion for selection being: "if I thought they could be republished." She adds: "Then friends say, be sure and have *that* story and make sure you have *that* story. They may not remember the title, but I know which one they mean."

A more inclusive volume, Gallant declares, "would be too expensive to buy, and I don't like a big book myself." (What she means is that at just under 900 pages, her new collection is still much less than the 1500-page foundation stone it might have been had her entire oeuvre been rounded up.) She expresses concern that readers assuming the book contains all her stories will be dismayed to learn otherwise. Then, seeming intent on finding something to worry about, she asks: "Do you think anyone will read it?" Assured there will be readers, she goes on to pooh-pooh the idea of a second volume to accommodate at least some of the remaining stories. "I don't think that anybody would dream of bringing out another."

Gallant's stories almost all take place in Paris—many of them in the Left Bank's 15th arrondissement near where she's currently chatting—or in her native Montreal. A fair number of the latter involve a young woman called Linnet Muir, whom the storyteller is quick to admit is "90% me." She explains that just as *Mavis* is a bird, so is *Linnet*. "I thought I might use *Merle*, because a merle is also a bird, but it made me think of Merle Oberon."

The Montreal about which Gallant writes has been and will continue to be the Montreal she knew as a child in the 1930s. "I can see St. Catherine Street as it was, with street cars." She makes a point of returning every year, but "when this generation dies," she says, "the young don't interest me. The young ones are like Americans living in Canada. I think [the cause is] television. I'm sure they make love like porn movies."

Conversation is interrupted when a sudden shower makes sitting outdoors a bad idea. Reseated inside, Gallant looks out the window at the rain running down in haphazard streams and says, "I like Montparnasse. The people are raffish." She scans the boulevard. "Grippes lives just down there," she notes. Grippes, as it happens, is not an actual human being but a character who began appearing in her stories around 1981 and who will show up in the novel Gallant is to publish next year called *Clowns and Gentlemen*. "That wraps up the male race," she quips.

Given the precise language and exacting ironies of her prose, one wonders just how rapidly she writes. Surely, there must have been times when Gallant was publishing so frequently she had to turn pieces out with great speed. "Oh, no," she says, laughing, but also shocked at the very idea. "It's fragile, fiction. It takes me a long time to write a story. From three months to three years." She likes to let them sit awhile before she goes back to them. "Then what is dead, you'll see it immediately," she explains. "You have to be ruthless. When in doubt, cut it." She also says: "I write every day. I get up early in the morning and do it. People say it's discipline. It isn't."

The content of those long-simmering stories undergoes a metamorphosis from her original inspiration, she says. She finds that fictionalizing an incident or a character gets closer to the truth she wants to convey than merely reporting unadorned observations. "It's better to sound plausible than merely in touch with the facts," she comments.

Fiction, which she composes on an old Brother AX 15 typewriter, isn't all she takes her time about. "I've been writing a book on Dreyfus for 20 years," she says. "The *New York Review of Books* has been waiting 10 years for my piece on Céline, because I want to get it right."

Gallant, now 74, prefaces her personal history by remarking, "I'm simplifying, because it's too complex to tell one's life, really." She was born in Montreal to a mother who was "basically American" and a father who was "a would-be artist," though he had a job his daughter only became aware of much later.

Raised a Protestant, she spent most of her student years at a Roman Catholic boarding school. She whiled away her early career as a journalist on the *Standard*, a weekly English-language newspaper. After ending a brief marriage, she recalls: "I decided I had to do something before I was 30." Though she had never written fiction, she determined she'd be a fiction writer. At the paper, she says: "Everyone thought I was completely nuts, and if I saw a young woman today, I would tell *her* it's completely nuts." But she knew what she wanted—"I can't remember a time when I wasn't writing, or making things up"—and she knew she wanted to do it in Europe. Just about the time the *New Yorker* started buying her stories, she headed for the Continent.

Her first submission was rejected, she recalls, on the ground that its subject matter—wartime marriages and breakups—had become "threadbare" by the early 1950s. Her second, however, was bought, and the good news came with a complimentary note from William

Maxwell. "I read it and I re-re-*re*-read it," she says. "No living editor, I think, could add an iota to its original charm and humor."

That kind of encouragement was the beginning of decades of shared admiration, and now Gallant characterizes Maxwell as a man "not in competition with other writers—and that is rare. He didn't interfere, or if he did, one didn't notice it." What did she think of Maxwell's own writing? "I think he should have won the Nobel Prize. I can think of two people who should have won—Maxwell and Eudora Welty."

Gallant also has nothing but kind words for subsequent editors like Daniel Menaker, who once said that tending her prose "was like editing ice cream." (She dedicates her collection to both Maxwell and Menaker.) About the late Joe Fox, her Random House editor, she remarks: "We were together for 35 years, and we never had a cross word." She's also grateful to Kate Medina, who became her editor when Fox died last year. "Did you know that editors are a legacy?' she asks, commenting with some quizzical delight on the unexpected ways of the publishing industry. Her association with agent Georges Borchardt has lasted more than 25 years. "I don't like changing," she says in typical understatement.

Almost no one who's crossed Gallant's path provokes harsh criticism. For instance, she chuckles when she thinks about Janet Flanner, the *New Yorker* colleague who, under the pseudonym Genêt, wrote a regular letter from France. Gallant does a gruff-voiced imitation: "'You don't know what you're talking about,' she would say, and I would say, 'I do, too.'" Gallant, who's known them all—or at least many of them—remembers a letter she had from statesman Pierre Mendès-France, whom she'd written when trying to collect information on the Dreyfus case and French anti-Semitism. She'd been told that over time it had abated, but Mendès-France wrote her he "couldn't understand how someone had told her that." (She claims she's finally ready for the Dreyfus book and jokes that she'd only resume research if "people come along and tell me one of two things—that he was guilty or that he wasn't Jewish.") Her opinion of Céline? She replies quickly: "What I don't like about him is that he attacked Jews when they were down and out. He raved away at people who couldn't defend themselves. That's what I think is swinish."

Gallant is prepared to comment on myriad subjects, and that includes revealing the details on many another real-life story she knows—"Most of them were told to me on this terrace," she says, gazing around the Select. Among stories she won't divulge, though, are reminiscences swapped by concentration camp survivors belonging to a local association called *L'Amicale de Auschwitz*, whom she often encounters at the cafe. They gather, she explains, because "they are afraid of being forgotten." Why does she remain silent on this topic? "Because I wasn't there," she says with finality. She pauses a moment. "My friends are a very mixed thing," she says. "You name it. I don't like being in a milieu. It's confining."

A waiter arrives to straighten out a tab that got confused after the table-shifting. Gallant confronts him about the outside waiter's bad behavior: *"Il pleuvait—on grincait* [it was raining—he made a fuss]." Despite her perfectly rolled French, Gallant almost never writes in the language. "I have to protect my written English. I can write 'Thank you for the exquisite lunch' or 'Thank you for the flowers.' But that's all I will do." Is she at all well-known in her adopted country? "No." She rethinks and revises: "The FNAC [a popular chain of discount stores] always has six or eight of my books, and they wouldn't if they thought it was wasting shelf space." She can and will elaborate on the subject. She considers that one of her French translators was foisted on her by an editor at her French publisher, Fayard, and that another, Suzanne V. Mayoux, gets "as close to the original English as one can get without being English-speaking."

It's time for Gallant to leave the Cafe Select. She retrieves her umbrella and starts to the streets, which are now drying in the late afternoon sun. Would she ever leave Paris for good? *"Americans* always go home," she replies, leaving an unspoken thought hanging in the rain-washed air as if it were a subtlety in one of her stories: she, of course, is *not* American.

DAVID FINKLE
October 7, 1996

OLIVIA GOLDSMITH

OLIVIA GOLDSMITH is in a hurry. She just got in this morning from her cottage in Vermont, where she had been working on her new novel between bursts of promotion for her current one, including satellite radio interviews. As we emerge from the elevator at her Upper East Side apartment building, a *Newsday* reporter, notebook poised, is sitting beside her on the sofa. Goldsmith glances up. "Go look in the bedroom!" she shrieks. There are clothes all over the floor, a garment bag half packed. It is just after 4 p.m., and at 7 she has to catch a flight to Paris, where she will confer with her French publishers. Then, on her return four days later, she's off on what she whimsically refers to, in a little blues ballad she has just written, as "Book Tour Hell."

Life was not ever thus. There are heartrending passages in *The Best-seller*, Goldsmith's bright-eyed bustling novel about the publishing business, just out from HarperCollins, that tellingly illuminate the loneliness, despair and outright neediness of the unpublished writer (one of her would-be bestseller writers even kills herself). And indeed it's something the author, however glowing her present career, has been through in spades.

Goldsmith is a bouncy, vivacious woman around the end of her fourth decade, with soulful dark eyes, a hugely infectious laugh, an air of comic self-deprecation and the ability to turn on a dime from outrageous mockery to sincere and passionate sentiment. She sometimes cultivates a sexpot image, flirts at the drop of an eyebrow and chooses to pose for author pictures with a flashy blonde wig. Another side of her is represented by the fact that she calls one of the business accounts she now employs to handle her very considerable earnings Plain Brown Wren Productions.

After a conventional New York childhood—the eldest of three sisters, Goldsmith was born in the Bronx, went to public school on the Upper West Side, then to New York University—she undertook a

121

highly unsuitable first marriage ("We were married for five years, then it took me seven, and every penny I had, to divorce him"). She also became a consultant for computer companies and subsequently formed an acute distaste for corporate America that has run through all her work so far. "I've always believed I wrote social satire, but of course there's no niche for that. People prefer to think of it as funny fiction, but there's another problem there, because that's not something women are supposed to do."

However it might ultimately be classified, the inspiration for her first and, so far, still best-known novel, *The First Wives Club* (S & S), came out of a combination of factors: her horror at her own bad marriage; the fact that many of the corporate CEOs she met would confide in her because she's a woman ("I developed a real understanding of these lonely guys who are raping the earth as a substitute"); and a cover story in *Fortune* magazine that described how many top corporate executives were marrying again. She refers to their new spouses as "trophy wives who were younger and much more glamorous than those poor worn-out ladies who had raised their children, helped them build their careers, and then been cast aside in favor of a newer, sleeker model you could show off to the other guys."

She wrote it partly in Vermont, partly in London, where she went to live for a couple of years while she tried to get the book out of her system ("I wrote a lot of it on top of the #22 bus, back and forth from Islington"). In *The Bestseller*, she says, she wanted to get across the anxiety of a struggling writer—"the worry about how to pay the damn bills." After a lot of knocking on doors with *The First Wives Club*, she found an agent "who said he could get me a million dollars, but he wanted me to make a lot of changes. As if these poor women didn't have enough troubles, I had to give one a retarded daughter, another a cat suffering from leukemia. And anyway, it didn't work!" she says with glee. The book came back from many publishers, and it was not until, in a development increasingly common these days, the manuscript found its way to Hollywood, that doors began to open.

"It was like an epiphany," gloats Goldsmith. "These three powerful women producers—women!—fighting over my book that wasn't even a book!" The three were Dawn Steel, Sherry Lansing and Paula Weinberg, and one day she had a call from an agent asking her to choose: "Who do you think shares your vision most closely?" Skeptical, and desperate for money, she replied: "Whosever check clears first." In fact, Lansing, then at Paramount, threw an extra $50,000 into the pot—"I think she realized how strapped I was"—and got the deal. After that, five screenwriters did various drafts ("People yell at screenwriters, and I didn't want anyone yelling at me!") and now, nearly six years after its 1990 publication, *First Wives* is set to open as a movie, with a stellar cast that includes Diane Keaton, Bette Midler and Goldie Hawn. No, Goldsmith didn't want "creative control," or a part in the script (though she does have a bit in the movie). "I figure if you put your kid up for adoption, you don't complain about the private school they send him to."

Suddenly, with word of the movie deal, publishers were eager to see the manuscript, but Paramount, Simon & Schuster's parent company, wanted S&S to have it. Michael Korda and Ann Patty were both keen, but meanwhile the book, which is told from several different viewpoints, went for line editing to an editor who virtually rewrote it, "what he called," snorts Goldsmith, "evening out the voice, getting rid of all the voices I'd achieved. I thought: He's been an editor for 20 years, and he doesn't understand POV? Give me a break!"

Next up was *Flavor of the Month* (1993), "which I guess you could call biting the hand that feeds me." The book was a study of how Hollywood, Goldsmith declares, abuses women, "who are never young enough or beautiful enough." Unfortunately it appeared just as Ann Patty, who had finally prevailed as her editor at S&S, lost her Poseidon imprint, and the book disappeared into a virtual void. "No ads, no promo, nothing." Meanwhile, Goldsmith had been exploiting her English stay for all it was worth. A fierce Anglophile, she says of the English: "They dig what I'm getting at much better over there; they understand that satire is in fact something people do." Her English agent introduced her to Eddie Bell, who runs HarperCollins in London, and the two hit it off. "He took me to lunch to talk about what I was going to write for them, and I thought he'd be perfectly horrified at the thought of a book about publishing." Here, she falls into a perfect imitation of Bell's dulcet Glaswegian tones: "'Olivia, we believe you can do anything you want to; no one has a finger on the pulse of women today like you do.' 'What about Terry McMillan?' I asked him. 'Who's Terry McMillan?'"

In fact, her next book, which she wanted to call *Designer Jeans* but which was published as *Fashionably Late* (1994), was again a take-the-lid-off-people-who-are-screwing-women-book, about the fashion industry. It did well enough, but Goldsmith's heart was set on a publishing saga, and fortunately for her, Jack McKeown, Harper trade chief in New York, gladly signed on, and executive editor Larry Ashmead became the good shepherd. "You couldn't have a better editor than Larry, because he loves publishing gossip and knows where all the bodies are buried. He shared lots of wonderful stories with me, but of course he always puts his own twist on them."

The Bestseller is at once a sharp-tongued look at some publishing types—there is a ne'er-do-well scion of a famous publishing house who is fudging the sales on his own tired books to support an extravagant lifestyle; a ruthless female editor-in-chief who uses sex as a weapon and keeps a vodka buzz going all day with the spiked Snapple in her office refrigerator—and an affectionate tribute to the power of publishing to transform lives.

"I was one of those kids who could never read enough, and I see the book as a kind of Valentine to the book world. I'm so grateful to be a part of it, but at the same time there's a lot of bullshit around." The Frankfurt Book Fair, the ABA convention, the role of *PW* reviews in a book's success, even independent booksellers' problems with the chains all play roles in *The Bestseller* and, for people who can't wait to see if they're among the real-life people who play bit parts in the book, there's an index listing several hundred names. Be warned however; fewer than one out of 10 people who find their names in the index will actually find a presence in the book.

It's all a bit of a game, like the cover of the British edition, which shows members of the Harper London staff and the author herself as a wickedly conniving party group, waving champagne glasses. This pleased Goldsmith considerably more than the New York effort, which shows the book at the head of a clearly recognizable *New York Times* bestseller list and prompted an immediate demand for its withdrawal from the newspaper. "I'm the Ford Pinto of authors!" cries Goldsmith. "They send me out with my gas tank next to the ignition, to see if it explodes!"

The latest party game in publishing, among those who have secured advance galleys of the book, has been to try to figure out who is who among the remorseless comptroller (who suggests taking 10 pages out of each new title as an economy move), the embittered senior romance novelist living on past glories, her greedily duplicitous agent and so on. Goldsmith is understanding but impatient. "These are archetypes, not stereotypes," she insists. "Nobody is drawn entirely from one person"—though she acknowledges that some of the harsh things said at a particularly acerbic editorial meeting were reliably reported to have been uttered at one of Richard Snyder's sessions at S&S.

Yes, movie rights to *The Bestseller* have already been sold. But she notes: "If it takes as long to reach the screen as *First Wives,* there won't be many of us left to see it by then." A much faster movie deal (they're already casting) was inked for the book she is still struggling to finish, bought by Hollywood on the basis of a five-page outline. This is to be called *Marrying Mom,* and "it's all about aging and death and sexuality. What else is there, after all—except perhaps food?" Seriously, or jokingly, it's Goldsmith's attempt, her first, to do what she calls "a real door-slamming family farce, with a sunny ending like— well, *All's Well.*"

Which leads to a few moments' earnest discussion—about the maximum she can sustain—of just what it is Goldsmith does. "I don't think it's art; maybe I didn't start early enough for that. But I do think of myself as a good craftsman—craftsperson?—with a sense of morality that I'd like my readers to feel. Okay, it's soup, but it's nourishing, well-prepared soup. Sure, I wish it were more, but it pays the rent."

It's now less than two hours to flight time, and the limo driver is already waiting outside as we leave, carrying a copy of Goldsmith's "Book Tour Blues"; and it's easy to imagine her belting it out, much as her heroines did in the very successful *First Wives* movie:

> What do I wear? What do I say?
> How can I do this every day?
> They're very kind, the bookstore folk,
> But they're all slowly going broke.
> I'm here to sign what they call "stock."
> It's seven books, and I'm in shock.
> Oh, I've sweat blood and tears
> But when that pub date nears
> No way to still my fears
> Of Book Tour Hell.

JOHN F. BAKER
August 5, 1996

WINSTON GROOM

UNLIKE FORREST GUMP, who would have run all the way from Point Clear, Ala., to Los Angeles, Winston Groom took the train. He boarded the Sunset Limited in nearby Mobile with his laptop computer and settled his rangy 6'6" frame in a sleeper cabin for the two-day trip. Away from telephones and the celebrity hoopla associated with the Academy Awards, where he was expected to make an appearance, Groom was free to work feverishly on the final edit of the much-anticipated sequel to his phenomenal bestseller, *Forrest Gump*.

It would be the only quiet time he would have, these 48 hours before the train reached its final destination. Upon arrival, there would be speeches, a flurry of media interviews and a private dinner party with the cast and crew of the blockbuster movie. He would be personally feted by Tom Hanks, who wasn't Groom's first choice for the part of Forrest Gump but who so wonderfully proved him wrong. And, of course, there was Oscar night at the Los Angeles Shrine Auditorium, where the film garnered six top awards, including the trifecta of Best Movie, Best Actor and Best Director.

The day after the star-studded night of celebration, the 51-year-old Groom is still chuckling. The Academy Awards are "Hollywood's version of Mardi Gras," he observes in his deep-South drawl, "with just a bunch of dressed-up folks having a grand ol' time." And to think much of the attention orbited around a comic novel he wrote in six weeks nine years ago about an idiot who unwittingly stumbles into stardom.

That Forrest is being touted as an American icon and has triggered a multimillion-dollar sideshow in T-shirts, chocolate and cookbook sales will always surprise Groom. He's not complaining. "If you get hit by a load of hay, you better make hay, because the time will come when they'll forget you and move on," he comments, with no trace of rancor. "I'm not naïve. I know that in New York or California, you're only as good as your last book or movie." Still, he admits he's somewhat irked by pundits who have used his fictional character's platitudes to make a point. "The funny thing is, I was only trying to write a book, not send a message," he says.

Groom is the first to credit the smash movie for the resurgence of his 1986 book, which garnered good reviews and respectable sales of 40,000 when it was first published by Doubleday. But the situation changed in the summer of 1994, when the film was released and Pocket Books reissued *Forrest Gump* in paperback. Sales to date are 1.7 million and climbing, followed by the hastily written spinoff, *Gumpisms: The Wit and Wisdom of Forrest Gump.* "It takes something to make a book a bestseller, and just being good doesn't always guarantee it," he admits. *"Forrest Gump* is the same damn book I wrote years ago, only it took a movie to get it discovered. And that's okay with me."

Whether history repeats itself with his newest book, *Shrouds of Glory* (Grove/Atlantic), remains to be seen. This time around the ever-experimental Groom switched gears and constructed a nonfiction account of the last great campaign of the Civil War, detailing the Confederacy's final, desperate struggle to turn the tide after the fall of Atlanta.He had always been intrigued with General John Bell Hood's doomed attempts to preserve the Confederacy—particularly after discovering that his own great-grandfather had been involved in some of the events—and knew he could translate his excitement into a readable book.

"My intention was to write something that appealed to a wider audience than Civil War nuts. This story was perfect because it had all the elements: sex, violence, honor," Groom says. Just in case people didn't make the connection, the decision was made to put "author of *Forrest Gump*" under Groom's name on the cover. Just in case.

Although the character he made famous has become a household word, Winston Groom is not, which suits him just fine. His demeanor is much like his name: that of a pure Southerner who spent enough years in New York to know he's more at home among shrimpers and swampy bogs than among Wall Street power brokers and gleaming skyscrapers. What he likes to tell people is that he did his stretch of time in the big city, and now he's out on parole. And what better place than Point Clear, pop. 2,125, a sleepy inlet on the eastern shore of Mobile Bay where he and his wife, Anne-Clinton, are overseeing construction of a maintenance-free home among stately magnolia trees.

"It still has its charm, but I can remember this place when it wasn't so chi-chi," Groom reflects. He grew up in Mobile, where his father was a lawyer, and he always looked forward to the summer months when the family would come across the bay to their vacation home to enjoy the cooler breezes and slower pace. Here is where he learned how to hunt and fish, two sports that followed him into adulthood. Those gentle memories are what drew him back to this coastal community in 1986, after living in revved-up places like Washington, D.C., New York and Vail, Colo. And when encroaching development invades their idyll, the Grooms will move on to yet another undiscovered paradise. "I give it 10 more years," he predicts.

Groom was expected to follow in his father's footsteps as a lawyer. With his striking resemblance to Franklin Delano Roosevelt, as observed by the *New York Times,* the red-haired Groom could have cut quite a figure in the courtroom. But at the University of Alabama, he edited both the literary and humor magazines. After that, the legal profession was never a consideration.

After college, Groom went to Vietnam in 1966, serving a 13-month stint as a second lieutenant in the infantry. He doesn't dwell on his wartime experience, only to say "I did my job and got the hell out of there." He also brought home enough memories to parlay into his debut book and two others down the road. "I suppose I've made a half a specialty of writing about war," Groom says of his battlefield books. "But if you're going to do something that nuts, you might as well find a way to turn a dollar on it."

In true Forrest Gump fashion, Groom landed his post-Vietnam job covering police and courts at the now-defunct *Washington Star,* though he had never worked as a reporter and didn't even know how to type. He almost didn't survive that first year, recalling the "terrible hours, low pay, distasteful work." Eventually, the disciplined Groom became good at journalism, earning a reputation for his smooth prose and comic timing. They caught the eye of the *Star's* writer-in-residence, former *Harper's* editor Willie Morris, who convinced Groom to quit the business and write the book he had long talked about. Morris would later say his advice to Groom was one of the smartest things he had done.

In retrospect, Groom admits it was risky to walk away from a steady paycheck so he could move to New York and write his book—especially since his focus was Vietnam, which at that time was a pretty unpopular subject. But the beauty of being naïve is not knowing any better, so once again, in Gump fashion, Groom took the plunge.

With the encouragement of Morris and writer James Jones, Groom wrote *Better Times Than These.* It wasn't a personal memoir of the kind so many returning vets are inspired to write, but rather a view of the war as seen through the eyes of an entire rifle company.

Morris brought the manuscript to agent Theron Raines, who immediately sensed raw talent. His hunch proved right. In 1978, Summit Books brought out *Better Times Than These* to critical praise. Some 60,000 copies sold in hardcover, an impressive figure for even a veteran novelist.

Groom hung around New York for the next eight years, immersing himself in the Manhattan-Hamptons literary set. Aside from the partying, he learned a thing or two about writing from colleagues like Kurt Vonnegut, George Plimpton, Joseph Heller, Irwin Shaw and Truman Capote. During this time, he wrote several books, including *As Summers Die* (Summit, 1980), a novel set in Mobile, and *Only* (Putnam, 1984), a memoir about his beloved dog, Fenwick (both will be reissued in paperback by Pocket); as well as *Conversations with the Enemy* (Putnam, 1984), the Pulitzer Prize-nominated collection of interviews with former Vietnamese soldiers that he wrote with Duncan Spencer.

Coming back home to Alabama in 1986 was a good thing for Groom. It is where he wrote *Forrest Gump*, inspired by a story his father had told him about a retarded man who could only do one thing well, and that was play the piano. Sequestered in what used to be slave quarters on a friend's property in Point Clear, Groom wrote fast and furiously, completing the manuscript in just a few weeks. "I had a few notes jotted down in the afternoon, and by midnight the first chapter was finished," he says, recalling the day he began *Forrest Gump*. "What I've learned about writing is that it either goes quickly, or it goes badly."

Perhaps an even better consequence of returning was meeting Anne-Clinton Bridges, an effervescent Mississippi beauty whose grandmother had been historian Shelby Foote's first girlfriend. They have a lot in common—literature, antiques and enjoying good times with friends—so that their 23-year age difference isn't noticeable. Besides, Groom knows he wouldn't find many women who would share their beds with their lovable but large sheepdog—Forrest Gump.

Their temporary residence, a rented wood farmhouse built in the early 1800s, is a shrine to all things Southern, from Confederate memorabilia to larger-than-life oil paintings of a distant relative in a velvet hunting cloak. Groom is clearly at home among his antiques and family heirlooms, and he's fiercely proud of the history and culture that define him.

"There's a reason Southerners make good storytellers," he says. "We're surrounded by big families and old friends, and we spend a lot of time talking. Those stories we live by may get embellished over the years, but they make it into our interior and become part of what we are."

The next few months will be a whirlwind for the author. He's got the Point Clear house under construction, as well as a new home in the North Carolina mountains. There's the promotion for *Shrouds of Glory*. In the fall, Pocket Books will publish the Forrest Gump sequel, an undertaking that follows Forrest's life with his son for the 15-year period that begins with the ending of the original. After that, Forrest Gump will be retired for good, and Groom will be tackling yet another genre. Right now he's toying with the idea of a five-generation historical potboiler set in Central America.

"Agents, publishers, critics, they all get upset when you do something different. If you make it big with something, they want you to write the same book over and over again," he says. "Well, I'm an eclectic anachronism, so I'm going to write what I damn well please. And when it stops being fun, I'll stop and practice law."

That's pure Groomism. But if he were to borrow a turn of phrase from the character he created, Groom would probably turn to the final thought in *Gumpisms*. "Always be able to look back and say 'At least I didn't lead no humdrum life.'"

MICHELE BEARDEN
April 17, 1995

RON HANSEN

WHEN RON HANSEN talks about writing, his normally warm demeanor takes on an air of solemn intensity. Meeting for lunch in a hotel on Washington's Embassy Row, he is glad to dispense with small talk, preferring instead to expound on the deeper ideals that motivate him as a novelist.

"The goal of writing is to be as clear and beautiful as possible, trying to produce symmetry and harmony out of chaos—like medieval carvers who were trying to imitate what angels would do on earth," he says.

Hansen's faith is indeed a palpable presence. He is in town from his home in Santa Clara, Calif., to meet with a group gathered in Washington to translate Catholic baptismal prayers from Latin into English. At 48, he is appealingly boyish looking, a handsome man who exudes a Midwestern wholesomeness and friendliness.

His five novels have encompassed such far-flung themes as the cloistered world of nuns in an upstate New York convent (*Mariette in Ecstasy*) and the violent lives and deaths of outlaws in the American West (*Desperadoes,* and *The Assassination of Jesse James by the Coward Robert Ford*). In *Atticus,* his spare and forceful new novel from HarperCollins, Hansen writes of a father, 67-year-old Atticus Cody, a Colorado cattle man and widower, who receives an unexpected visit from his estranged son, Scott, an artist and alcoholic, who was responsible for his mother's death in a car accident many years before. Atticus subsequently finds himself in Mexico to claim Scott's body, after his son's apparent suicide. There, in a town called Resurección, Atticus must reckon with his son's old girlfriend and their seemingly lawless compatriots and relive painful memories from his family's past. The novel, with its unexpected twists, is at once a moving character study, a murder mystery, a portrait of expatriate life south of the border and, ultimately, an examination of the mysteries of the human heart. Its achingly beautiful portrayal of a difficult father-son relationship is rendered with the sensuous detail and the grace that characterize all of Hansen's writing.

The novel is "about forgiveness," says Hansen. "That's a key concern for me. What I really like is the loyalty and relentlessness of the father's love. I think that kind of love is what makes the world work; there are a few key people who have it, and they keep everything going, and that is what allows other people to be as scattered and rebellious and full of loss and wreckage as Scott is and yet have the world struggle on. It's visited on people in different ways, but we see it perfectly exampled within a loving parent."

An homage both to Atticus Finch of *To Kill a Mockingbird* and to Hansen's own grandfather, the novel is based, in part, on a family story about Hansen's uncle, an Iowa farmer. Hansen's uncle had a brother, a dealer in Las Vegas, who was found dead in the middle of the desert, shot in the head. "So Uncle Ray, when the harvest was in, went out to Las Vegas with his son Jimmy, who was also a farmer, and scouted around, trying to figure out what had happened to the brother. As a kind of coincidence, Jimmy's wife had left him, gone off with a highway patrolman and ended up in Las Vegas. So for Jimmy to go to Las Vegas was to revisit that whole past."

Hansen has long been fascinated by such sudden, life-changing events and coincidences. "I wanted to replicate our own experience of life: You settle in and say, okay, this is what my life is going to be like, and something comes and slams you, and you're totally taken by surprise and tilted off balance.

"That's my perception of the world. Sometimes I think that other people are really settled in their lives. But it feels to me like I'm always in pursuit of something, trying to figure out what's next. So for me a mystery is closer to our own experience of what life is."

Hansen says that *Atticus* was a difficult book for him to write and that he stopped several times. Describing his relationship with his own father, an electrical engineer, as "painful," he found the father-son material hard to deal with. An identical twin, Hansen was born and raised in Omaha, Neb. He attended parochial schools, received a B.A. in English from Creighton University in Omaha and went into the army, spending his Vietnam years in charge of the casualty branch at Fort Huachuca, Ariz. He entered the Iowa Writers Workshop on the GI Bill and immediately fell in with the 30-year-old John Irving, his first workshop leader. The two became friends, and Hansen became a live-in baby-sitter for Irving's two young sons.

132

After completing his M.F.A., Hansen worked as a college textbook salesman for Random House and began *Desperadoes.* Having written two unpublished novels, he decided that writing within a genre would increase his chances of placing a novel with a major publisher. He spent time on fellowships at Stanford and the University of Michigan and taught itinerantly for several years (placing *Desperadoes* and *Jesse James* with Knopf in the meantime), then took a position at the University of California at Santa Cruz, starting a week before the 1989 earthquake. "In Nebraska, there were blizzards and tornadoes all the time, so I was used to natural phenomena that could destroy your life," he laughs. His book of short stories, *Nebraska,* came out the same year, and by that time he had done a children's book, *The Shadowmaker,* as well.

Since settling himself in California ("a very congenial place to write"), he has acquired an M.A. in Spirituality from Santa Clara University and has been married and divorced. He is the Gerard Manley Hopkins Professor of Writing at Santa Clara, a Jesuit institution.

Hansen started off his publishing career with agent Liz Darhansoff, who placed both *Desperadoes* and *Jesse James* with Robert Gottlieb at Knopf and *The Shadowmaker* with Robert O. Warren at Harper & Row. After Gottlieb moved to the *New Yorker,* Darhansoff submitted *Nebraska,* at Hansen's suggestion, to Gary Fisketjon at Atlantic Monthly Press. He had met Fisketjon at a writers' conference (the two share a penchant for golf). Hansen declines to discuss why he switched agents, but he sent the manuscript of *Mariette* to Peter Matson at Sterling Lord Literistic, and Matson sold it to Ed Burlingame at Harper-Collins, who has since left. Now his editor there is Terry Karten, who also saw him and his friend Jim Shepard through the editing of *You've Got to Read This* (1994), an anthology of short stories.

Hansen was inspired to write *Mariette in Ecstasy* after reading *The Autobiography of St. Therese of Lisieux,* about a French woman who joined a convent at an early age and had an "incredibly ardent relationship with God. I wondered, why is it that nobody writes novels on subjects like that?" In editing the anthology entitled *You Don't Know What Love Is* (Ontario Review Press, 1987), Hansen had also come upon *Letters from a Portuguese Nun,* a novel written by an 18th-century male author under the pseudonym Mariana Alcoforado, about a nun who protests the tranquillity of her relationship with God. "I liked that idea of somebody being so passionately in love that everything else seemed second-rate in comparison. I wanted to work with those kinds of materials." So Hansen invented his story about a nun's relationship with Jesus, which is ultimately expressed through stigmata. "I then dealt with the very real phenomena [of] what happens with human beings when that sort of privilege is visited on another. There are rivals who feel like they've been ignored when they are equally worthy, so there's jealousy and hatred, and there are those who hope to piggyback on her experience; they consider her a saint and hope to use her as an intercessor with God."

Hansen was dubious that the book would ever reach publication. Matson did a multiple submission, and, Hansen says, "some people raved about the quality of the prose, but they didn't know how they could publish it. One person said, this is probably going to be a classic, but, sadly, we don't publish classics any more."

In a situation no one anticipated, the book did very well for Harper-Collins, going into seven printings, selling 55,000 copies in paper and hardback and appearing on several bestseller lists. "People don't have to be Catholic to wonder what the life of a nun is like," observes Hansen. He wrote the script for the film, directed by John Bailey and due for a spring 1996 release from Savoy Pictures.

Hansen writes screenplays "as a break from writing fiction," he says. He has recently completed a script for his short story "Sleepless," for director Joseph Ramirez. A screenplay based on *Atticus* by Richard Kletter is under development.

Still, it is fiction that beguiles him. He is not a fast writer, and in fact began work on *Atticus* in 1983. "Lots of drafts have to occur before I even get close to what a story's about. I just don't see it for a long time. I'll write stories and put them in a drawer and pull 'em out 10 years later and do something with them. I never show them to other people."

Hansen says he doesn't think he's touched his major subject matter yet and intends to work on a novel or memoir about growing up a twin. "I notice that twinship comes up a lot in my novels," he says. "It's daunting material for me." He is close to his twin brother, who lives in their hometown of Omaha; they speak to each other at least once a week.

Many of Hansen's books concern the clashes between lawless individuals and respectable society. "For me, the historical novels, the books about the West, were about moral evil. What are the abuses, the terrible aspects of ambition, which is what *Desperadoes* was all about. What is forgiveness about? What about revenge and all the ways we eliminate our enemies, or hope to, and whats the comeuppance of that—which is what *Jesse James* is about."

Hansen points out that *Atticus* is "more personal than a lot of my books have been. In a lot of ways, I think Atticus and Scott represent dual sides of my personality. Maybe Atticus represents what I hope to be and Scott is what I could be, unless there are all kinds of checks and balances. There's a sense that I have about myself of being as totally out of control as Scott is and needing some armature, some kind of root. Atticus is that for me, a model figure of rectitude and integrity and truth that is a corrective to my impulses.

"I'm in some ways a lawless person myself. It doesn't appear that way. I'm really not very comfortable with laws and strictures of society. I've always felt like an outsider in that way. But I know that acting it out and being a rebel will just get me into trouble and restrict my freedom, and I'm always looking for ways to have freedom. So I hew pretty closely to the line of what's allowed while letting it be known that that's a constraint.

"For me the process of writing is the joy of writing. It's the putting down individual sentences, making them fit together, making the story interesting. Once you've completed a book, you realize how ramshackle a thing writing a novel is. You've somehow made it seem like it was always coherent. That's the satisfying aspect of writing, the really affirming thing about it."

AMANDA SMITH
February 5, 1996

ROBERT HASS

As POET LAUREATE of the United States, Robert Hass has a mandate to raise national awareness of the importance of poetry and the written word. Such a task, at a time when most households have 70 TV channels and many others are plugged into the global village prophesied 30 years ago by McLuhan, surely is daunting. But being the frontman for a quaint art that barely has a profession tied to it—unless it's called teaching—does not faze Hass. Rather, it is a task to which he has taken naturally. In fact, there may not be a better poet today working with such catholic tastes, boundless energy and open aesthetics as Hass.

Perhaps this sense of openness is grounded in Hass's California roots. Born in San Francisco of German and Irish stock, he grew up mingling with kids of myriad backgrounds and then found himself in his impressionable teens living in the suburb of San Rafael, reading Kerouac and watching the rise of the Beat movement nearby. Having attended graduate school at Stanford in the heady 1960s, Hass emerged with a sensibility that is pan-poetic and insatiably curious, at once as alive to the poetry of Japan as to that of Eastern Europe, as much a devotee of the California poetries of Rexroth and Jeffers as the austere wintering of Robert Frost.

Acclaim came early for Hass. His first book, *Field Guide*. won the Yale Younger Poets competition in 1973 and was lauded by one reviewer "as a means of naming things, of establishing an identity through one's surroundings, of translating the natural world into one's poetry." Since then, he has built upon that early promise, prompting Carolyn Kizer to observe in the *New York Times Book Review* that "to read his poetry or prose, or hear him speak, gives one an almost visceral pleasure."

Hass, despite the peripatetic nature of his poetic interests, has stayed close to his roots. The father of three children from a first marriage, he still lives in the Bay Area, with his second wife, the poet Brenda Hillman, and her daughter.

Somehow, Hass manages to write and to think deeply about his craft despite his Laureate obligations in the nation's capital, his full-time teaching position at Berkeley and his participation in poetry and literacy events all over the country. When *PW* catches up to Hass, whose latest book, *Sun Under Wood* (Ecco Press), is an NBA finalist in poetry, he is lecturing to hundreds of poetry teachers and would-be poets under a large tent in New Jersey. The venue is the Geraldine R. Dodge Poetry Festival, and Hass's gentle, impassioned presentation lays out the depths of his engagement with the questions of poetry and what he sees as its place not only in the culture but in the development of self.

"History," he says, "can be reclaimed in the rhythms of a poem." As a person who has thought deeply about such issues, Hass offers a wonderfully winding exposition of the idea: "In the history of writing in the European tradition, as I understand it, what happened is that, up until the 1780s, the idea was that truth and knowledge came from reason or revelation and poetry was an attractive way to say those truths. But with romanticism the idea that poetic knowledge precedes reason came to the fore. Now, if the source of all knowledge is poetic insight, where does it come from? Inside or outside? The mind or the world? And why does the question matter?"

The audience stirs, perhaps a bit unaccustomed to pondering such elemental questions, perhaps more accustomed to seeing poetry as simply heightened self-expression.

"The issue," Hass continues, "is literally a matter of life and death to poets like Czeslaw Milosz," one of Hass's mentors at Berkeley and with whom, in true mentor-student fashion, Hass still jousts. For Milosz, "the only purpose of poetry is a perfect description of reality. The adequacy and presence of the physical world is something I wanted to believe in," Hass confesses. He takes a long sip of coffee standing at the podium. "But is this just mere record-keeping?" he asks, more of himself than of the audience.

Hass will continue for another hour, discussing his beloved haiku poets—Basho, Buson, Issa—who, like Milosz, describe only the real (or as Hass puts it, "the frog, the hyacinth, the pond"), eschewing metaphor and interpretation, the reach for a meaning beyond the images. But Hass will give equal time to poets in the romantic tradition who seek out metaphors in order to transform reality, like Wordsworth, or create something to stand in its place, like the modernist romantic Wallace Stevens. Hass would have it that the movement away from the "realism" of William Carlos Williams ("no ideas but in things") is dangerous if it leads merely to a solipsism. He wows the audience with an anecdote about a Stevens poem: "The palm at the end of the mind/beyond the last thought/rises in the bronze distances," pointing out that when Stevens crossed out "bronze distances" and replaced it with "bronze decor," he entered a troublingly hermetic impressionism. Hass concludes by wondering at the extremes of a poetry bent upon transforming rather than describing, asking, somewhat on Milosz's behalf (whose work was censored in his native Poland): "Why did so many surrealists become communists?" Metaphor, in this instance, has taken up arms as revolution.

The talk is a brilliant performance, but delivered in such a humble, self-effacing manner by the lean, tanned man in a pony tail that some teachers in the crowd may not remember the disquisition on Roman Jakobsen, or that Hass, in the course of extolling the relevance of figures like Whitman and Frost, also praised Language poet Lyn Hejinian ("Her *My Life* is a work of genius") and young Chinese-American poet Li-Young Lee. Hass, whose essay collection, *Twentieth Century Pleasures* (Ecco), won the NBCC award for criticism in 1984, represents the best in literary intelligence, blending an ecstatic tolerance with discriminating judgment. Sitting at a picnic table over black coffee and a cigarette, Hass would clearly be happy to talk about the intricacies of his chosen craft all day; but when asked about literacy and poetry, he musters his characteristic enthusiasm and does not speak in vague generalities or without passion.

"When I got the [Laureate] job," he says, "I did a lot of reading about literacy and I went to a lot of places poets don't normally go, speaking to corporations, for example. And one of the things that struck me was just how powerful a presence poetry has had in the culture.

"You have to remember that, at the beginning of the 19th century, less than 60% of American males could write their name, and that was far higher than in most of Europe. If you were black, you could get killed for reading. Once the ideals of puritanism transferred to the ideology of democracy, the engines of literacy geared up. Capitalist investment in printing presses led to the widespread agitation for the establishment of public schools and public libraries, just as now we have similar forces pushing for computer literacy and access to cyberspace. And the goal of advocating literacy was to expand audiences, to expand markets."

And poetry, says Hass, was very much a part of this push. "It was everywhere: in newspapers, magazines; businesses did poetry pamphlets. You can see Burma Shave signs as a relic of a public poetry, leading people down the road with the promise of soap. To have access to the culture, to get the jokes, you had to be able to read."

Although one can sniff beneath this analysis a certain anti-corporatism, Hass believes that, in the end, "as a democratic experiment in building literacy, there is no equivalent to the U.S."

He notes, however, that the landscape appears to be changing. "At the beginning of this century, the new media began to break the hold of the publishing business as the monopoly purveyor of information and entertainment and celebrity creation. Today, there are so many faces in other media that there is little room for a culture of writerly celebrity."

Even if poets aren't among America's celebrities, issues of fame and mainstreaming have always riven the poetic community. Jealousies, turf mentality and a sense of privilege in marginality enliven discussions wherever poetry lovers meet. At the moment, there is, if not a poetry war, at least a lively skirmish, with one side being the American Academy of Poets and its new formalism, and the other being those poets who see themselves as inheritors of a tradition that overthrew the constrictions of form years ago. Hass has alliances in both camps, and for good reason, he says: the conflict rages within. When *PW* asks him where the poetry wars are being fought, Hass responds: "In the guts of the living," quoting Auden, but declines to say more.

"I don't have too much interest in choosing up sides" Hass says, careful to steer clear of poetry politics. "But something I am very concerned about is what's happening with bookselling. Everyone is getting clobbered right now," he says of publishers large and small, "with all the expansion on the retail level. Clearly, the bet is that the superstores aren't just poaching on the small stores—some independents have been hurt badly—but expanding the readership. However, it seems they have expanded before the market did. And the danger is that, after this ordeal, we'll just return to the mall-store model. I just hope everyone can be patient, and, of course, I hope they are right: I hope the creation of attractive, booklovers' bookstores does expand readership and that bookselling remains healthy."

Hass, who is 55, describes his childhood in Northern California as a battle against the "ferocious anti-intellectualism" of the time as well as the Catholic grade school he attended. If not for the encouragement of his older brother, Hass says, he would not have been able to pursue his fantasy of being a writer. "I started out imagining myself as a novelist or essayist, but then Gary Snyder and Allen Ginsberg came along; and poetry, imbued with the whole lifestyle of the Beats, was so much more exciting." Hass could go down to the Surf theater and see Ginsberg standing in line for a Kurosawa film; the poetry community in San Francisco was national news, and as an aspiring writer, Hass wanted to be part of it.

After earning an undergraduate degree at St. Mary's College, he got his doctorate in English at Stanford in 1971, where he audited courses given by haughty and exacting Yvor Winters. Hass then went on to a teaching job in the English Department at SUNY Buffalo, where Robert Creeley was laying out a counter-cultural poetics with an enchanting metrical music and an austere precision. There, someone told Hass about the Yale Younger Poets competition; he sent in his manuscript for *Field Guide*. Stanley Kunitz selected it as winner.

Since then, Hass has published exclusively with Daniel Halpern's Ecco Press. *Praise* came out in 1979, *Human Wishes* in 1989. *Sun Under Wood* is his first collection in seven years. Halpern has also published four Hass-edited volumes on Milosz, the classic *Essential Haiku: Versions of Basho, Buson and Issa,* as well as the award-winning *Twentieth Century Pleasures.* "I've been lucky," says Hass. "New Directions was my model of what a publisher should be and Dan has stepped right in."

As to how poetry, or good literature, will fare as we enter the 21st century, Hass is hopeful, or perhaps trusting is the word. "For all the talk of the time of the 'gentleman publisher' of yore, what I have learned is that publishing has always been predominantly an urban phenomenon clustered around cities and capitalists and entrepreneurial places; the spread of literature as well as literacy has been market-driven. As these things go, that makes sense. I'd love to see a comparison of how 'literary' the publishing was in economies that weren't market-driven. Did they publish only the best literary work, being free of the market? Or is it the market that in some ways tells us what is important to people?" It's a good question. As a poet skeptical of how truths are formulated, Hass leaves the answering to the reader.

MICHAEL COFFEY
October 28, 1996

Seamus Heaney

THERE IS a Gaelic superstition still associated with Seamus Heaney's ancestral home in County Derry in Northern Ireland. According to Heaney, a St. Muredach O'Heney once presided over a monastic site affiliated with his family. It's said that if soil is dug from the ground of that site by a Heaney, it carries an aura of magic and beneficence.

Heaney, too, has an aura, if not a star power, shared by few contemporary poets, emanating as much from his leonine features and unpompous sense of civic responsibility as from the immediate accessibility of his lines. Since Robert Lowell dubbed Heaney "the most important Irish poet since Yeats," his poems have entered the core curricula of schools around the world. Listeners jam the rafters at his readings. He has published more than 10 volumes of poetry in 30 years, as well as three collections of essays, one play and a host of translations, chapbooks and other ephemera.

Commanding a great range of voices, idioms and metric conventions, Heaney's poetry nevertheless remains rooted in the soil of his native countryside, in the clash of ancient myth and modern politics, in domestic rituals and elegies for friends, family members and those lost to sectarian violence in Northern Ireland. Despite his oft-invoked pet name, "Famous Seamus," Heaney prefers the solace of his phoneless Wicklow cottage and the toilsome pleasures of teaching to the glare of the limelight. His new volume of critical prose, *The Redress of Poetry*, out from Farrar, Straus & Giroux, is a collection of lectures delivered at Oxford, where he is the Professor of Poetry.

Citing Heaney's "works of lyrical beauty and ethical depth, which exalt everyday miracles and the living past," the Nobel committee announced on Oct. 5 that Heaney is to receive this year's prize of $1.1 million. On that day, however, the 56-year-old poet was vacationing with his wife, Marie, in Greece, well beyond the reach of the international media. "We had just passed from Argus into Arcadia," he recalls, when—two days after the announcement—he happened to phone his children in Dublin (there are three, Michael, Christopher and Catherine, all in their 20s). "They were under siege."

When *PW* meets Heaney in Cambridge, Mass., a month later, the public's enchantment with him is unabated. The previous night, 2000 admirers waited in the rain in Harvard Yard to see Heaney read at the centenary celebration of the Harvard art museums.

There's a clandestine air to our late-morning rendezvous. Slouched in a chair in a heavy tweed suit in his secluded room in the Harvard Inn, Heaney looks a bit haggard. Under his unruly plume of white hair, his face is tinged with apprehension. As a vacuum cleaner sounds in the hall, he confesses a "weariness" about the "pure publicity" associated with the prize, preferring instead to discuss the poetry itself and the landscape from which it emerged.

The eldest of nine siblings, Heaney was born at Mossbawn, a farm in Derry, 30 miles outside of Belfast. "It was a farming household," he recalls, "with enlightened values [and] a special sense of worth." He attended boarding school from the age of 12, and there he met Seamus Deane, now the Keough Professor of Irish Studies at the University of Notre Dame and the editor of *The Field Day Anthology of Irish Writing.* The two became fast friends, both entering Queen's University in Belfast in the same class. For 10 years, that intimacy shaped and sustained both writers' formative love of the written word ("Deane was the star in our literary firmament," Heaney recalls). In the early 1960s, Heaney taught literature at Queen's University and began placing poems in the *New Statesman,* whose editor was Karl Miller ("one of the great editors of our time," notes Heaney), leading to a solicitation from Charles Monty, an editor at Faber & Faber in London. The publisher of Eliot, Auden, MacNeice and Lowell, Faber "was a much more translunar address in 1965," Heaney points out. "It was like getting a letter from God the Father."

Faber brought out *Death of a Naturalist* in 1966; it won several prizes, including the Somerset Maugham Award. Evincing the influence of Frost, Hopkins and Ted Hughes, these poems evoked his early years at Mossbawn, the tactile fluidity of the farmland, a fascination with buried things and the delights and terrors of childhood. He was to revisit that landscape often in subsequent books, but with *Door into the Dark* (1969), *Wintering Out* (1972) and, especially, *North* (1975), another Heaney emerged: an allegorist of national politics and mythology. In a series of "bog" poems, Heaney wrote of the mummified, iron-age corpses exhumed from the bogland, emblems of Ireland's first conquerors and martyrs. Other poems dealt with the politics of Ulster, its ethnic humiliations and poetry's role in confronting its terrible history.

In 1972, Heaney moved his family from Belfast to a cottage in Wicklow in the Irish Republic. As *North* took shape, he stopped teaching for three years. It was then, he recalls, resolutely raising his fist, that the full import of a life devoted to language and poetry grew clear. "I felt that I had vindicated poetry in myself and vindicated the word 'poet' for myself, and when I stood up, it was with the full force of my being," he says. The critic Helen Vendler, among the academy's staunchest Heaney fans, believes *North* is "one of the greatest of 20th century books of poetry, right up there with *Prufrock* or *Harmonium.*"

Heaney marked the 1970s with teaching stints at Berkeley and Carysfort College in Dublin, and in 1981, he became a visiting professor at Harvard. Early on, he notes, "I made a choice, for better or worse, to work in the university in order to preserve a kind of nonchalance with regard to publication. I have an old-fashioned ethic of earning my keep. I also have a kind of poetic, protective notion that the poetry should not be a meal ticket."

Heaney also turned out prose—lambent memoirs of Mossbawn and critical essays on poetry—the first collection of which, *Preoccupations* (FSG), appeared in 1980. Asked about the difficulties involved in switching gears from poetry to prose, Heaney shrugs. "It's a different part of your being. That's what the muse means. To some extent [the essays] are my persona as teacher. They're my job. Poetry is completely different. It's a force that feeds off everything else," he says.

Tenured in the halls of academe, however, Heaney was not insulated from the unrest in Northern Ireland, which came to a head in the hunger strikes of the early 1980s. Prompted by the staging in Derry in 1980 of Brian Friel's play, *Translations*, which showed English surveyors traveling through 18th-century Ireland, Anglicizing all the place names, Heaney cofounded the Field Day Theater Group with Friel, Deane, the actor Stephen Rea and others. "That play was a play of wondrous discovery and renewal," recalls Heaney. "It did what theater should do in a society. It was an intravenous shot for people." A pamphleteering campaign followed, as Heaney and Deane began publishing Field Day chapbooks on Irish politics and culture. One of the first pamphlets was an essay by Deane called "Civilians and Barbarians," "about how Irish culture was marginalized by the conquerors." Heaney, in turn, published an open letter, in verse, to the editors of a Penguin anthology of contemporary *British* poetry, who had heedlessly included him in their book ("be advised/My passport's green./No glass of ours was ever raised/To toast the Queen").

While cautiously optimistic about the ongoing peace process, Heaney credits Ulster's poets with a subtler grasp of the dualities of Irish history than the diplomats in Dublin and London. "I think the poetry is ahead of the peace. If you take writers like [Paul] Muldoon and [Ciaran] Carson who live there, their language, their plays and their ploys as writers have to do with outstripping the binary condition that they were offered," he says. "Through changing the language, opening trap doors inside every statement and going into a postmodernist double-take, they have in a sense prefigured the kinds of society that's called for."

If the vitality of Northern Irish literature springs, in part, from political friction, does Heaney worry that the poetry will slacken, as ancient enmities are soothed? "Peace talks don't necessarily mean the disappearance of the causes of the collisions," he says. "It means the onset of civilized ways of handling it, you know, rather than barbaric ways of handling it." He pauses. "I think that every writer in Ireland, North and South, has gone through elegy and tragedy. Stylistically speaking, the challenge is to move it on forward into adept and skeptical playfulness. A post-Beckettian poetics is called for."

It is in the context of Heaney's vexed relationship to art and politics that *The Redress of Poetry* is best appreciated. When Heaney's tenure at Oxford began in 1989, he says, "I know I was expected to do a kind of postcolonial resentment of English literature, which seems to me predictable, and other people are doing it better than I can."

Heaney chose instead a less fashionable plan: to redeem a few canonical, British and Irish poets from the simplifications and neglect of academic ideologues. Heaney's thesis: that poetry of the highest order shouldn't be fettered to political crusades. Through its "fine excess," its power to outstrip the circumstances it observes and broaden the horizons of its readers, great poetry redresses the profounder spiritual imbalances of its age. This credo is delineated in *Redress* in chapters on Herbert, Wilde, Yeats, Dylan Thomas and others.

"I think literature is there to open the spaces, not to erect tariff barriers," Heaney explains. "The notion of balance, of one form of life redressing another, of the imagined redressing the endured, that is just a central trope. But it also seems observably true that the sense of proportion, the sense of joy, the sense of irony, depends upon a certain amphibiousness between what we can conceive of and what we have to put up with."

His favorite chapter, on Christopher Marlowe, recovers *Tamberlaine* and "Hero and Leander" from critics whose sole interest has been to read these texts as complicitous in the bloody legacy of English imperialism. "It's just a corrective to a kind of constricting panic in people that they will give offense," Heaney says. "The language that people are offered in the academy is totally a language of suspicion. Of course, that was a very salubrious language from my generation. But if you teach suspicion to people who have nothing within their minds to suspect, I think it proceeds toward the nihilistic." He pauses, his eye atwinkle. "The idea that anything that amplifies the spirit can be tied down with a dainty, politically correct label—it's damning, it's deadly. Rapture is its own good."

In the U.S., Oxford published Heaney's first five volumes before he was approached by FSG, which now handles all of his work. His editor is Jonathan Galassi, who succeeded Michael di Capua and Pat Strachan. Faber serves as his American agent. No appearances are planned to mark publication of *Redress,* but come January, Heaney, who teaches at Harvard one semester each year, will again be stationed in his office at Widener Library, and wending his usual way through Harvard Square. "I keep dropping in on the Grolier Poetry Bookshop, run by Louisa Solano," he says. "She valiantly keeps going in what I think is a perilous enough situation for poetry-only [booksellers]."

Meanwhile, he hopes that the Nobel Prize money (which is untaxed in Ireland) will buy him solitude. With five days a week at his Dublin home and two at the cottage in Wicklow, "I have a fairly constant domestic life," he says. But the creative spirit demands sufficient time for germination and slow revision. "I'm not a kind of spillage system of verse," he laughs. In May, FSG will issue *The Spirit Level,* Heaney's first volume of poetry in five years. The poet is only middle-aged, after all, and the level of *his* spirit remains very high, indeed.

JONATHAN BING
December 4, 1995

Ursula Hegi

IN THE YEARS after Ursula Hegi's arrival in the U.S. at the age of 18, she intentionally turned her back on Germany, the country of her birth. She married an American, became an American citizen and chose America as the setting for her first two books. Now in her late 40s, Hegi finds that it's not possible to reject one's origins, especially in the case of 20th-century Germany. "The older I get," she says, "the more I realize that I am inescapably encumbered by the heritage of my country's history."

Hegi began revisiting that heritage in *Floating in My Mother's Palm*, a highly praised novel published by Poseidon in 1990. In it Hegi introduces various inhabitants of a fictional German town called Burgdorf. Like Hanna, the narrator of *Floating*, Hegi grew up in a small town near Düsseldorf in the 1950s, observing the foibles and flashes of generosity of people within a tight, small community. With Poseidon's publication of *Stones from the River*, Hegi extends her portrayal of Burgdorf's characters and the exploration of her own heritage to include the several decades preceding her birth: the years leading up to World War II, the war itself and its immediate aftermath. The stories in the two books are interwoven with such seamless ease that readers will find it difficult to believe that the new book was not written first.

Stones from the River is Hegi's attempt to understand the conspiracy of silence in towns like Burgdorf throughout Germany—a conspiracy that countenanced persecution of Jews during the war and enabled a community to quiet its conscience once the truths of the Holocaust were revealed. "When I came to this country," Hegi says, "I found that Americans of my generation knew more about the Holocaust than I did. When I was growing up you could not ask about it; it was absolutely taboo. We grew up with the silence. It was normal and familiar; these are terrible words considering the circumstances." Like the narrator in *Floating*, Hegi wryly recounts how history lessons in school started with the classic Greeks and Romans, ended with World

War I and began all over again with ancient Greece and Rome. "We knew a lot about those old Greeks and Romans," she says.

Hegi weighs her words carefully and often asks if there isn't a better term to describe this or that emotion, as if entreating her interviewer to respect her words and not give them nuances she doesn't mean them to have. She speaks English flawlessly but with a pronounced accent, and her long blonde hair and rosy complexion reveal her Teutonic ancestry. Hegi says that sometimes she dreads it when people ask her where she's from. "I wish I could say some other country, not Germany. As a German, I feel implicated by what happened."

Still, Hegi had no intention of digging up the unspeakable parts of her country's past in her third novel. In fact, she recalls emphatically denying, in an interview with National Public Radio's Bob Edwards, that she would be revisiting the inhabitants of Burgdorf in her next book. But, she recalls, as soon as she left the studio, the voice of Trudi, a character in *Floating*, began speaking inside her head, demanding her "own book." This almost mystical connection with Trudi continued: not long afterward, Hegi and her companion, Gordon Gagliano, were driving from Portland to home near Spokane, Washington, listening to Beethoven's Ninth Symphony, when she got the urge to jot down some notes. Soon she had filled half a legal pad, often with complete passages that appear unchanged in *Stones*. "Trudi was in that car with us—even Gordon felt her presence," she says.

Trudi is a *Zwerg*, a dwarf whose handicap sets her apart from the community. This "otherness" mirrors her refusal to take part in the complicity of silence and enables her neighbors to confide in her. She collects their stories and uses them to barter for information, divulging or withholding or changing details as needed and thus developing her own power in the community. Hegi says that Trudi did not become the protagonist of *Stones* because of her physical deformity, but because she was already a fully developed character in *Floating* whose voice cried out to be heard.

When asked about the inevitable comparisons with *The Tin Drum*, Hegi shrugs. "Yes, I know, 'another novel about a dwarf in Germany during the war.' It worried me in the beginning—well, it stopped me for about five minutes. But the character was so strong in her insistence to be heard that to stop writing wasn't possible."

A faculty research grant in 1986 enabled Hegi to return to Germany for the first time in 15 years to research background material for *Floating*. This was immeasurably helpful, she says. "It added a whole layer of sensuousness—the sounds, the smells, the tastes—that you can only get from being there." When she visited her hometown, she inquired about the *Zwerg* she remembered from her childhood, a woman whom she had barely known but who, she says, "obviously must have made a big impression on me." Having failed to find her, Hegi was sitting in a cafe when the object of her search appeared at her table, having heard that Hegi was looking for her. Instead of replying to Hegi's tentative questions about some of her relatives, the woman shot back, "I hear you've been divorced." Only after Hegi had shared the details of her marital breakup would the gossipy *Zwerg* tell her about her grandparents. It was this bartering for information that contributed to the development of Trudi's character.

Although Trudi's voice presented itself to Hegi "whole and complete, like a gift," the process of fleshing out the narrative was much more difficult. Hegi took a second trip to Germany before finishing *Stones,* visiting the concentration camp at Buchenwald and other similar sites. This time, research was not the purpose. Hegi was compelled to make what she feels was a pilgrimage. "I was afraid to go [to the camp]," she says, "but as a German-born woman I felt I had to. Writing the book was what gave me the courage."

To provide details of the period, Hegi immersed herself in historical material on the Holocaust, reading dozens of books and collections of journals written by concentration camp inmates. "There were many, many times when I wished I could leave the research alone, but I couldn't. It was an important part of my own journey, of integrating the past within myself."

Serendipity had a hand in furnishing some of the most helpful details. A German-American writer named Ilse-Margret Vogel, who called Hegi to congratulate her after the publication of *Floating,* was able to provide much material about the Resistance movement during the war; she was the first person who talked openly to Hegi about that time. Their conversations gave Hegi the courage to write to her godmother and ask for information, despite the fact that the older woman had previously refused to talk about the war years. Her godmother complied by recording her memories on tape. To Hegi, this constituted a gift of major proportions. "One sentence would become an entire story," she says.

She continues to be pessimistic about the interest of the German people in their tarnished past. Although she'd like *Stones* to be published in Germany "more than anywhere else in the world," she expects that it would make her the target of criticism there. "I would be tearing open the silence," she says, "something that even now many people aren't ready to face. I've come a long way in the past five or six years. Three years ago, even, we couldn't have had this conversation." In fact, it is an attraction-avoidance dynamic that fuels much of her writing: Hegi says she is drawn to write about things that she doesn't dare look at but needs desperately to figure out—"the things that won't leave me alone."

Hegi's development as a writer came in fits and starts. While growing up in Germany, she wanted to write but lacked craft and encouragement. She wrote a novel after arriving in the States but collected enough rejection letters from publishers to convince her to destroy the manuscript and stop writing altogether for three years. At the age of 28, with two sons, aged five and one, Hegi enrolled at the University of New Hampshire for a B.A. and then an M.A., and she stayed on to lecture in the English department until her divorce in 1984. On arriving at UNH she found herself within a community of writers and impulsively wrote "writer" as her occupation on a passport application. Soon thereafter, agent Gail Hochman sold her first novel, *Intrusions,* for publication by Viking in 1981. The University of Idaho Press issued a decade's collection of her stories in 1988. Hegi favored a university press because she surmised they would keep a short-story collection in print much longer, "and they did—it's still available in hardcover after six years."

Kathy Anderson at Poseidon was the first editor to make an offer for *Floating* and ironically lost her job the week the novel received a glowing review in the *New York Times Book Review.* Poseidon editor Ann Patty subsequently signed Hegi to a two-book contract and edited *Stones.* Hegi was uneasy about the transition, but when Patty called after reading the manuscript and said, "Trudi is the dwarf in all of us," she knew they would work well together. Now that Patty, too, has left Poseidon and the imprint is closing, Hegi has been assigned to Mark Gompertz at Simon & Schuster, at Gail Hochman's request. Hegi is approaching her 15-year anniversary with Hochman and says that the consistent connection with her agent has been invaluable while dealing with a procession of editors.

Hegi lives in Nine Mile Falls in eastern Washington with an architect and a black mutt they named Moses ("as in, found by the river"). When weather permits, she kayaks on or swims across the Spokane River in front of their home. She is tenured at Eastern Washington

University, where she teaches courses in fiction writing and literature in the M.F.A. program; she also serves on the board of the National Book Critics Circle.

For someone who feels so strongly about human rights, Hegi became politically aware relatively recently. Citing one incident that spurred her activism, she recalls a demonstration against a neo-Nazi group across the border in Hayden Lake, Idaho. She had decided not to participate in the event, believing it was a mistake to attract more media attention to white supremacist agendas, and was in her car driving elsewhere when a sudden insight flooded her mind. She realized that this was "exactly what happened in Germany—the silence. In the beginning everyone considered the Nazis a bunch of thugs; no one took them seriously." She phoned Gordon to meet her, and they joined the thousand people who had gathered in protest. "It was important that each and every one of us was there," she says.

Hegi has finished her next novel, called *Salt Dancers,* which is set in the Pacific Northwest. She is currently working on two new projects, waiting to see which will take over. *The Passion of Emma Blau* is the third novel with origins in Burgdorf, beginning with the immigration of Helene, a character who appears in *Stones,* to the U.S., and tracing the stories of successive generations of German-Americans. She is also developing a nonfiction work on the experience of being German in America.

When asked if she considers herself a German-American, Hegi hesitates, and it is the German side of the designation that gives her pause. "I don't really know," she says. "It doesn't have to do with choice. America is my country of choice, and I feel a connection to it even though it's not perfect. I have very little connection to my country of origin."

And yet Hegi says that in writing *Stones* her relationship with her native land altered more than she expected, and it will probably continue to change. "In the early years here, I went out of my way to avoid meeting other Germans," she says. "Now I seek them out in order to understand."

KITTY HARMON
March 14, 1994

ANDREW HOLLERAN

ANDREW HOLLERAN'S real name is Eric Garber. When Holleran's first novel, *Dancer from the Dance*, was about to be published by Morrow in 1978, he was unsure whether to use his real name on the frankly sexual, unashamedly "out" novel about the glamour and emptiness of the Manhattan gay life—because of his parents to whom he had not come out, because of the small Florida town they lived in, because of the small-minded people he imagined might make trouble for everyone. The book was about to go to press when he called his editor, Pat Golbitz, to discuss his worries. "She confirmed my sense that the people I feared were always the first to figure things out. She said that was the risk I had to decide to take. Or I had until five o'clock that day to come up with a pseudonym if I wanted to use one." Eric Garber had always liked the name Andrew, and he had gone to school with a boy named Romer Holleran, whose name he remembered as unique.

So the author of one of the landmarks of contemporary gay literature is known by a pseudonym that might never need to be invented today, nearly 20 years after its late 1970s, pre-AIDS publication. *The Beauty of Men*, Holleran's third novel and his first in 13 years (*Nights in Aruba* was published in 1983), is now out from Morrow.

But 20 years is a long time, and not only because AIDS intervened, killing most of his friends in New York. Holleran left the city over a decade ago to live in Florida and to care for his mother, who was paralyzed in a fall. Since then, he has lived in the small town near Gainesville that led him to invent his pseudonym. His mother died in 1994.

The history of those years is told in *The Beauty of Men*, the story of Lark, a 47-year-old gay man cut off from his past by AIDS, which has taken away the friends and the life he knew in New York. Lark is also isolated from his own present by his mother's illness, which consumes his time because he allows it to, and by his own fear of aging, which he perceives has made him invisible in the sexual competition that once defined his life. Like *Dancer from the Dance* and *Nights in Aruba*, both about a young man dividing his time between a promiscuous Manhattan milieu and visits to his elderly parents in Florida, Holleran says, *The Beauty of Men* is autobiographical—but not memoir.

"Have you ever read *Stan Mack's Real Life Funnies*?" Holleran, now 51, asks, referring to the cartoon strip that formerly ran in the *Village Voice.* "Everything is 100% based on something he really heard or overheard in conversation. That was the headline in every strip. When I began this book, I said to myself, 'I will make up nothing,' but as you work on it, it becomes a book, and is no longer you, or your life. I had the joy of putting myself into Lark, but a book objectifies things and it isn't your life."

Deep in the background *The Beauty of Men* also tells a parallel story of gay life in the 20 years since *Dancer.* Holleran says, "There has been an extraordinary assimilation, and it's freaky when you are someone who remembers when it was not always that way. AIDS accelerated this opening up. I think it was a means of making people aware of gay life, gay politics, gay art. I remember I was riding a bus in about 1985 or so, when the Mineshaft [a notorious Manhattan sex club] was closed by the Board of Health. There was a woman across the aisle from me reading the *New York Post* and I thought: it's all out there, they know everything if it's on the front page of the *Post.*"

Any salutary visibility of gay life has happened in a world Lark has left behind; it's on the edge of his awareness, and the brighter horizon for others seems only to make his own isolation more intense. "The novel is about the gap between the glory life, the *Out* magazine stuff, and the real life of most people," says Holleran.

The book is definitively about AIDS, though AIDS is a plague depicted at a distance imposed by geography and cast against a background of death by emotional isolation (Lark's) and paralysis (his mother's). "I've lost friends. I feel disoriented," Holleran says. "There is a sense of unreality about life. For me, it became easier to write about AIDS this way, rather than tackling it head on, because there are so many stories to tell, stories that I had either lived through with friends or heard about. It was a question, for me, of how do you get it down. How do you get it organized? It was possible for me to write about AIDS from my rural perspective. I narrowed it, I confined it, but the book still had to be about AIDS."

AIDS is the story of his generation, the generation of gay men that Holleran wrote about in *Dancer from the Dance.* "I see that I've written a trilogy of novels that is completed now with *The Beauty of Men.*

Nights in Aruba was the story of what happened to my characters before *Dancer;* this is the part of the story that came next. It was not conscious, but when I looked back on *Beauty,* I saw this does finish it." The new book, he says, "is where they end. This is that generation, the next story. The names are different, the characters are different, but it does continue a story by a writer with the same obsessions. So differences and all, it's a continuation of the same narrative."

In Holleran's mind as he wrote about Lark were other novels—*Mrs. Dalloway, Herzog, A Single Man* and the Rabbit books—that "follow a character around in his daily morass. It's a narrower canvas than in *Dancer,* but it is a broader view of life."

As Holleran sees it, *"The Beauty of Men* is, I think, a reflective novel, but about a man who is not able to reflect successfully. It's about his cell, his prison. I don't think his mind helps him. He seems to be intelligent, but he doesn't see. Lark seems a mystery to me. I was not going to comment on him. His depression is continuous, but I didn't want to explain it. I was reading the book last night and I wondered why I didn't open it up, lighten it up. You have an illusion that you could have done something different, but that's just self-laceration."

Holleran has doubts about how the narrative's pervasive sadness will affect readers. "It's a book I wrote for strangers," he says, wary especially of how his friends and family will react to such a personal story. "At first, I was apologetic about writing" such a personal book, he says. "But I've got Lark's inner voice, his cranky inner voice, and the pleasure of his language kept me going. I loved the vocabulary, the humor." There are flashes of sparkling wit in the novel—all recovered memories of that long-ago New York—and Holleran wishes there were "more than quips, more than one-liners." The real laughter in *The Beauty of Men* conspires to make the intoxicatingly claustrophobic landscape of the novel even more mesmerizing and bleak.

"Dancer went out into the world in a state of ignorant bliss. It's a bit more neurotic when your third book comes out. It's that spooky feeling you get, a form of mysterious communication with a reader you'll never see. This book is my nasty little *Walpurgisnacht,* where I put in every negative belief I have about gay life. Now I have to write a comedy. I've got to write the same story from a completely different angle. I feel guilty about the gloom." The assertion of guilt carries conviction; the impulse to write comedy is wistful.

"A person with a pessimistic frame of mind wrote a novel in which life provided the pessimistic facts," Holleran says "After [a friend's]

153

suicide, I realized there are a lot of bodies on the floor, and not all of them died of AIDS."

Thirteen years between novels is a long time, Holleran acknowledges, but the years were spent caring for his mother, writing a column for *Christopher Street*, abandoning several novels in various stages of completion and "reading magazines." "I wrote outlines of books I wanted to write, and this is a book I never wanted to write."

Holleran explains: "My trouble after writing *Dancer* was, that was my book. It was a blessing and a curse. I had done it, but what would I do next? *Dancer* came out with a wholeness that has made it very tough to add to. Maybe that's why I haven't published more. I took the lives of all my friends and put them down on paper. It's not easy to put things down on paper; you need a gimmick, you need an angle, a viewpoint. A lot of people who don't write think that you just type out what you're thinking, but of course you don't."

Holleran's agent, Ron Bernstein, notes that this is technically the second novel in a two-book contract signed just after *Dancer from the Dance* was published (Morrow accepted *Ground Zero*, a 1988 collection of essays first published mainly in *Christopher Street*, as the second book in that contract and made a new deal for the novel).

After Pat Golbitz, who had acquired *Dancer* and published *Nights in Aruba*, retired, Will Schwalbe, now the editorial director of Morrow, was eager to take on the new book. For years, Schwalbe and Holleran corresponded and talked on the phone without ever meeting; they met only after *The Beauty of Men* was finished. Holleran says that Schwalbe's encouragement and belief were vital. "The novel was utterly shapeless. He encouraged me, even when it was a heap of rubble. Somehow it came out, but he midwifed it." Schwalbe was the only person to read the novel while it was in progress.

Just as Lark can't admit his homosexuality even when his mother questions him beseechingly, so Holleran, despite a decade when his life was intertwined with his mother's on a daily basis, never spoke to her about being gay. About Lark, Holleran says: "His mother offers him the chance to be open, but he refuses it. I don't know why." About himself, he explains: "It was one of those things that was known but couldn't be discussed. It's painful to talk about. Even when someone does come out—and I suppose I did come out in some way—it's still a tragedy that there is this gulf between you and your family. A difference. It's like you're a foundling. You're gay and they're straight. There's no papering it over." Holleran graduated from Harvard in the late 1960s, served in the army in West Germany and studied writing at the University of Iowa after abandoning law school.

Holleran says his parents "knew I was a writer, but they didn't read my books. It was my choice. They were a good family in the sense that they respected privacy, didn't press, didn't inquire, they allowed others their boundaries." After his parents died, Holleran says, "I discovered things about them that I hadn't known, and which didn't offend me. They had their secrets too.

"Really, I thought it was wonderful. It was something human. Each of us had something they didn't want the others to know." Families, Holleran says, "are very sad. Events don't always let us communicate to people what we want them to know in the time we have. Death takes people away before you can tell them everything you hope to. It is torture not to be able to speak to people after they are dead."

Holleran, who still keeps an apartment in New York, returns infrequently to the city he first moved to in 1971. "The thing you can't reproduce from New York is the conversation," he says. "But most people I know overlook the enormous sustenance of solitude. I talk to friends on the phone, which makes me see that not living in New York is not that important, really, because everyone there talks on the phone anyway. The schizophrenic thing about New York is that you want the city and also the house in the country, reading Henry James in the garden. Here, I don't have the city but I do have the Henry James."

He is also resolutely single. "When I lived in New York, I would get into bed and sometimes I would say to myself, 'Why are you going to bed by yourself?' and I'd force myself to get up and get dressed and go cruise. It used to bother me a lot that I was alone. The question was 'What are you doing in New York if you're going to sleep alone? Why else did you come here?' That is water under the bridge. Now, the highest compliment I can pay to a book is to take it to bed with me. We have such a negative image of getting older, especially gay men, but all of us. There are so many nice things about it. None of which are in my book."

BILL GOLDSTEIN
June 17, 1996

KAZUO ISHIGURO

THE JACKET OF Kazuo Ishiguro's new novel, *The Unconsoled,* is a re-
production of a painting by the artist John Bowman. It's a scene in a
vast auditorium. Three figures on a stage are spotlighted, and muted
light falls randomly on people standing and sitting in the audience, but
all are faceless, anonymous. A ghostlike presence (a once-clear figure
subsequently painted out by the artist) stands behind the lectern,
barely visible in a dim spotlight. The chiaroscuro shadowing, the sense
of chaos and lack of communication, keep the viewer at a distance,
confused about what is going on. Yet there is the feeling that perhaps,
if one looks more closely, the meaning will become clear.

Ryder, the narrator of Ishiguro's long-awaited fourth novel, out
from Knopf has this feeling, too. A pianist of international reputation,
he arrives in an unnamed European city confused about what he is to
do. Everyone he meets alludes mysteriously to a mission more important than the concert he (perhaps) is to perform. They assume he is
aware of the crisis to which they refer; but, instead of enlightening
him, they burden him with their personal problems. Increasingly agi-
tated, Ryder nonetheless feels an obligation to console them: "People
need me. I arrive in a place and find terrible problems, and people are
so grateful I've come," he says. Yet everything he does leaves the lives
he touches more miserable than before.

In this way, Ryder resembles the protagonists of Ishiguro's three
previous novels, *A View of Pale Hills, An Artist of the Floating World*
and *The Remains of the Day*: he is completely unaware of the effects
of his words and his behavior, which are, ironically, entirely opposite
to what he says and intends. He is, like those earlier protagonists, emotionally crippled and unable to act spontaneously or to achieve intimacy with others.

In most other ways, however, Ishiguro moves into new territory with
this mesmerizing book. Long, deliberately opaque and disorienting,
with a large cast of characters whose identities are only gradually re-

156

vealed, it is a more difficult read than his other novels, and, Ishiguro himself agrees, not easy to characterize.

"This book will probably produce a large variety of interpretation" he admits. "And it involves a lot of exploration on my part as well. I felt that I had to move forward as a writer, or I should be trapped by a lot of things I had been praised for in the past."

Slim, intense, but still looking boyish at age 40, the author meets *PW* in the lobby of a Chicago hotel; he has just done a reading in that city. Oversized spectacles emphasize his quick, dark eyes, and he is dressed entirely in black: turtleneck, jeans and sneakers. Ishiguro speaks earnestly about the risks he took in writing this novel, in which he has eschewed a linear story in favor of an elliptical narrative with the atmosphere of a surrealist nightmare.

"This way of telling a story was something I've been wanting to do for some time," Ishiguro says. "I wanted to have someone just turn up in some landscape where he would meet people who are not literally parts of himself but are echoes of his past, harbingers of his future and projections of his fears about what he might become. I wanted to write about someone who doesn't have a schedule but is too embarrassed to admit it, so he pretends he does, and after a while forgets that he is pretending.

"These few days are supposed to be emblematic of the way we go through our whole lives," he adds. "Other people's agendas crowd in on our circumstances and we're just stumbling through. But occasionally we stop and look back and pretend that we actually made the decisions. And in that sense, it is a book about our world."

In contrast, Ishiguro himself appears composed, well-organized and unneurotic. Born in Nagasaki in 1954, he was five years old when his father, a scientist, came to England to work for the British government. After graduating from the University of Kent in 1978, Ishiguro did social work, first in Glasgow, then London. While studying for his M.A. in creative writing at the University of East Anglia, he began *A View of Pale Hills*; an advance from Faber & Faber editorial director Robert McCrum (who remains his editor there) helped him to finish it. Though the novel was well received when it was published in 1982, Ishiguro continued to work with the homeless for two more years, giving up that occupation only when he began earning more from writing than from his "day" job.

In 1986, *An Artist of the Floating World* was shortlisted for the Booker, won the Whitbread award, was a best-seller in England and put an end to any financial insecurity. By the time *The Remains of the Day* won the Booker in 1989, enjoying a second spurt of sales when the movie was released, Ishiguro had become a celebrated author.

All the more reason, then, to admire his sangfroid in deliberately writing a far more challenging work than he had attempted before, and in taking almost nine years to complete it. He spent quite a long time, he says, just working out the rules that might apply in the alternative landscape he was creating, one in which time is distorted in the manner of a dream where events occur in slow motion or with dizzying swiftness. As preparation, he wrote a series of short stories, "tryouts," he calls them, not to be published but "to have a go at creating a dreamlike landscape."

A talented musician himself (he plays jazz on the piano and the guitar and once aspired to make music his profession), Ishiguro decided to make his pianist protagonist "a messiah in musical terms." He wanted Ryder to step into a crisis—"but not a *political* one," he stresses—so he decided that the people of the city in the unnamed but vaguely Teutonic country where Ryder finds himself are miserable because, some years in the past, they had made a terrible mistake in celebrating the wrong artistic values.

"This kind of crisis arises out of a sense that in a democracy people feel a sense of responsibility that they should be able to do something about the issues that face them. On the other hand, there's a sense that the issues are so difficult and complicated that they can't discharge their duties as citizens adequately. They have to look to some expert," Ishiguro explains.

The author himself confesses to the same feelings of ineptness. "Although I'm supposed to be a reasonably well-educated person, I feel increasingly inadequate to the issues in our world that are supposed to be key to our well-being. I don't know how international business works, or the arms trade or the military or foreign policies of various countries. Although I might cultivate various areas of expertise, still I feel rather helpless."

Frustration, misunderstanding and inability to communicate also characterize four dysfunctional child/parent relationships in *The Unconsoled*. Ishiguro, pointing out that he started to write the book "in earnest" right after his now three-year-old daughter Naomi's birth, speculates: "I guess it is a time when you try to connect the young child to people you know who bear emotional scars from their childhoods." Noting that his wife, Lorna MacDougal, is a social worker, he says:

158

"We may have come across damaged people more frequently than most others have."

And in another sense, his feeling of being an outsider in England undoubtedly influenced his way of understanding the world. "I was brought up to look at British values and customs very respectfully. I was aware that a lot of my friends believed things were intrinsically *right,* but to me they were just British customs. Rules like children never being allowed in the drawing room. My friends accepted them as the rules of life, but I thought they were rather peculiar." In the novel, this "cold emotional distance" between parents and children becomes hauntingly evident in terms of blighted lives.

Sonny Mehta was another ethnic outsider in England, and although the two did not work together while Mehta was head of Pan/Picador, they established a strong relationship once Mehta became Ishiguro's editor at Knopf. "Sonny has been tremendous for me in the States," Ishiguro comments. Though he remains "very grateful" to Faith Sale at Putnam, who bought his first two novels, "nothing happened" with them in America, he says. "With *Remains,* Sonny had just come over and he was keen to publish me. He was absolutely terrific. He put me up in his apartment all the time I was here publicizing it. He briefed me on where I should go, whom I should meet. He involved himself in the minutiae of publishing. He made phone calls to booksellers across the country to say I was coming.

"The key to Sonny," Ishiguro says, is that he works like an Indian politician. "He once described to me the experience of following his wife Gita's father around during an Indian political campaign. Her father is one of the grand old men of Indian politics. He is always reaching out to people in tiny villages in remote locations. That's how you must do politics in India; you must forge the bond. And this is the way Sonny sees publishing in the U.S. It's not good enough to send out reps and faxes. You've got to get out there and start something going.

"The U.S. is unique that way," Ishiguro continues. "In England, you can do virtually all your press from London. You can pop over to Italy, France and Germany for a few days. But here every area has its own cultural history. There's a kind of American attitude: not wanting just to be *told* but to *see,* which is one of the good things about America."

Also unique in Ishiguro's experience is the film version of *The Remains of the Day*; he says, to his surprise, he really liked it. The movie casts its own kind of authority. I found myself watching it almost forgetting that I knew the story. In fact it's a slightly different story that the movie tells. In technical terms, it's a faithful translation, but it is a different work altogether," he muses.

"I had a go at TV writing very early in my career," Ishiguro adds, "and after that I felt a challenge *not* to write anything that could be translated to TV or a movie. So I try to write a novel completely unique to the reading experience. I try to use purely literary techniques. I thought *Remains* was entirely unfilmable, since it's entirely internal."

Ishiguro says he "can't possibly see" a film being made from *The Unconsoled.* He throws back his head and laughs. "The Hollywood people will get to that elevator scene [on page three] and throw it down!"

Nothing in *The Unconsoled* approaches a conventional Hollywood denouement. Yet it ends on a vaguely hopeful note. In the last scene, after a series of missed connections and emotional disasters, Ryder tells himself that things are not so bad after all. "I wanted to show that sort of hopeless, slightly pathetic kind of optimism, which in the end is something that we all have to resort to in order to keep going," Ishiguro says. "In a sense, all of my books end on that same note—after the character discovers how empty life is. Here Ryder is trying to gain something profound from what normally would be a superficial contact with other human beings. He's looking for some kind of *consolation.*

"I do feel it is somehow pathetic, that kind of cheering up of oneself. But on the other hand, I have a certain kind of admiration for the human capacity to do just that. There's something admirable and courageous about it, even if it seems completely futile."

Though Ishiguro fills his fictional world with self-deceiving people trying to surmount failed lives, in the end he grants them the dignity to endure their sorrow.

SYBIL STEINBERG
September 16, 1995

THOMAS KENEALLY

IN ANCIENT TIMES, Tom Keneally would have been a Celtic bard, such is his gift for wielding narrative and anecdote, witty quip and resonant observation. While his books never scant on storytelling brio, however, his work also reflects a concern for life's ambiguous challenges, glancing ironies and opportunities for moral behavior.

Keneally's power to move and persuade is not confined to his books; he is equally impressive in person. We first glimpse the charisma of this rumpled word-magician during his tour in conjunction with the paperback reissue of *Schindler's List*. Speaking without notes for more than an hour, he holds a large audience rapt, often eliciting shouts of laughter, then raising moisture in many a listener's eye.

A tête-à-tête in his unassuming office on the campus of the University of California at Irvine, where he is a Distinguished Professor of English, convinces us that Keneally is no less a natural raconteur with an audience of one. Rotund and ebullient, he sports a shiny bald pate somewhat balanced by an unruly white goatee. He has an inexhaustible supply of stories, a hearty belly laugh and an inclination to see everywhere the interdependence of life and art.

Real events have been the imaginative sparkplugs for many of Keneally's novels. His 21st work of fiction, *A River Town*, (Doubleday/Nan Talese), is based on his grandparents' life. "There is in our house a picture of the second general store my grandparents owned," Keneally says. "The first store—where most of the action of the book takes place—bore a sign in blue and gold that said T. Keneally, for Tim Keneally. In the picture of the second store, the sign says K. Keneally, after my grandmother Kitty." His laugh booms out. "I've always thought there was a book in that change of initial."

"I questioned the father," Keneally continues, using the Irish-inflected article *the* rather than the pronoun *my*. "The story began to emerge." And so did the character of Tim Shea, who Keneally says is "a construct about what I know about my grandfather. 'Ah, the old fella

161

got into trouble with the supply houses,' my father told me. He fed half the bloody town and never got paid. He fed the nuns and they gouged him. He was such a sucker."

Not surprisingly, this trait is Tim Shea's undoing. Wishing to lead a quiet life as husband, father and provider, he is thrust into the role of town hero against his instincts. Just as suddenly, as a result of his dogged code of honor, he becomes public enemy number one in the little community of Kempsey in Australia's Macleay Valley in 1900.

A painting on the office wall offers another version of events. It's Keneally's own work, what he calls "Tim and Kitty descending from Ireland on the Australian landscape." Rendered in bold primary colors, it's sort of a Celtic Chagall: Tim and Kitty float in mid-air, contemplating their new country with aplomb. Like Mary Poppins, Kitty holds an umbrella; a harp rests on a cloud, and, Keneally points out, "there's the priest playing rugby outside the pub, the ringbark trees, the hero ancestor."

Keneally says his grandmother Kitty was a pragmatic woman who often had to assume the authority her softhearted husband was loath to assert. "When Tim had trouble with drunks or toughs, Kitty would hear the ruckus and come put them in their place. She was a forceful little squirt. I like spunky little women," Keneally says, "and I like to write about them."

He's equally enthusiastic about sports. A cricket ball on his desk reminds him of how difficult it was to write a clear description of the game in *A River Town* for readers who have never seen it played. "I'm a bit of a failed jock, myself," he adds.

Family, women, sports, painting—Keneally's conversation ranges untidily over the things that please him. But all his books, both novels and nonfiction, bear the mark of careful research and the graceful organization of details. While the central situation of *A River Town* came from family stories, Keneally pored over turn-of-the-century newspapers for the minutiae that ground a narrative. He found all sorts of treasures, including a piece about the man who inspired the character of Bandy Habash, the Indian herbalist. Called before the magistrate in Kempsey for riding recklessly in C Street, "which is where I lived when I was a little boy," Keneally says, the man defended the need to exercise his horses somehow, since he was not allowed to join the Turf Club. Keneally uses the incident in *A River Town*, allowing him to portray the pervasive racism of the period.

A grisly item in a Victorian newspaper jolted his imagination. A young woman had died undergoing an abortion; her severed head, preserved in a large flask of alcohol, was being carried from place to place in the hope that someone could identify her. In the novel, the sight of this unfortunate woman's head, and the knowledge that her soul cannot rest until she is properly buried, throw Tim into a purgatory of anguish.

He thus joins the parade of Keneally's typical protagonists—decent, ordinary men and women who become impaled on the horns of an ethical dilemma, compelled in one defining moment to follow a personal code of conduct no matter how difficult it becomes. It's such complications of human nature that interest Keneally. "It makes living messy but it makes writing a delight," he says.

Oskar Schindler's moral ambiguity, of course, inspired the fact-based novel with which Keneally will always be identified. Although *Schindler's List* was awarded the Booker Prize in 1982, the year it appeared, it was the movie version that created a new demand for the book. Touchstone's reissue in 1993 introduced Keneally to the delights of the bestseller list, and to large audiences avid to hear the man who calls himself "a dumb guy looking for a briefcase who found a good story." He has related over and over again the circumstances of wandering into a leather shop in L.A. and being buttonholed by the proprietor, a Holocaust survivor who was among those saved by Schindler, the German who risked his own life by sheltering hundreds of Jews in his factory.

"I was convinced of the moral force of the story," Keneally says. "Stories of fallen people who stand out against the conditions that their betters succumb to are always fascinating. It was one of those times in history when saints are no good to you and only scoundrels who are pragmatic can save souls."

Keneally himself has a strong sense of civic duty and an old-fashioned patriotism. "The big question in Australia is always: Are we British or are we Australian?" he asks, with evident bias toward the country of his birth. Some of the best moments in *A River Town* occur when characters make pompous and vainglorious appeals to their countrymen to send regiments of Australian men to aid Britain in the Boer War. A century later, Keneally is actively involved in trying to wrest Australia out of the British Commonwealth. As founder and past chairman of the Australian Republic Movement, he goes back and forth to Australia frequently, a punishing schedule of international flights, short visits and hectic itineraries. Though he says he will miss the "brilliant students" in his writing classes at UC Irvine, he is somewhat relieved that his four-year tenure there will be over in June so he can be planted once again on Australian soil.

"The irony is that I've got to come back here," Keneally says. He's immersed in researching a nonfiction book that will take another year to write. Again inspired by several family legends, Keneally began looking into the stories of political prisoners whom the British transported from Ireland to Australia. Many of them later escaped and went on to make new lives—and sometimes brilliant careers—in America. His own great-uncle, a Fenian, was transported in 1865 and later pardoned in a political tradeoff. He ended up in California, where he became city treasury clerk of Los Angeles. "I found his memoirs," Keneally says triumphantly, "and I even found a picture of him in the Huntington Library!" Keneally is astonished at the dramatic stories he has discovered. "But the research is a killer; it's on three continents," he says.

Once that book is completed, Keneally is yearning to get back to the characters in *A River Town,* whose lives he sees stretching into a trilogy. "I will take Tim and Kitty up again in 1908," he says. Then the third book will follow their son Johnny as a soldier on the Western Front in 1914.

Aside from the teeming demands on his time and imagination, Keneally expresses satisfaction with his life. Touchstone currently has 1.4 million copies of *Schindler's List* in print, and sales of his previous novel, *Woman of the Inner Sea* (1992), "are bobbing along nicely," too. He's had a special kind of gratification from his 1990 novel, *To Asmara,* which told of the Eritrean people's struggle for independence from Ethiopia. When Keneally and his wife, Judy (they've been married 30 years and have two daughters), went to Eritrea in 1993 to observe the referendum, they found that all the UN representatives had been required to read *To Asmara.* "That's *better* than being on the bestseller list," he says.

Another satisfaction is working with two capable women: his editor, Nan Talese, and his agent, Binky Urban. His relationship with Talese goes back to *Schindler's List,* but she left S&S before the book was published. "When an editor leaves, it's sort of like having your wife shot on your honeymoon, and you have to get married again," he says. At that point, Keneally had already endured the loss of editors elsewhere—Viking, Harper & Row, Harcourt Brace. He went to Warner, lured by a promise of a new program to publish important fiction. But between *To Asmara* and *Flying Hero Class*, that rationale disappeared, he says, and Warner was not enthusiastic about *A River Town*.

By that time Keneally had also become convinced that his London agent, Tessa Sayle, could no longer represent him adequately in America. He had been introduced by a friend, the director Fred Schepisi, to Urban. She showed the book to Talese, who snapped it up. "What I like about both those women," says the 59-year-old author, "is that they think I have an unlimited time ahead of me, as if I'm just embarking on a long career."

About Urban he adds, "No job, however menial, is beneath her attention for her girls and boys. I like her so much that the last time I was in New York I bought her a backpack," he says, in the same tone in which he might announce the purchase of emeralds.

Meanwhile, Keneally hopes that critics will see what he's driving at in his new novel. "*A River Town* is much more characteristic than *Schindler's List* of the kind of book I write. Yet there's a continuity of theme, if not subject matter, between the two. We ruined priests, we never get out of the habit of parable telling," he confesses, referring to the fact that as a young man he studied for the priesthood. Disillusioned, he left before ordination. "I wanted the church to be better than I was," he observes wryly.

Instead of using a pulpit, Keneally has expressed his ethical perspective in books. "Moral tales are the best tales," Keneally says. *A River Town* is the best kind of moral tale, where the message of the story is displayed through a believable, admirable human life. Apparently the Keneallys do it that way.

SYBIL STEINBERG
April 3, 1995

JAMAICA KINCAID

A TEENAGE GIRL in the mid-1960s abandons her home on Antigua, a tiny island in the West Indies, bound for New York and not to return home for 19 years. She becomes an au pair for a family in Scarsdale, N.Y., then for a different family in New York City. She breaks off all contact with her mother, takes photography courses at the New School, dyes her hair blonde and changes her name. A few years later, in her early 20s, she convinces *Ingenue,* a girls' magazine to allow her to interview Gloria Steinem. The article is a success, and soon she's writing pop music criticism for the *Village Voice* and "Talk of the Town" pieces for the *New Yorker.* She writes her first work of fiction— "Girl"—a hectoring monologue in the voice of her mother, which is published in 1978 as one incandescent page in the *New Yorker.* By the time her first collection is published in 1983, she's being hailed as one of the most important new fiction writers of the decade.

Jamaica Kincaid's life story sounds a bit like a cross between Charlotte Brontë's *Jane Eyre* and Jean Rhys's *Wide Sargasso Sea,* except in this version, the woman from the West Indies triumphs, working her way through governess jobs to become a renowned author. Her biography also sounds more than a bit like one of her own novels, because, as Kincaid puts it, with characteristic irony, "everything in my writing is autobiographical—down to the punctuation."

The Autobiography of My Mother, Kincaid's third novel (and fifth book) with Farrar, Straus & Giroux, adds a dazzling new chapter to the ongoing fictional autobiography she is composing. Narrated by the 70-year-old Xuela Claudette Richardson (Kincaid was born Elaine Potter Richardson), *Autobiography of My Mother* extends the themes of her earlier work: mothers and daughters; sexuality and power; and the way the legacy of colonialism—"a common history of suffering and humiliation"—leaves indelible traces on the imaginations and emotional lives of those born in places like Antigua and Dominica. It is in no danger of being described as a "charming book," as was Kincaid's first novel, 1985's *Annie John* ("you're in trouble when you're called charming," Kincaid likes to say). It is unrelenting and emotionally devastating, though still written in the elegant, luminous prose that her readers have come to rely on.

Annie John, a coming-of-age tale about a young girl growing up in Antigua, ends with the 17-year-old protagonist leaving the island for good, on her way to study to be a nurse in England; 1990's *Lucy*—whose protagonist is named for the Lucifer of Milton's *Paradise Lost,* a poem Kincaid was forced to memorize large chunks of as a child—tells the story of a slightly older young woman working as a nanny in the States. Clearly, Kincaid was tracing a trajectory closely following the course of her own life. But *Autobiography of My Mother* departs from that pattern, going back to imagine what her mother's life on the island of Dominica would have been had she never given birth to children: the novel is a re-imagination—an impossible one, since it presupposes the negation of her existence—of her own personal history.

There's something quite perverse about this novel, as if Kincaid, tired of seeing her work characterized simply as thinly veiled autobiography, had decided to create an entirely new literary form—that of the invented autobiography of one's parent. One of the most harrowing takes on motherhood since Toni Morrison's *Beloved,* the novel treats family history as a dark mystery to be plumbed. "I would bear children, but I would never be a mother to them," Xuela pronounces. "They would hang from me like fruit from a vine, but I would destroy them with a carelessness like a god's." "My impulse is to make everyone uncomfortable," Kincaid comments simply.

A beautiful woman who stands nearly six feet tall, Kincaid must have made quite a splash in those early days in New York City as a proto-punk West Indian nanny with dyed blonde hair. Although she's no doubt mellowed since becoming a mother of two, an instructor at Harvard, an obsessive gardener and an eminent author, she still projects an attitude. She greets us in her office in the African American studies department at Harvard, where she's currently teaching for one semester a year. Her desk is piled with books: *Jane Eyre* ("my favorite novel"); Jane Austen's *Mansfield Park*; the narrative of Mary Prince, a 19th-century Antiguan slave. She explains that she's teaching one fiction-writing class and an English class on "literature and possession," "an account through literature of how we claim things, how we come to possess things."

Speaking in the proper British accent only the best colonial education can impart, Kincaid says of her apprenticeship in fiction writing: "I remember before I wrote 'Girl,' every New Year's Eve for several years, when you're supposed to make a wish at midnight, I used to wish that that would be the year I'd start to write fiction. And then one year it really was the year. That year somebody gave me a book by Elizabeth Bishop with that poem 'In the Waiting Room.' And I read that, and I just knew how to write. It was a tremendous gift for me. I felt as if someone opened the door and showed me my own tools, the things that I needed. I just knew how to write after that."

She is amazed and grateful for that gift. "It doesn't come easily, but I don't expect it to. I never understand when people complain that it's so hard to write. I think it *should* be hard. Because what are you doing when you write? You're doing something so complicated, so unpredictable, it deserves to be hard. I wouldn't trust it if it came easily."

Kincaid's route to authorship was, obviously, an unusual one, and she feels, fortunate in the mentors, editors, agents and literary friends she found along the way. She first began writing for the *New Yorker* after spending some time as a sort of informal assistant to her friend George Trow, who took Kincaid with him while researching pieces for the magazine's "Talk of the Town" section. One time she took some notes for Trow on a West Indian carnival. Trow showed them to the magazine's legendary editor, William Shawn, who spotted her talent and decided to print her notes as the piece itself. (Kincaid is now married to Shawn's son Allen, a composer.) Once she started writing fiction, she signed on with FSG for her first book, the short-story collection *At the Bottom of the River.*

"FSG offered me the least money, so I took them! I had always wanted to be published by Farrar, Straus. I can't imagine, I would never dream of having another publisher." After editor Pat Strachan left to join the *New Yorker,* Kincaid became one of Jonathan Galassi's authors. For the past eight years, her agent has been Andrew Wiley, whom she describes as an invaluable figure in her career: "In a certain kind of writer's life, he is crucial. When Mr. Shawn left the *New Yorker,* many of his former writers needed the protection of an agent. Mr. Shawn had been a cornerstone of publishing and he was our protector—he protected us from horrible people. And when he was gone, we were really in the clutches of horrible people, and so a lot of us needed Andrew Wiley." Members of the media who have dubbed Wiley "the Jackal" might well be surprised by the ingenuousness of that statement.

168

Autobiography of My Mother forcefully engages with the inequities of a world divided into "the big and the small, the powerful and the powerless, the strong and the weak"; when Kincaid discusses the publishing world, she returns to these themes. Kincaid conveys deep and abiding distrust of those who treat literature as just another business and in her telling, figures like William Shawn and Andrew Wiley stand between authors and the rich and powerful who control the industry: "Mr. Shawn used to protect us, used to try to get us enough money at the magazine, and to make sure we did the best kind of writing we could. It was sort of a tragedy for American literature when he was removed from the *New Yorker,* and it killed him, I think. He was treated very brutally. I think American literature is really changed for it. A lot of us got hurt when the *New Yorker* fell apart. Now it's the property of a rich man—and I'm not a rich man, nor do I want to be."

She says she feels no particular bitterness over the new course of the *New Yorker,* only regret that "that nice place to write was upset. It's not something I can do anything about. I just have to move on and hope I can find somewhere else to write."

Kincaid's one nonfiction book to date is 1988's *A Small Place,* a scourging meditation on tourism and colonialism inspired by a visit to Antigua. Its piercing refrain, "you are a tourist," was described by one reviewer as "backing the reader into a corner," a judgment which amuses and mystifies Kincaid. She apologizes for not making her readers "feel all bundled up in a warm blanket," but says she herself only likes to read writing which dares to make a reader uncomfortable. The *New Yorker* declined *A Small Place* for publication, saying it was too angry—and indeed, it may have come as a shock to those readers who read *Annie John* and *Lucy* as no more than girls' coming-of-age stories, ignoring their references to questions of power and its abuses.

Kincaid is left-of-liberal, and as if to prove it, she declares that she deeply wishes Newt Gingrich had died in the place of the radical lawyer William Kunstler, whose death she is still mourning. Even when she's denouncing the world's many evildoers, her voice is gentle and engaging. The effect is not so much a softening of her anger, but an intensification of it by contrast. She makes anger and outrage completely compatible with good humor.

Kincaid's passion for writing is at least matched by the fervor she brings to a second obsession. Living in Vermont with her husband and their children, Annie and Harold, she has plenty of space for gardening, an occupation which she describes as "an absolute luxury. You've eaten, you're clothed, you have a house, you look out and you re-arrange the landscape. It's an aesthetic decision. It's all exaggerated, it's luxurious, it's a kind of excess." Kincaid has written regularly about gardening for the *New Yorker* for several years, and FSG plans to publish a collection of these writings in 1997.

Pondering the relationship between gardening and writing, Kincaid muses, "When I'm in the garden, I'm actually also writing, I'm always going over the sentences—so by the time I actually write, I've written what I'm putting down on paper many times in my head. I don't revise my writing at all. But I do the equivalent of revising in the garden, continuously. I never stop digging up beds, rearranging everything."

She adds that she has no routine of any sort for her writing. The word processor is always there, as she puts it, but she only goes to it when she's ready. "It would kill me if I had a routine. I cannot stand routine, and I cannot stand fixed ways of doing things. If I cannot do it my own way, differently each time, then I can't do it at all."

At moments like this, it's easy to imagine the young Kincaid as a brilliant but disobedient student in Antigua—like her own Annie John, whose report card reads: "Annie is an unusually bright girl. She is well behaved in class, at least in the presence of her masters and mistresses, but behind their backs and outside the classroom quite the opposite is true." Kincaid has never forgotten what it felt like to be small, young and without power, and she uses that feeling of powerlessness as the material for her novels. Even as she's become a respected author, mother and professor, she continues to write behind the authorities' backs—where she feels most at home.

IVAN KRELKAMP
January 1, 1996

MICHAEL KORDA

IN THE AFTERMATH of his two-year battle with prostate cancer, Michael Korda's already eclectic career has taken a surprising twist. As the editor-in-chief of Simon & Schuster since 1968, he has brought more glamor and visibility to trade publishing than any book editor since Maxwell Perkins. Yet in *Man to Man,* his unflinching cancer memoir (Random House), he sheds his flamboyant public persona, revealing himself as frightened, vulnerable and hostage to the unpredictable ravages of a disease that few men are willing to discuss with candor.

Self-help guru, globetrotting memoirist, commercial novelist, editorial wunderkind. The chameleon-like Korda has courted these roles, making it abundantly clear he's no commonplace book editor. The nephew of legendary filmmaker Alexander Korda, educated at Oxford, veteran of the Royal Air Force and the Hungarian revolution of 1956, he's raced Ferraris, is an active NRA member and hosts an annual cross-country event on the Hudson Valley horse farm he shares with his wife, Margaret, a former model. Deal-maker and pitchman par excellence, he has edited Larry McMurtry, Graham Greene, Jacqueline Susann and, for a brief but demanding stretch, both Jackie *and* Joan Collins.

But in *Man to Man,* Korda emerges as a proselytizer and poster boy for an illness that, experts estimate, will afflict one in five men. Witty, compact and matter-of-fact, this book recounts the physical and emotional devastations of his cancer, unabashedly inviting the reader into his bedroom, bathroom and hospital room, spanning the prostate troubles that preceded his diagnosis and the slow convalescence that followed his radical prostatectomy in 1994.

It is a gutsy departure for Korda, until now best known as an author of lightweight, commercial blockbusters, who has long projected an image of adventure and cosmopolitan sang-froid. In fact, the book did not begin to germinate until weeks after his surgery, Korda explains. "I found myself shut in and brooding about what happened," he says.

171

"As I got into it, I thought to myself, this is really a story that ought to be told." In particular, he was compelled by the paucity of literature on the subject and the difficulty men found in discussing it. Among those with prostate cancer, he wrote in *Man to Man*, "to the fear, which is perfectly natural, of death, loss of virility, and incontinence is therefore added a dreadful loneliness; for unlike women, who tend to bond together in distress, men—certainly in the face of *this* disease—tend to retreat into silence. For many of them, prostate cancer is a *private* battle, and because of that, it is all too often lost."

In a conversation spanning two afternoons, Korda revisited the 10 books he's written, the highlights of his 40-odd years at S&S and the major personalities and changes that have shaken the industry in that period. At 62 in a flamboyant, custom-tailored shirt and tie, he bears little resemblance to the steely, talking head in the 1970s spectacles whose photo appears on his book jackets. Though he admits to fatigue at the end of the day, it's not evident. So lavish, in fact, are his charm and vitality that one tends to accept at face value even those remarks that on later reflection sound improbable. A short, coiled spring of a man who emanates a congenial, ferrety air, he often twists excitedly in his chair at his own most outrageous anecdotes, told in a soft voice with the cadenced, English inflections of an old Hollywood star.

When Korda arrived in New York in 1958, joining S&S as Max Schuster's assistant, the landslide of corporate consolidations, cutthroat agentry and escalating advances had not yet made a dent in the industry. Korda contends, however, that it was not the golden age of publishing, as it has been romanticized. "I've always thought it profoundly wrong to say that it used to be better in the old days," he declares. "The old publishing houses were run like family grocery stores by people who owned them without stockholders. Bennett [Cerf], Donald [Klopfer], Max [Schuster] and Henry [Simon], Alfred and Blanche Knopf. They were pretty stingy with money, because they thought that if they gave you a dollar raise or put an extra bar of soap in the men's room, that the money was coming directly out of their own pocket. Publishing salaries were phenomenally low. People were ashamed to discuss how much they were making, and there was a sort of perverse pride in the fact that manual laborers—plumbers—were paid more than people who worked in book publishing."

Driven less by a need for extra income than by a desire to stake his own claim in the literary scene, the ambi-talented Korda had begun to write in earnest by the time he succeeded Robert Gottlieb as S&S editor-in-chief, contributing splashy articles and film reviews to such magazines as *Newsweek, Playboy, Vogue* and *Glamour.*

Few book editors find time to write books, but Korda had a knack for deft and speedy copy, bringing particular wit and insight to a subject that was not unfamiliar to him in his early years at S&S: office politics. Lynn Nesbit, who remains his agent to this day, sold his first book, *Male Chauvinism! How It Works* (1973), based on a *Glamour* essay on sexual discrimination, to Nan Talese at Random House. It was followed by *Power! How to Get It, How to Use It* (Random, 1975) and *Success! How Every Man and Woman Can Achieve It* (Random, 1977). Radically unromantic how-to manuals for the managerial class, written in an anthropologist's deadpan, they fared poorly with critics. But both were major bestsellers, launching the young editor-in-chief as a kind of self-empowerment savant on the TV talk-show and lecture circuits.

Korda attributes the enormous sales of *Power* to shrewd packaging by Jim Silberman, who inherited the book from Talese. "I had in mind a kind of C. Northcote Parkinson, tongue-in-cheek book about the way Americans do business," he posits. "By subtly moving me in certain directions without walking me, which is what good editors should do, he turned it into a book that actually sold itself as a self-help book.

"It was heady and exciting," he says, though he soon grew tired of his inspirational shtick. "I think by the time I got to write *Success,* I had already worked out in my mind that it was a bridge too far," he explains. Unhappily, Korda was already under contract to Jason Epstein, his third editor at Random House, for another book, in the same vein, called *How to Be a Winner 100% of the Time.* "I phoned Lynn and said, 'I am terribly sorry. We are going to have to give back all this money, because I just can't do this anymore.' What I'd really like to do is write a book about my family."

Nesbit then persuaded Epstein simply to switch the contract from one book to the other, Korda recalls. "Without Jason's instinctive feel that I could write that book and his generosity in taking that gamble and not tearing up the contract, I might never have written *Charmed Lives.*"

Eschewing the frosty ironies of his previous books, *Charmed Lives* was a tender and gossipy biography of the brothers Korda (Alexander, Zoltan and Vincent, Michael's father), émigrés from a Hungarian peasant village who jump-started the British film industry of the 1930s. Alexander, the dominant brother and the most famous of the three, takes center stage, playing Prospero, Pygmalion and surrogate father to Michael, who vividly details the celebrities and the atmosphere of heady decadence that surrounded him.

Despite Korda's flair for line editing, he admits that his own books have occasionally required a crash diet under the supervision of his editors. Of *Man to Man's* editor, Bob Loomis, Korda says "there is not a single line in this book that has not in some way been massaged by Bob." Mildred Marmur, who assisted Epstein with *Charmed Lives,* performed a similar service. "Millie came to me one day and said, *'Bubbe,'*" recounts Korda, "it's too long. We're going to sit in my office day and night until we have a book that the BOMC will take as a full selection.' And we sat down, the two of us on the floor of her office with sandwiches sent in from time to time, and we hacked that book down until finally Millie said, 'that's it.' And lo and behold, she sent it over and a week later they phoned back and said it was a full selection. It was the most exciting moment of my life."

Charmed Lives was certainly the first time that Korda succeeded in joining his stylish prose to a subject he found to be truly important. "It was a book that helped me define myself. It was probably my way of seizing control over the Korda family, and its myths and legends, and putting them in as much order as I can. Having been somewhat on the periphery of the family, I compensated for that by being the chronicler of the family. They may or may not have wanted a chronicler. They probably would not have wanted me."

Korda was then free to try his own hand at commercial novelwriting, a vocation to which he'd long aspired. His debut was *Wordly Goods* (Random House, 1982), a lurid novel about a power struggle between two multimillionaire financiers and the woman who was mistress to both. Sales were modest, and Korda himself calls the book "an apprenticeship." Under pressure from S&S publisher Dick Snyder, who found it unseemly for Korda to publish successfully with a rival house, he brought out his next novel with Linden Press, the S&S imprint of Snyder's wife, Joni Evans. *Queenie,* a pot-boiler based on the life of Merle Oberon, Alexander Korda's second wife, earned out its $250,000 advance, becoming a hardcover *PW* bestseller and a TV miniseries.

When Evans left S&S (her divorce proceedings underway with Snyder), Korda grew increasingly uncomfortable with the idea of publishing with his own house. He released three more novels with S&S imprints (*The Fortune*/1988, *Curtain*/1991 and *The Immortals*/1992) but does not intend to publish there again. "I never had a desire to leave Random House," he explains. "In retrospect, it was a mistake. With Joni on your side, it's like a three-ring circus of excitement, and Linden really was a world apart. But the other imprints never had quite that independence."

Reporting for three decades to the redoubtable Snyder, Korda himself managed to avoid the kind of personal collisions with Snyder that for some of his colleagues ended in bitter departure from S&S. The two remain close friends. "He's one hell of a publisher and one hell of a friend," declares Korda. "Dick's reputation for bite is much less real than his ability to bark," he says. "Our interests did not overlap. I had no desire to do the sales, the management and executive stuff and be CEO of a larger S&S. He had no desire to be editor-in-chief."

A canny businessman, Korda nevertheless has long sought a degree of detachment from the corporate end of the business. "It's in part Dick's genius and Carolyn Reidy's smartness that I've always been used for what I want to do and what I do best. I am pretty much a pure editor. I'm not unsophisticated in terms of business and numbers, but that's not really what I do. What I do best is working with authors and working with books."

At S&S, Korda has ridden the crest of mass market hardcover publishing, while the company expanded in leaps and bounds from a small publisher of distinguished nonfiction and crossword puzzles into a $2.2 billion consumer group. To many, Korda personifies that growth. The editor of NBA and Pulitzer Prize winners, he is still renowned more for presciently taking under his wing the commercial authors, like Harold Robbins, Mary Higgins Clark, Jackie Collins and Clive Cussler, who've driven S&S trade's net profit.

In his recent *New Yorker* profile of Jacqueline Susann, Korda tells of transforming her manuscript of *The Love Machine*, written in eyebrow pencil on pink stationery, into a major bestseller. One suspects he'd therefore have had little sympathy for Random House's efforts to wriggle out of its contract with his own former author, Joan Collins. In fact, Collins asked him to testify in her behalf, but he declined. "The last thing I wanted to do was be on Court TV testifying against my own publisher." Preferring not to discuss the case in more detail, he reflects: "It can be a difficult situation to inherit a complex project that has a lot of problems that you would perhaps never have bought if you had the opportunity. That's a very difficult position to be in for an editor, and it's an awful position for a writer."

He notes that he never could have sustained his long tenure at S&S if it weren't for his lightning-fast editing skills (he has been known to turn a 700-page manuscript around in a weekend) and his dedication to the basics. "With the right book, I can find spiritual peace doing line editing. I wonder if it isn't a dying art. If you look at a really good editor's treatment of a manuscript, the handwriting, the notes, the little lines, it's like a tapestry. It's monkish."

Korda insists that among New York's top book editors, he's "probably the only person left who reads unsols. It seems like a dumb waste of time. Very seldom in my life have I ever bought anything that way. But I'm haunted by this weird feeling that there are all these people out there writing books and that some sentient human being will not at least look at a few pages.

"You can't rationalize this industry," he continues. "Because statistically we just know that somebody out there we've never heard of is writing a book that is going to knock everybody's socks off two years from now. So I have this curious elemental thing, which is that every time I open a manuscript I start with a sense of hope. Hope often dashed, I must say. But in the final analysis, that's what the business ought to be about. And not about how you package bestsellers.

"Part of what's so wonderful about this business," Korda says, reflecting on the hundreds of books that he's published, "is being able to look back at what worked and what didn't work." Asked to name the 10 books of which he's the proudest, he reels off an eclectic list, beginning with Colin Turnbull's *The Forest People,* his first as an independent editor. "I paid $3000 for it, with great misgivings on everybody's part; 38 years later it's still in print." His 10th was his favorite flop, *Shardik,* Richard Adams's second novel after *Watership Down.* "It went from 60 miles an hour to zero in one second. We couldn't give it away. And this is the book after one of the greatest publishing successes of all time." The other eight are as follows: Carlos Castañeda, *The Teachings of Don Juan,* Jacqueline Susann, *The Love Machine,* Larry McMurtry, *Lonesome Dove,* Mary Higgins Clark, *Moonlight Becomes You,* Richard Rhodes, *The Making of the Atomic Bomb,* Justin Kaplan, *Walt Whitman,* David McCullough, *Truman,* Martha Weinman Lear, *Heartsounds.*

Korda is a "compulsive workaholic," and his industriousness has scarcely abated. According to S&S senior editor Chuck Adams, "through the whole trauma of the operation, he was calling from the hospital, he never stopped." He works in New York three days a week, dividing his days at home carefully between editorial and writing projects. "I used to get up around five in the morning and write for a couple of hours. I don't do that anymore. Now I take two days a week to write when I'm writing a book. Magazine articles I tend to do in little bits of spare time, rather like knitting."

In *Man to Man,* Korda is skeptical of macho bravado about health and well-being exemplified by John Wayne's remark that his proudest achievement was that he had "licked the big C." ("Of course he hadn't," Korda writes. "The big C came back, and licked him, in the end.") Does Korda believe that he's overcome his cancer? There are no signs that it has returned, he notes, but "you never win totally. Cancer is a lot more powerful than me or you. You survive it, but that's the most you can say, and you hope that the survival will last for a long period of time."

Certainly the larger-than-life aura that's surrounded Korda since his early days at S&S has diminished. As he has, at least for the moment, doffed the old, invincible, swashbuckling mystique, does his crusade against prostate cancer—which doesn't discriminate between the rich and the poor, the powerful and the powerless—signal a contrition on Korda's part for the preoccupation with power, success and celebrity that propelled his earlier books?

"I don't know that I feel that I have anything to requite for. But *Man to Man* is much closer to the person I really always have been. My writing is a screen that obscures me most of the time rather than clarifies me. *Man to Man* may be the first book that lets in a view of the person that I am."

JONATHAN BING
April 29, 1996

GUS LEE

LOOKING BACK on his life, Gus Lee, at 49, says: "I'm very lucky in my background because the muses could have given me a much more pedestrian environment."

Growing up as a Chinese-American boy in the poor, predominantly black San Francisco neighborhood called the Panhandle, Lee yearned to be black. Later, he attended West Point, became an attorney, investigated corrupt U.S. Army recruiting officers and transformed himself into the author of the acclaimed autobiographical novels *China Boy* and *Honor and Duty*. A third novel wrenched from his experiences, *Tiger's Tail*, a political thriller set in post-war Korea, is out now from Knopf.

In each of these novels, the protagonist wages a relentless search for moral truth, for a way to live that reconciles Chinese roots and American ways. Lee's unswerving need to honor his personal past is manifested in the story of how, after a hiatus of 30 years, he was reunited in 1991 with his childhood friend, Toussaint, an African American descendant of Caribbean pirates, who taught young Gus how to defend himself. The boys had lost track of each other when they entered different high schools, but Toussaint was vividly rendered as a major character in *China Boy*, the fictionalized tale of Lee's childhood.

His need to resume contact with Toussaint was a compulsion for Lee, who had, over the years, checked records of the U.S. Army, the Motor Vehicle Bureau, the FBI and Social Security without success. Toussaint seemingly had vanished.

Lee and his wife, Diane, take up the tale of their search with *PW* at their five-bedroom, stucco-and-frame home in Colorado Springs. Three years ago, they and their two preadolescent children moved from the posh Bay Area suburb of Burlingame so that Lee could be a full-time writer without the need to augment their income with his legal work. They are now preparing to move into a smaller house nearby that will be more manageable for Diane, who does her own housework. The packing boxes are out of sight, however, and the dining room is an oasis of calm. A portrait of Lee's beautiful mother hangs on the wall, along with framed displays of his first two book covers and an antique calligraphy scroll inscribed "longevity and prosperity."

Diane, a psychiatric nurse and editor "numero uno" on all Lee's books, talks about her determination to help her husband maintain the search for Toussaint. When one of her nurse's aide students, an African American, mentioned having seen Gus Lee discussing *China Boy* on television, Diane told her about the book's black characters, including nine-year-old Toussaint. The aide replied that she knew a Dr. Toussaint "Streat," who had moved from the Bay Area to Fresno, where he was in charge of family practice at the Kaiser Hospital.

"All my old prejudices came out," recalls Diane Lee, a WASP from Kansas City. "I thought: there is no way that a little black boy from a slum could be a doctor!" One phone call to the stunned physician erased her stereotypes. A wildly excited Mrs. Lee sped home to her husband, whose computer searches had been off by one letter: Toussaint's surname was Streat, not Street. The subsequent reunion between Dr. Streat and Lee reaffirmed their old friendship.

"Toussaint was the Good Samaritan," Lee says fervently, recalling his boyhood in the Panhandle. "I appreciated anyone who wasn't trying to kill me." Today, almost six feet tall, Lee still has the strong, broad shoulders he developed by studying boxing and lifting weights. "I'm not a natural warrior, just as I'm not a natural boxer. I'm not a fighter," Lee notes with the ease of a man finally at peace with himself.

While the bodybuilding was a means of survival, Lee preferred books, devouring the works of Twain, Dickens and Jane Austen. However, he was pressured to prepare for West Point by his father, Tsung-Chi (aka T.C.) Lee, a former major in the Kuomintang army.

It was a major disappointment to T.C. that Gus flunked out of West Point after three years because he couldn't pass the engineering/math requirements. Gus went on to get his B.A. and LL.B. degrees from the University of California, Davis, before serving in the army as a criminal defense lawyer and command judge advocate.

That achievement was small consolation to T.C. The elder Lee had arrived in San Francisco in 1939 to work at the Bank of Canton as an assistant to T.A. Soong (Chiang's brother-in-law), a former classmate at Shanghai's prestigious, pro-Western St. John's University. Those connections—and the sale of Mrs. Lee's jewelry (she came from a powerful family of Suzhou scholars) finally helped her and their three young daughters to make an arduous journey in 1944 across war-torn China to India and the U.S.

In San Francisco, Mrs. Lee gave birth to their long-hoped-for son, Augustus. When Gus was five, Mrs. Lee died of breast cancer. Two years later, T.C. married a Pennsylvania Dutch woman whose severe discipline was to haunt Gus for years. His stepmother, Edith, has reappeared as a formidable, ghostly presence in all Lee's books.

He points out that both of his parents were rebels, considering the times in which they lived. When his father joined the Kuomintang army, it was an "unthinkable" act for a wealthy young man. His mother—who had received a formal education, rare for a girl—converted to Christianity and refused to consent to an arranged marriage. She had her eye on T.C. Lee, the adventurous boy next door in Shanghai.

Lee believes there was even a bit of a rebel in his stepmother, Edith. Before she met T.C., Edith had left her close-knit Pennsylvania Dutch community and married a young Oregon law student who was killed by Chinese Communist soldiers while serving with the 2nd U.S. Infantry near the Imjin River in Korea. Ironically, 20 years later, Gus Lee himself served with the 2nd U.S. Infantry on the Imjin River during his first tour of duty in Korea in 1977.

His new novel, *Tiger's Tail*, was inspired by his second Korean assignment. Lee was among 10 Army attorneys in the Connelly Commission, set up by the U.S. Senate's Armed Forces Committee, to investigate illegal recruiting practices. Korean nationals—many of whom had served in the South Korean army—were paying up to $10,000 to bribe their way into the peacetime all-volunteer American army as a means of becoming citizens. A "couple of hundred" recruiters were pocketing payoffs for enlisting them.

The investigation in 1979 and '80 began like an adventure story, Lee recalls. Eventually, hundreds of recruiters and senior commanders were relieved of their duties, massive reforms were instituted and suspect enlistees were separated from the service.

Jackson Hu-chin Kan, the army's investigating prosecutor in *Tiger's Tail*, resembles Kai Ting, the autobiographical hero of Lee's first two novels, but his suspenseful, fictitious mission is far more complex and dangerous than Lee's real assignment. Jackson is asked to find a colleague who has disappeared along the Demilitarized Zone (DMZ) between North and South Korea. Jackson also exposes the base's power-mad commander and finds a way to release an American soldier from a Korean prison. The action is brisk, but more urgent still are the various characters' moral imperatives, which drive heroes and villains alike to dog at their respective missions despite all odds.

Although *Tiger's Tail* is fiction, the army atmosphere in Korea is real, Lee emphasizes. Reflecting on the Korean experience, Lee says he had met officers who believed the North Koreans were planning to cross the border again. "Some of our guys thought, 'Why not hit them first? Why should we wait to take the first blow?' The U.S. military," he says, "is premised *not* to deliver the first blow. We'll take a savage first blow often unaware and unfortunately unprepared, but attacking another country in your own self-defense is what Hitler claimed to be doing when he invaded Poland.

"That kind of first strike talk exists," Lee says. "I didn't have to invent it." He is forthright in admitting that invention doesn't come as easily to him as describing his own experiences. "*China Boy* wrote itself in three months. It was like going down whitewater rapids. The other books took much more navigation and thought," he says. In 1992, he took four months of unpaid leave from his executive job with the California State Bar Association to write *Honor and Duty*.

Lee hadn't even considered writing until his then seven-year-old daughter Jena asked him about her Chinese grandmother. Lee realized he had no vivid memory of her, so he interviewed his three sisters, keeping a record of their diverse recollections. He thought that his family journal might be the basis for an article, but Diane declared, "It's a book!" Both neophytes to the process of getting published, they discovered that they had to find an agent. Lee, then a deputy district attorney in Sacramento, was referred to Jan Dystel by a colleague, William F. Wood, author of *Rampage, Stone Garden* and *Court of Honor.* Dystel, who is still his agent, put *China Boy* up for auction, and Dutton brought out the hardcover edition in a first printing of 75,000. Signet published the mass market paperback, and Plume has the trade rights. The book is still in print, and is being translated in the People's Republic of China. Twelve publishers bid for *Honor and Duty.* It and *Tiger's Tail* were bought jointly by Knopf and Ballantine. Lee is grateful for the advice of Knopf editor Ashbel Green and Ballantine/Ivy editor Leona Nevler.

Writing the books based on his life was more than a career change for Lee. Talking to his sisters about the family opened a window into his past and occasioned often painful insights. "I discovered my mother, not only who she was but also what she wished for me and how far away I had traveled from her hopes. The last thing she wanted me to be was an agnostic and I was. The last thing she wanted me to be was a stern father and I was with my son. I had begun preparing him for a hard life. I was yelling at him and acting as if I were putting him through boot camp."

When Diane challenged him to get some professional counseling, the therapist pressed Lee to explain the source of his severity toward his son. To his dismay and astonishment, Lee recalls, he replied, "It's not me he has to worry about, it's Edith"—and burst into tears. "She had died 15 years earlier," he says, "but her strict parenting pattern and my father's was deep in me.

"My journeys as a boy and man have been chronicled in three books, but my most difficult journey was as a father," Lee continues. "I thought that once I understood my emotions, I would change." But his stern behavior persisted. Rather than give up, Lee joined, albeit reluctantly, a small male covenant group at the First Presbyterian Church in Burlingame. Five men would meet every morning and pray for each other. Though he admits that at first he thought it was "asinine," he eventually became a believer in Christianity. The entire experience, Lee admits, went "against all my intellectual will and training."

In Colorado Springs, he attends the First Christian Church. "It's still hard for me to talk about this," he says. "But Christianity gave me a sense of genuine humility and hope for my children. I no longer have the things I feared most in myself, attitudes that I saw in my father and stepmother. Without my faith, I couldn't have done it. In my original culture, Chinese fathers literally have the power of life and death. What I found through faith is that children learn respect if you respect them."

JUDY STONE
March 18, 1996

182

JIM LEHRER

ON A WARM November day, Jim Lehrer strides into his home in Washington, D.C., a few blocks from the National Cathedral. Tie loosened, suit jacket open, he settles himself on the sofa in his pretty sunwashed living room. Lehrer's familiar face, as ordinary and noble as a farmhouse on a Western plain, composes itself in a look of alert waiting.

Lehrer's brown eyes are steady with practiced attention, but they light up like a boy's when he talks about his new novel, *White Widow*, out from Random House, and about his love of fiction writing, which began when he was a young reporter with visions of Hemingway dancing in his head. In the course of our conversation, he comes across as a forthright, decent man, who has been motivated to publish 10 novels, two works of nonfiction and three plays out of a boyishly exuberant sense of the "sheer pleasure" of writing, coupled with a drive to leave something behind that is rooted in a very adult sense of his own mortality.

"Writing is a real joy to me," he says. "I really enjoy making up stories, making up characters and writing it all out. I don't do it to satisfy anything other than my own sense of what I want to do."

Lehrer gives the impression of having stopped on a dime, having just rushed from his Arlington, Va., office where he was preparing to interview FBI Assistant Director James Kallstrom, head of the federal investigation into the crash of TWA Flight 800. Lehrer is used to quick changes, accustomed to living in the present moment under intense scrutiny. He talks about a tense moment he endured as sole moderator of the first of the two 1996 presidential debates.

"The responses were timed," he says. "During one of Dole's responses, I suddenly realized that I didn't know how long he'd been talking. I was concentrating on what he was saying and I forgot to keep track of the time." He remembered in a heartbeat. Being under the gaze of the President and millions of others collects the attention with amazing speed.

The debates made Lehrer news himself—a paradox, since he was undoubtedly chosen as sole moderator precisely because he could be trusted not to strut or intrude. His resolutely civil, even-handed interviewing style, honed over two decades of nightly broadcasts on PBS (first with his longtime co-anchor and close friend Robert MacNeil, then, after MacNeil's retirement in 1995, alone on *The News Hour with Jim Lehrer*), made him a gatekeeper to history, soberly ushering in as many facets of the truth as could be gathered in the available time.

Lehrer is proud of his and MacNeil's PBS way of doing things. Indeed, his 1995 Random House novel, *The Last Debate,* is a broad, bitter indictment of celebrity journalism. He recalls driving his adult daughters to Hartford for the first debate. "I told my girls in the car," he says, "if people remember the questions, I haven't done my job."

Yet Lehrer does want people to remember his writing. When his television work is done, he gives himself completely to whatever project is gripping his interest at the time. "My job is unusual in the sense that when it's over for the day, it's over," he says. "I can try to do better the next day, but there's nothing more I can do about what I did that day. It's over."

In fiction, Lehrer is anything but restrained. He writes every morning and evening, working in stray bits of time on one of a number of computers he uses while traveling, in his office, his home or his country house in West Virginia. In all of his books, including *White Widow,* a dark tale about a Texas bus driver, the prose and plotting have an unpretentious, composed-on-the spot quality. In its second half, *White Widow* rolls from one shocking development to the next like a bus careening downhill without brakes. Getting the story down, letting out that part of himself that doesn't get expressed on the air, seems to be the important thing. It's not surprising that the wildly prolific author Georges Simenon is one of his inspirations. Lehrer writes like there's no tomorrow.

In 1983, Lehrer tasted what it would be like to have no more tomorrows when he suffered a heart attack and underwent double bypass surgery. Five days after the attack, he sat up in bed and wrote in a small spiral notebook a list of priorities for the rest of his life—writing fiction was at the top. While his first novel, *Viva Max!* (1966), was driven by a young man's dream—"I'll write a novel and it will change my life"—his attitude changed after his heart attack. "I really have to do it now. It is as natural and essential a part of my life as eating or collecting bus signs." (Lehrer has a passion for buses and a world-class collection of bus signs).

Lehrer soaked up material as a young newspaper reporter in Dallas in the late 1950s and '60s. On November 22, 1963, he was dispatched to ask the Secret Service man in charge of President Kennedy's security whether the President would be riding with the bubble-top on his limousine on or off. "Take off the bubble top!" Lehrer heard the man say. Later, the heartbroken agent whispered the same words again to Lehrer inside the Dallas police station. By the time Lehrer had worked his way up to city editor of the *Dallas Times Herald*, everyone around him seemed to be writing a novel. "It was the surrounding atmosphere. It was like water. It was everywhere."

That atmosphere helped Lehrer, then 32, write *Viva Max!*, a comedy about a Mexican general who retakes the Alamo in modern times. He sold the novel to Duell, Sloan and Pierce without an agent but engaged Peter Matheson of Sterling Lord to negotiate a deal for the 1969 film version, which starred Peter Ustinov and Jonathan Winters. (Lehrer's current agent is Timothy Seldes of Russell & Volkening, Inc.). Lehrer quit his job as city editor to write full time but soon inched into public broadcasting with a part-time job in Dallas. His PBS star rose quickly, but even as he moved with his wife and three daughters to Washington, D.C., he churned out four novels and a lengthy proposal, all of them, he says, too "terrible" to kindle any interest in publishers. Finally, in 1975, the same year Lehrer teamed up with MacNeil, Atheneum published *We Were Dreamers*, a nonfiction account of his father's attempt to run his own bus line.

Lehrer insists that it was his brush with death that brought him back to writing fiction. "Would I be writing fiction if I hadn't had a heart attack? That's a good question. The answer is I don't think so." His face creases in a smile as he paraphrases Samuel Johnson: "Depend upon it, sir, when a man knows he is to be hanged in a fortnight, it concentrates his mind wonderfully."

During his long recovery, Lehrer tried his hand at playwriting (his friend Eudora Welty sat with him in the theater while two of his plays were given readings by the New Stage Theater in Jackson, Miss.). A daydream about a Kansas kid who gets an eye torn out by a tin can gave rise in 1988 to *Kick the Can*, the first of the One-Eyed Mack novels. Mack, shut out by his partial blindness from his dreams of being a highway patrolman or driving a bus, dons an eyepatch and heads south to become a pirate. His good-natured if far-fetched adventures finding missing people, cracking crime rings, becoming lieutenant governor of Oklahoma—fill six novels, including *Crown Oklahoma* (1989), *The Sooner Spy* (1990), *Lost and Found* (1991) and *Short List* (1992), all published by Putnam, and *Fine Lines* (1994), published by Random House. Lehrer explains that in 1992 he left Putnam for Random, over *Blue Hearts* (1993), a somber thriller starring an ex-CIA man, because Putnam wanted him to stick with One-Eyed Mack. A new Mack novel is currently under contract at Random House, to be edited by senior editor Suzanne Porter.

Lehrer confesses that his wife, the novelist Kate Lehrer, has told him he ends his books "too soon," and that some at Random House have advised him that he may as well slow down, since they don't intend to market more than one Jim Lehrer title a year. Since his steady editor there, Peter Osnos, has departed Random and Times Books to create his own house dedicated to publishing serious nonfiction, Lehrer is uncertain about his long-term publishing future. It's certain, though, that he will keep writing. Lehrer gestures towards the built-in bookcase behind the sofa. His current books fill most of one shelf. "I want that whole bookcase to be filled when I'm gone," he says.

Asked why fiction so captivates him, Lehrer explains: "I'm a written-word person, a page person, a paper person. I love television and I get great satisfaction out of those moments when things go really well. But those moments pass. The moments in books never pass and that's why I write novels."

Lehrer has a great life. Every day he says he gets the "buzz" that comes from connecting with something important that is happening in the world, even though the world usually comes to him in his PBS studio as he interviews the participants and observers of great events. Yet, if people come seeking to sample Lehrer's fiction now that he is being heralded as a broadcasting institution, they are in for a surprise. All of his previous novels have sold modestly, and Lehrer seems free of any self-conscious desire to please the multitudes. *White Widow* is a haunting tale, strikingly different from the picaresque whimsy of the One-Eyed Mack novels. It is a simple, at times contrived story that has the shivery feeling of a nightmare about suddenly having everything you loved and took comfort from wrenched away.

The catastrophic loss in *White Widow* echoes events in Lehrer's past. Born in Wichita in 1934, the young Lehrer watched his father, a bus-station manager, struggle to live his lifelong dream of owning an independent bus line, the Kansas Central Lines, with three rattletrap buses: Betsy, Susie and Lena. The line failed after only one year of operation. The next year, 1948, the family moved to Texas. The sting of that lost dream—along with Lehrer's sense of the everyday beauty of buses made an indelible mark. In his memoir, *A Bus of My Own* (Putnam, 1992), he admits that his father's bankruptcy caused him a recurring nightmare about waking up to discover that he has lost his job and been busted back down to the obit desk on the *Dallas Morning News*. (He himself worked as a Trailways ticket agent while he attended Victoria College in Victoria, Tex.)

Lehrer insists that *White Widow* did not grow out of any conscious fear or pain. "It didn't start out as a dark story. It started out as the story of a bus driver. Once I told the story of his backing over and killing those people, which was based on an incident that actually happened, then the consequences of that took over. And the dark things grew naturally out of that and my own view of things.

"My wife says, and I agree with her, that *White Widow* pushed me beyond where I've gone. It's my favorite book because it breaks new ground for me and at the same time it's about things I'm very familiar with. I think there are hidden things in me that come out all the time when I write, including dark things. And that's what makes writing so exciting."

Driving to Washington's Union Station after the interview, Lehrer suddenly exclaims, "I had a revelation about my life the other day. I realized that I'm living my dream. I wanted to be a journalist and I wanted to write fiction and I'm doing it." We discuss how it would feel to have a dream and not be able to achieve it. What if Lehrer had burned to be a great shortstop? As the marble monuments of Washington glide by, he ponders his destiny, but at the station, he snaps out of it, eyes alert, ready to take on the cares of the day.

TRACY COCHRAN
December 30, 1996

MARK LEYNER

MARK LEYNER'S first memory of television is of watching a ticker-tape parade for astronaut John Glenn. It was an epiphany for him, fueling an ambition that would shape his fantasy life for years to come. "It was the first time I had that frisson of 'if only that could be me,' " Leyner deadpans. "I probably said in my inchoate language, 'I want a blizzard of adulation, right through the greatest city in the world.' "

That narcissistic dream has since transformed Leyner into one of the most flamboyant, warped and ingenious authors of humorous fiction. Since publication of his first short-story collection in 1983, Leyner's work has increasingly focused on the fictional, fabulous, and cartoonish antics of a single character: author and media icon Mark Leyner. Set in a dizzying universe of television, rock music, high technology and advertising, Leyner's wired, disjointed prose has captured both the fidgety attention span of collegiate readers and the acclaim of prominent critics.

Long considered a cult author, Leyner's literary standing is now well established and his work is avidly sought by magazine editors and film producers, allowing him to write full-time while raising a family. It is no coincidence that his new book, *Tooth Imprints on a Corn Dog*, (Harmony) lacks the abrasive, experimental edge of his previous fiction. An upmarket, highly accessible short-story collection (half are reprinted from magazines like *The New Yorker* and *Esquire Gentleman*), it nevertheless exhibits all the whimsy, irreverence and biting satire of his best work. The protagonist is still, much of the time, Mark Leyner; yet his persona is gentler, more circumspect, given to tender reflections about the pressures of fatherhood and professional freelancing.

In reality, the 39-year-old author resides with his wife, one-and-a-half-year-old daughter and "codependent" golden retriever in a nondescript brownstone apartment on the main drag of Hoboken, N.J. At 5'7" and sleekly attired, with slicked back hair and a gym-toned build visible beneath an unbuttoned white shirt, Leyner welcomes *PW* into his small living room from which we head downstairs to his fastidious basement office. A framed poster of Bruce Lee hangs above his desk, which displays a stack of notes from his current project, a "parody of tell-all autobiographies," tentatively called *Let's Not and Say We Did.* One can't help but notice the Jekyll-and-Hyde-like irony that this orderly, subterranean study is where Leyner composes his most anarchic work.

"There's a stunning contrast between my discipline and organization and the unpredictability of my writing. But I think one is necessary for the other," he says, adding "this is where, each day, I go to war with my imagination."

Drinking Coke from a tall Bugs Bunny glass, Leyner tells of attending high school in suburban Maplewood, N.J., and forming a rock band that rehearsed in his parents' basement. Despite his dreams of rock stardom, the band was short-lived. Still, he insists, rock music, at its loudest, most intoxicating and garish, continues to influence the way he writes. "There's an unmodulated volume and intensity to [rock] which is not supposed to be a part of writing," he explains. "I work endlessly on these sentences because I'm really after that unmodulated intensity." He adds archly, "I am just completely committed to being funny all the time."

Rock 'n' roll is in fact one of many extraliterary resources propelling Leyner's iconoclastic style. He claims not to be especially interested in modern fiction. "My aesthetic is much more influenced by what I call the grammar of television. I'm also very fascinated by biology. I have a number of books now about basic surgical skills. . . . I'm really trying to educate myself to the point where I can do my own surgery. Were it not for some choices made along the way, I would have become a surgeon or at least a forensic pathologist, like Quincy," he quips, referring to the TV character. "I'm interested in rock 'n' roll insofar as it's a wonderful spectacle, and I'm interested in all spectacles. That includes sensational trials, wars, unusual surgical procedures, the Olympics."

Since his undergraduate days at Brandeis, however, Leyner has dedicated himself to writing. In college, he published a poem in *Rolling Stone* dedicated to Tina Turner, and eventually obtained an M.F.A. in creative writing from the Univ. of Colorado, where he met members of the Fiction Collective, which would eventually publish his first short-story collection, the ingenious but helter-skelter *I Smell Esther Williams.*

Returning to New Jersey in 1982, Leyner took a succession of odd jobs, including a stint as editor of *The Hoboken Reporter,* and a longer stretch as a copywriter for a medical advertising company, while struggling to write fiction in his free time. He recalls that, while driving to work, he would compose in his head. "I learned how to remember about two pages worth. And I'd get to the office and run straight to the computer and type it out." As it turns out, the peculiar art of medical advertising aptly suited the surrealist, densely allusive texture of Leyner's first novel, which was just beginning to take shape. Writing ad copy allowed Leyner to "spend a lot of time musing about language and doing research in arcane medical books" he says, while seeing, in sharp relief, the rich absurdities of the ad industry. "Watching a client's face light up because you said 'the greatest balloon angioplasty catheter tips ever,' and they know that no one's ever put it that way, there's something sublimely ridiculous about it."

The turning point in Leyner's writing career came in 1988, when McCaffery published his story "i was an infinitely hot and dense dot" as the lead item in the *Mississippi Review* special Cyberpunk issue. *Harper's* excerpted the piece, and shortly thereafter, editor Michael Pietsch offered Leyner a book contract at Crown. The result, *My Cousin, My Gastroenterologist,* is considered by many to be Leyner's best book. It is a brash, free-associative odyssey across suburban America, blending the physical mayhem and absurd antics of a Chuck Jones cartoon, the grittiness of pulp fiction and the randomness of late-night cable TV. Adroitly packaged by Crown as a trade paperback original with a bold, comic-strip cover and cutting-edge layout, it soon became a major hit at campus bookstores. Pietsch's only editorial changes, notes Leyner, were to add punctuation in a few places. "I really thought it was interesting to see how the language acted unmediated by punctuation, to have a continuous stream of information," Leyner explains, adding with deadpan immodesty that "my work has always been somewhat immune to editing. I'm very much the world's expert on how to do it."

When Pietsch left Crown for Little, Brown, Leyner felt he needed a formidable agent to represent his next novel. Although Martha Millard sold hardcover rights to what was to become *Et Tu, Babe* to Harmony editorial director Peter Guzzardi and paperback rights to Vintage, Leyner switched agents again, before the book was published. To this day, Leyner is represented by ICM's Amanda Urban, whom he extols as "the agent of agents."

In retrospect, Leyner admits that the celebrity culture parodied so extravagantly in *Et Tu, Babe* was beginning to go to his head. Taking his writerly will to power to its most illogical extreme, *Et Tu, Babe* chronicles the rise and precipitous downfall of international superstar Mark Leyner. A disjointed collection of megalomaniacal adventures, written in a style of boundless exaggeration, it simultaneously skewers and revels in the spectacle of celebrity authordom. "At the time I was intoxicated with my own portrayal of myself. But also I was very proud of having accommodated my very unhinged style to a narrative. . . . For the first time in my career I really felt like there was no material that I couldn't somehow bludgeon into whatever form I wanted."

Ironically, by casting himself as the protagonist of this grandiose spoof, Leyner jump-started his own career as a celebrity author. *Et Tu, Babe* generated considerable publicity, including an appearance on *Late Night with David Letterman* and a *New York Times Magazine* profile featuring Leyner on the cover. "The *Times Magazine* cover is still somewhat astonishing to me," he admits. "It's probably one of the handful of things I'll always remember about this career of mine. That night I went out to a restaurant frequented by media celebrities because I thought that there would just be pandemonium when I entered the room. Because I thought that all of New York would be talking about nothing else but me. But no one noticed me."

Leyner acknowledges that he has had to learn "to carefully balance my delusions on paper with my delusions in life." He is the first to admit that publicity has its disadvantages. "You end up waiting for the phones to ring to hear who's going to come and take your picture next. You have to slap yourself around a little bit and say, 'Listen you're just a writer.' "

Nevertheless, Leyner's new collection mischievously continues to elide the boundaries between fiction and nonfiction. "The membrane between my books and the reader's life is very thin and porous," he says. "What I get the little frisson of risk from is fictionalizing facts. There's something very appealing to me about just making things up. About lying." In fact, when one story, "Oh, Brother," a clever, albeit ludicrous, parody of the Menendez trial, appeared in the *New Republic* last year, it precipitated a flurry of letters from journalists seeking more information about the case, and one angry professor who had unwittingly assigned it to his class without realizing it was a satire. "I've written things where I intended the credulity of the readers to be tested a bit," Leyner notes, "and this was not one of them. I never ever thought anyone would take it seriously."

Asked if his hypertrophied sense of irony is a bulwark against charges that his fiction is not really serious literature, Leyner shrugs. "The level of irony tends to be more a function of my psychopathology than anything else," he says. "I don't know if it's faux-literature or not. But I think that's one of the charming things about it, wondering if he's for real, and how we should take it."

Leyner concedes that, as he is an experimental fiction writer, the renown he's enjoyed over the course of three books is remarkable. Looking back at the last few years, he grows uncharacteristically earnest. "Beyond anything that's ever happened to me, the most wonderful thing is to wake up in the morning, have coffee, then come down here and this is my job. I never ever thought that I could consider this as going to work." He laughs self-consciously. "I sound like one of those baseball players who says, 'They're paying me for this?' I just feel so lucky and privileged."

Given the lure of the limelight and Leyner's fascination with hype, we wonder aloud if other careers wouldn't hold more appeal; say, that of the talk-show host or elected official. To which Leyner responds, "I will definitely do other things. But the primary thing I'm going to do in my life is write books. I could never host a talk show, because I'm too much of a misanthropic loner. But I'm the sweetest misanthrope in the world."

JONATHAN BING
March 6, 1995

BARRY LOPEZ

STRUGGLING TO DEFINE himself, Barry Lopez says: "Someone once asked me: 'What kind of writer are you?' and I said: 'I am a writer who travels. Some writers stay at home or inside a room. I am a writer who travels.' " To which one hastens to add: when he's not at home, writing, of course, along the MacKenzie River, 40 miles outside of Eugene, Ore., where he's shared 25 years of relative seclusion with his wife, Sandra.

For all that, Lopez travels—to the North Pole, South Pole, Africa, Asia, Australia, bringing back his reports in such nonfiction classics as *Of Wolves and Men* and the National Book Award-winning *Arctic Dreams,* essays that appear widely in magazines from *Outside* to *Harper's* (where he's a contributing editor) and short-story collections such as his new books from Knopf, *Desert Notes, River Notes* and *Field Notes.*

Born 49 years ago in Port Chester, N.Y., Lopez recalls "walking out into Long Island Sound as a three-year-old, up to my neck, and the longing to go farther. The space out over the water, and the light out over the water, was an *attraction* to me. I wanted to go out in the morning and *be* in that."

He grew up in a semirural suburb of Los Angeles, where the grandeur of the western landscape formed his fascination with time and space. After high school in New York City, he went on a three-month tour of Europe, and by the time he graduated from Notre Dame in 1966, he had traveled to every state except Oklahoma, Alaska and Hawaii.

No romantic posturing sentimentalizes Lopez's tales of his adventures: there's rigor in his approach to the open road, his grasp of scientific knowledge and his poetic use of metaphor. Wonder and curiosity animate his brown eyes. He's trim and fit, black hair combed back, and his tan face is that of a young man, still open, wiser, sadder, perhaps, but with no trace of the stereotypical hardened explorer's creased ruddiness. For Lopez, the world is there to behold and reveal, through the art of storytelling. Asked about the incipient dangers of colonial presumption that some Western travelers carry as baggage, he explains his credo: "I think there are two ways to travel. One is to travel for who you are, the other is travelling for what you do. When you travel for what you do, you're the servant of the people you're with, and the servant of the information you encounter."

That word "servant," and the phrase "in service to" pop up frequently in Lopez's conversation. A life principle, no doubt a mix of personality and what he calls a "first-class classical Jesuit education," the idea of service goes to the heart of Lopez as a person and a writer. Beyond self lie "my people—all of us," or "the community." Beyond books, subject, style, literary imagination, the work—sits "the reader." Together with the lessons of responsibility, inquiry and humility absorbed from the luminous side of Enlightenment thought, Lopez carries the imprint of other writers and teachers whose influence has chiefly been moral.

An early mentor was Barre Toelkan, a teacher at the University of Oregon, who gave Lopez a method, a way into his subjects, and, perhaps more importantly, introduced him to the world of folklore and cultures outside the European tradition.

Another was Wallace Stegner, who "taught me how to *behave* as a writer," Lopez says. And of a chance meeting with writer Jorge Luis Borges, he recalls: "I was mesmerized by the man because he had a bearing at the age of 80—40 years blind—that told me, who was half his age: if you conduct yourself well, if you work hard, and if you write well, it's possible to be 40 years older and have this kind of dignity."

In an artistic age characterized by the cult of personality, self-dramatization and confession, Lopez is an anomaly. Having published a handful of stories and freelance articles during his senior year in college, and having decided to pursue a life of writing, he headed for the University of Oregon in 1967.

Once enrolled, however, Lopez became disenchanted with a program that had "too much of a sense of the writer, and not nearly enough sense of the reader." He soon switched to journalism, a move that would further consolidate his idea of the writer's mission. "In journalism, to write an editorial, for example, you sat down at a table that had a typewriter bolted to it, and the task was to write in 600 words something that was coherent and convincing. And you sat there until you did it. I like journalism because it's a grown-up world—deadlines, responsibilities. Freelance writing forces you to focus on the responsibility you have to write cleanly and clearly. It inclines against self-indulgence."

This overwhelming consideration for the reader accounts for the almost invisible narrator in much of Lopez's nonfiction, where the intent is to give voice to the landscape itself. Nor do his short stories find a personal center. "One of the strictures that I placed on myself in fiction is that I would never write about a situation that I had experienced," he states. Asked to summarize his literary philosophy, he adds, "I like to use the word *isumatug.* It's of eastern Arctic Eskimo dialect and refers to the storyteller, meaning 'the person who creates the atmosphere in which wisdom reveals itself.' I think that's the writer's job. It's not to be brilliant, or to be the person who always knows, but it's to be the one who recognizes the patterns that remind us of our obligations and our dreams."

A piece in *The Georgia Review* called "Replacing Memory," a deeply personal essay about his mother's death, seems to contradict Lopez's notions of authorial anonymity. But, he explains: "It has been my belief for a long time that nothing very important happened to me, but that I was fortunate enough to have witnessed things that were important and worth talking about. I think now at the age of 49 I have for the first time turned around and looked at my life. I must say, however, that I'm not certain I will continue with the form of the personal essay. You must pose the question: How does this serve the reader? What is it about yourself that is really of use to the reader?"

Whatever forms Lopez's work takes in the future, it will be anchored to the questions of landscape and culture that have obsessed him from youth—an inquiry he finds unique to the North American literary tradition. As he expands on his theme, Lopez's speech takes on the tones of a moralist whose anger is without cynicism and fueled more by sadness than rage. He speaks of a Western European mindset that is divorced from the elements of *landscape,* a word that includes people, animals, weather, topography. And in pursuing this question he's had to take a long look at the dark side of the Enlightenment thought, which shaped his sensibility. "We treat the world in a utilitarian way," he says. "It has always to be doing something, it has to prove itself, it has to make itself valuable.

"We don't have a spiritual relationship with landscape," Lopez continues, "and in that way we're different from all other groups of human beings, as far as we know, back tens of thousands of years. We don't include landscape in the same moral universe that we occupy . . . and that's imperialistic to me. When you don't have equitable relationships with landscape, I think it's hypocritical to say you have equitable relationships in your life. You can call it a spiritual crisis or an ecological crisis, but the root of it is the problem of hierarchical relationships. We have a culture that has a colonial relationship with landscape, and until it changes I think we're writing our own death warrant."

How all this plays itself out can be seen in the *pattern*—another favorite word of Lopez's—of each work. *Arctic Dreams* moves from the scientific to the imaginative, and then to the historical dimensions of human encounters with the far north. In his short fiction, his style has changed to suit the subject. *Desert Notes* is as spare and lyrical as the environment it reflects; *River Notes* is mellifluous as gurgling water; and *Field Notes* is full of dialogue and dramatic tension. The latter trilogy further finds a writer moving from a certain innocence in his mid-20s, then through his mid-40s, in which his stories, rather than centering on place or topology, focus on individual characters in shifting, international contexts, nearly all of whom share with Lopez an "insistence on privacy and independence," the conditions necessary for magic and personal transformation.

Yet despite Lopez's need for solitude—his nonfiction work can occupy him 10–12 hours a day for weeks on end—there's nothing of the egotist in his outlook or method. Central to his literary concerns is his impulse to break with "authoritative voice" and to embrace a "Renaissance perspective"—he sees each work as a collaboration that involves everybody from the guides, native peoples, scientists and artists he travels with to the editors who help him polish the final manuscript.

Having read a scholarly article on wolves by wildlife biologist Robert Stephenson, Lopez wrote to him requesting a visit, and *Of Wolves and Men* began to take shape. In this way correspondence, chance meetings and shared concerns about "spatial perception, of placement in space," have put him in touch with such figures as the landscape photographer Robert Adams, expatriate British writer James Hamilton-Paterson, Uruguayan novelist Eduardo Galeano, Estonian composer Arvo Pärt and the American writers Wendell Berry, Gary Snyder and Peter Matthiessen, among many others. In fact, Lopez speaks of his discovery and involvement with the larger community of artists and thinkers as the fundamental change of his life of late.

Editors, too, have played important roles in Lopez's working life. Elizabeth Sifton, friend and mentor; Laurie Graham, his editor at

Scribner's; now, Bobbie Bristol at Knopf—these relationships have been mutual and rewarding. Looking back, he finds that he's worked better with women editors than men, and he ascribes this to his sense that men often bring their own adventures to the work, rather than an interest in the specific story he's trying to tell. This latter virtue best defines his agent, Peter Matson, whom he describes as "a good listener . . . with an ability to relate to anyone he's working with in a way that suits that person." "I can't say enough good about Peter," Lopez adds, "he has known intuitively exactly what I needed from an agent."

Lopez is poised at mid-career, though with a shelf of books behind him many would consider a life's work. Looking forward, he speaks of a "big nonfiction book," a formidable work in the wings, but is quick to add: "As a writer I could probably be reduced to a handful of ideas. Ideas that will be our salvation are ideas that have been around for thousands of years. My themes will always be dignity of life, structures of prejudice, passion, generosity, kindness and the possibility of the good life in dark circumstances.

"I'm always writing," Lopez concludes. "There's no difference for me between my life and my work: they're completely of a part, totally related. I'm reading when I get up in the morning and I'm reading when I go to bed at night. I'm walking and traveling and doing all that feeds my work during all my waking hours, and I'm certain that during my sleeping hours stories gestate.

"I think that the world desires to be beautiful," Lopez goes on, with deep feeling. "I have found that beauty in mathematics. I have found it in the hunting behavior of wolves, and the way men and women touch each other. I think the world's keenest desire is for beauty, and that our knowledge of how to achieve that is the various forms of behavior and expression that we apply a single word to, which is love."

DOUGLAS MARX
September 26, 1994

ROBERT MACNEIL

Robert MacNeil is one of the most familiar faces that could appear on the jacket of a novel—though as a novelist he's still a novelty. The co-host for two decades of PBS's *MacNeil/Lehrer Newshour,* the man with the familiar face, the earnest and resonant Canadian tones and a lifetime's experience as a newsman has only just brought out his second novel, *The Voyage,* published by Nan Talese at Doubleday.

Prominence on the printed page has been a long time coming for MacNeil, though from his earliest days he had wanted to be a writer—specifically, at first, a playwright. He actually began, after college in his native Canada, as a radio actor, for which his rounded baritone ideally suited him. He was also, for a brief, hilarious period, an all-night radio deejay who once accidentally locked himself out of the studio during a visit to the john. During his early days in London, where he cut his journalistic teeth as a subeditor at Reuters News Agency's Fleet Street offices, he wrote a play that was considered for a time by the then up-and-coming Royal Court Theatre. "I had this vision of it being accepted and being a huge success, so that the Reuters editors would hear about it, and I could walk in and grandly quit," he says, with a rueful grin for the naïvely ambitious young Turk he had been. (In a remarkable turn of fate, his son Ian is now a stage designer working at the Royal Court.)

Although his TV persona is almost uniformly grave, as if he brooked no levity, MacNeil in person is a keen-witted, lively conversationalist, quick to chuckle and thoroughly informal. He is also remarkably self-effacing. MacNeil is famous, in Kennedy assassination legend, for being one of the few newsmen (he was then working for NBC) present with the initiative to hit the street when the shots were fired at the President in Dallas, and to have actually spoken to Lee Harvey Oswald within minutes of the shooting. Indeed, he approached Oswald, who had just emerged from the Texas School Book Depository, to ask him where there was a phone he could use, and Oswald pointed inside. Oswald, in police custody later, confirmed the exchange. Instead of dramatizing the encounter, as most men would, MacNeil brushes it off: "When William Manchester wrote his book, he worked out that it must have been me," he says now, but declines to make more of it.

His memories of that day are still fresh, however—including an extraordinary moment in the press bus following the motorcade when, drowsy after an early awakening and a drink on the brief flight from Fort Worth, he dreamed of shots being fired at the President and wondered uneasily what, as a newsman, he would do. When it actually happened minutes later, MacNeil leapt from the bus—the only reporter to do so—and followed policemen running up the grassy knoll from which they believed the shots had come. In doing so, he lost what he thinks of as an amazing opportunity to talk to the people lying on the ground at the moment when they had experienced the shooting. But he still covered himself with journalistic glory, getting out the first word that shots had been fired, and then seizing and holding on to a phone at Parkland Hospital to tell NBC the news of the President's death.

It's one of the many highlights of MacNeil's journalistic career, all described in a book called *The Right Place at the Right Time*, published by Little, Brown in 1982, and paperbacked by Penguin in 1990. (When we expressed interest in reading it, MacNeil mailed us a copy that carried the inscription: "Here's one of the many remaindered hardcover copies.") That was not his first book, however. Ever a thoughtful observer of the impact of TV on the public mind, he first appeared in print with a book called *The People Machine: The Influence of Television on American Politics* (Harper, 1968), which now seems remarkably prescient.

But although he had always wanted to be a writer, he found that "you need a lot of discontent to write on the side. When someone's sending you around the world to exciting places it's hard to say that you're not really doing what you want to do."

It was an abiding fascination with language, particularly his native English, that inspired his next book, *Wordstruck*, published as a tie-in with a PBS-BBC series (*The Story of English*) five years later by Viking. Even as he wrote it, however, his fictional imagination was stirring. Like many newspeople, he had written some in his 20s: "There were two early novels. No, I didn't throw them away, but I daren't even show them to my wife."

Wordstruck took MacNeil back to his Canadian roots, recounting the love of language he developed while growing up in Nova Scotia.

"It liberated me a bit, and the fictional stuff began to flow," he recalls. He actually sought a delay on *Wordstruck* while he worked on what was to be his first published novel, *Burden of Desire*. This is a romantic triangle set during the First World War in Halifax, Nova Scotia, where an accident aboard an ammunition ship in the harbor caused the biggest man-made explosion in the world before the Manhattan Project.

But the Viking editor who had encouraged *Wordstruck*, Elizabeth Sifton, had meanwhile moved on to Knopf, and when MacNeil turned up with a novel manuscript that in this initial, uncut stage measured 1200 pages, he was turned down. "That was a bad time, and I wondered whether I was going to make it as a novelist after all." But he took heart in an unexpected quarter. "The assistant to my agent, Bill Adler, told me how much she loved it, and that really cheered me up." Adler showed it to Nan Talese at Doubleday, and a novelist was born. Adler remains his agent to this day.

MacNeil is awestruck at Talese's professionalism. "She called me into the office and talked in great detail about the book for two hours without notes. She understood all the characters; in fact, she seemed to know more about them than I did." She also helped cut and shape the book into the leisurely and haunting romance it became, luring the reader by moving the huge explosion up front (MacNeil had it in the middle) and urging him to expand on interesting factual sidelights like the material on the treatment of shell-shock by military doctors in those far-off wartime days.

Some of the critical praise *Burden* received commented favorably on MacNeil's success in writing passages of the book from a woman's point of view. That was part of his liberation from what he thinks of as the burden of objectivity imposed on a newsman. "I want to write more freely, with less control, less careful consideration." He was surprised by how much of the book emerged from his own subconscious mind, and part of his writing plans, now that he is free of the regular deadlines imposed by his five-nights-a-week TV appearances, is to let that subconscious take over again. "I'm both intimidated and thrilled by the prospect of settling down to writing. I'd love to go to a creative writing class." He's also thinking of getting back into the heads of his *Burden* characters, and taking them up through the 1930s and to the Second World War: "I'm very fond of them."

MacNeil is full of plans for his new liberty. Apart from the *Burden* sequel, he's also thinking about a contemporary New York story, revolving around a murder, and also about another shot at a play. And his sturdy Canadian consciousness still stirs, inspiring thought of a book he might call *Looking for My Country,* "which would describe what it is like to be a Canadian, and why we're neither British nor American." He offers a sardonic story of the prominent Canadian novelist Hugh McLennan, who, as it happens, also wrote a novel based on the great Halifax explosion. "When he sent it to a New York agent, the man said, 'Great, but couldn't you set it in some American city?' "

MacNeil declares: "There's a little demon in me that demands: Why shouldn't Canadians be as interesting as anyone else? Being Canadian isn't necessarily funny. We're simply not a written-about people. We're acutely conscious of literature, but we think it's British or American. It's something that's not about us." He says all this aware that he is himself in an anomalous position, as one who has made his life in one country while retaining his citizenship in another. "I keep a cottage up in Nova Scotia, but essentially my life is here—and I'll probably die here, which as they say concentrates the mind. I'll have to think more seriously about that."

His new novel, *The Voyage,* deals interestingly with the tensions between Canada and the U.S., but in mostly political terms. Its hero, David Lyon, is a veteran of Canada's External Affairs Department who is the Consul-General in New York. He is seen hosting former Canadian premier Brian Mulroney as he tries, with all his charm, to sell the country (not literally) to a group of hardheaded New York businessmen. There are also reminiscences, both fond and not so fond, of former premier Pierre Trudeau. "I wondered at first whether I should use real people, then I decided to go ahead, because I do think it makes it seem more authentic," says MacNeil. "I don't know, of course, how they'll respond to finding themselves in a novel."

What he hopes readers will respond to is a greater sense of pace and urgency than in the slower-moving *Burden.* MacNeil speaks with particular admiration of Simenon's Inspector Maigret novels. "He's been a major influence. He has this extraordinary ability to move the narrative along by every means possible, with dialogue, description, action."

His own novel, too, moves rapidly, as Lyon is confronted with the rash affair he conducted for years with Francesca, a beautiful young model—an affair that could bring down his honorable career. Francesca tests herself in a perilous journey, alone in a yacht, across a stormy Baltic at night. MacNeil, a skilled yachtsman himself ("I just sail along the coast of Maine for a while occasionally") has contrived to give her adventures gripping authenticity.

In a world where there seems all too little time, how does MacNeil manage to create long, carefully wrought books as a sideline to a demanding full-time job? He gets up early, writes for a couple of hours before going to the studio to prepare for the daily broadcast, does the rest on weekends and holidays. "But I'm nothing compared to Jim." In fact, his co-host, Jim Lehrer, already has seven or eight novels behind him and, as he confides at a party MacNeil hosts for Lehrer's latest a few nights later, was thinking of publishing even more frequently, using a pseudonym, until his publisher persuaded him otherwise. "I can only do one thing at a time," MacNeil says enviously. "But Jim can switch instantly, and pick up on his new novel wherever he is, without missing a beat." He discloses that the fellow novelists also discuss their work with each other constantly. "I think we talk more about our novels in progress than about the program."

In the end, what thrills MacNeil most about the freedom to wander in a world of his own creation is his ability to tell it exactly as he wants to. "Journalism is still euphemistic in many ways. It daren't show the worst." He recalls the edited TV footage from Vietnam—and the fact that in *Burden of Desire* he was able to describe the effects of the munition-ship blast more graphically than any newspaper account. "I can make it real *myself*," he exults. It's a liberation from a lifetime of careful, cautious objectivity.

JOHN F. BAKER
October 16, 1995

STEPHEN MARLOWE

THE *Death and Life of Miguel de Cervantes,* Stephen Marlowe's third fictional biography, is a teeming, picaresque work faithful in spirit both to the author of *Don Quixote* and to the unusual life and career of the man who has brought him to life. Born in Brooklyn, Marlowe has roamed across Europe for the last quarter-century, penning 50-odd SF and mystery novels under a half-dozen pseudonyms, finding inspiration for his writing by perennially immersing himself in new places and new experiences. In the early 1980s, Marlowe gave up pulp writing to try his hand at literary fiction. Subsequently, as recently as 1991, he found that he was "an American novelist with no hometown in America, no agent there, and no American publisher until his work had been brought out in Europe first."

That began to change in 1994, when Marlowe and his wife, Ann, moved to Madison, Conn., although they've kept up their packing skills by returning to Europe three times and by renting three different houses in a scant two years. ("I'll never own a house," the author remarks, "because if I did I'd feel trapped and wouldn't want to live in it.")

When Dutton published *The Lighthouse at the End of the World* in the fall of 1995, his surreal fictional biography of Edgar Allan Poe became Marlowe's first literary work to have its initial publication in the U.S. *The Memoirs of Christopher Columbus* was already an international bestseller and winner of France's Prix Gutenberg for best historical novel of the year before being published Stateside by Scribner in 1988. *Cervantes,* released here by Arcade, was published in the U.K. five years ago.

"I made the mistake of sending it around in the States without an American agent," says Marlowe, who clearly enjoys dissecting the ins and outs of publishing as much as expounding on his novels. "Publisher after publisher said they loved it, but said they were the only person in America who had ever heard of Cervantes," he recalls. Scribner editor-in-chief Christine Pevitt, who bought *Columbus,* expressed interest, says Marlowe. "But she finally said, 'You know, I love this book as an editor, but as a publisher I'm afraid that with the kind of advance you want it's going to lose money.' She nevertheless passed along the in-house report by Tim Bent, who was very enthusiastic."

Marlowe wrote a thank-you note to Bent, who in 1990 became an editor at Arcade, the literary publishing house founded by Richard and Jeannette Seaver in 1987. At the time, Bent's colleagues at Arcade deemed the book's length and resultant production costs too daunting, given a market unreceptive to novels of such epic breadth. By the spring of 1996, the situation had changed. Marlowe had an American agent, his former Scribner publisher, Mildred Marmur; *The Lighthouse at the End of the World* had garnered critical acclaim; and Arcade was prepared to back *Cervantes.*

Like *The Memoirs of Christopher Columbus, Cervantes* features an eponymous narrator who speaks in deliberately anachronistic language, using 20th-century slang as he jumbles together past, present and future in a zesty narrative. "My feeling is, if you're writing a novel set in a fairly recent period, it makes sense to try and capture the language of the time completely. That's what I did in the Poe book," comments Marlowe. "But if the historical period is farther back, you have a problem. Trying to capture the language, you end up writing what I call 'forsoothly,' and I don't think you can make that sound alive for the contemporary reader. So I chose to write those books in a contemporary, slangy voice, telling myself—I think with some accuracy—that this is the way people of the time sounded to each other."

Making a story come alive, for himself as well as the reader, is crucial for the author, a vivacious man who looks younger than his actual 68 years and whose conversation reveals a horror of boredom in any form. His research methods mirror his personality. "When I'm writing a historical book, I've got to do the research every day: it's much fresher to me that way, and if it feels fresher to me, it's going to feel fresher to the reader. Obviously, to write about Cervantes, I read more than one biography of him before I began. But the background, the places, the times, the things, the history, I research those as I go along."

Working out a novel's structure is done in a similarly impromptu fashion. "I only know the beginning and the end; there's all this vast unknown middle in between. If a book is to satisfy me, the characters have to work, and if they think inside their heads and interact with each other, all that space in between is somehow going to come out right. In a sense, I write on the basis of not knowing what comes next.

With a long project that takes two years, as *Cervantes* did, I might become a little bored with the book if I knew what was going to happen. I know people who write 60-page outlines of a 250-page suspense novel: what's the point of writing the book?

"I want to be surprised, and I also want the reader to work with me. I would never dream of writing down to my audience; if I develop as I go, then I hope I can take any readers with me. Some people have said, to my surprise, that *The Lighthouse at the End of the World* is a little difficult. It may be, but I don't care. I worked hard on it. Why shouldn't the reader work? I have fun, and perhaps the reader will have a little fun, too."

With the exception of a two-year army stint during the Korean War ("Uncle Sam's idea, not mine"), Marlowe has lived by the guiding principle of having a maximum amount of fun, which for him has always meant writing and travel. (This did not prevent him from paying for the education through college of two daughters from his first marriage). Though his parents weren't readers, an aunt and uncle "brought so many books to the house that we finally had to build bookshelves along one entire wall. At the age of eight, I wanted to be a writer and I never changed my mind."

After leaving Brooklyn to get a B.A. in philosophy from William & Mary, Marlowe came back to New York in 1949 and landed a job as executive editor at the Scott Meredith Literary Agency. "Scott himself really didn't have a great love for books—he might as well have been selling shoes—but his office turned out a lot of writers and editors. When I left because the short stories I wrote began to make money, I hired Evan Hunter to replace me; Don Westlake and Lester Del Rey worked there, too."

As a science fiction writer, Marlowe hit the ground running. In fact, all seven pieces in a 1950 issue of *Amazing Stories* were written by the 22-year-old author under a variety of pseudonyms. By the time he got out of the army, Marlowe had switched to mystery and suspense. "I was making a living—I've been lucky; I've always been able to make it as a writer—but I felt I'd done as much as I could in science fiction. The last thing you want is to feel jaded by or with your work, so I jumped to suspense novels. But at some point I had said all I wanted to say in that field as well."

The author doesn't have much to say about his decades of genre fiction; one senses he's a bit embarrassed by some of it. "The last three books are the only ones that matter to me," he declares. "I was too prolific before. When you're young, writing comes more easily because your critical faculty grows as you get older. As a kid, if you get it down on the page and it looks pretty plausible, that's great. But when you get into your 40s and 50s, you start thinking, 'Wait a minute; I can do this better.' The *New York Times* once called me the most prolific mystery writer in the United States; I said, 'Good Lord, I don't want to be the most prolific anything; I would love to be the best.' "

A few years passed after that insight; the Marlowes, who were married in 1964, continued their wanderings across Europe while he waited for inspiration. "Then one day I sat down and out of the blue wrote the first scene of *The Memoirs of Christopher Columbus.* I gave it to Ann, who said, 'Wow: what happens next?' I said, 'I don't have the slightest idea, but I'll find out.' "

Perhaps it's no coincidence that Marlowe's voyage of self-discovery culminated in a novel about the conquest of a new continent. Four American agents passed on the book, apparently because they were confused by the author's exuberant use of modern language to tell a 15th-century story. (One went so far as to carefully point out all the anachronisms that spoiled the book's "authenticity.") Happily, British publishers were more receptive. "With the enthusiasm of Liz Calder at Jonathan Cape and Sonny Mehta at Pan, suddenly everybody in the world wanted the book, including American publishers," Marlowe recalls. Scribner landed it with a $100,000 preemptive bid.

The international success of both *Columbus* and *Cervantes* enabled Marlowe to be sanguine about the latter book's initial failure to find a publisher in the States. "I hope I'm an international writer," he remarks. "I'm an American who feels most American when I'm abroad. Writers are either insiders or outsiders. The quintessential insider is Faulkner, who wrote about one milieu, one place, one environment. The way I write and think, I must see the world as an outsider, a stranger looking in. I'm not comfortable with the idea of nationalism or patriotism."

Although he followed his pair of wandering Renaissance protagonists with a novel about a 19th-century American who never left the States, *Lighthouse* enabled him to continue his project of plumbing the nature of writing through fictional portraits of real-life authors. "If Cervantes was a crucial fiction writer in the sense that his work is where the novel as we know it began, Poe was crucial in a very different way. He literally invented science fiction and mystery, but he also invented the idea of the disintegration of human personality, which is so crucial in 20th-century fiction. So Poe in his own way is as seminal as Cervantes."

When Milly Marmur stepped down in 1987 as Scribner publisher to open her own literary agency, she took on the Poe manuscript, eventually placing it with Dutton, which will also publish Marlowe's novel-in-progress. About that he will say only, "there's a real-life writer in it, but he's not the main character; the main character is one of his fictional characters who would like to be real."

His many different publishers have made only minor revisions in his manuscripts, says Marlowe, for whom there is only one editor who counts: Ann Marlowe, who published a few novels in the 1960s before giving up writing to blue-pencil her husband's books. "For better or worse, I rely primarily on myself and secondarily on Ann; the editor at the publishing house really is a distant third. If Ann wasn't so good, I don't think I'd feel this way, because you need input from somebody, but she is a tremendous line editor. She freelances for both Arcade and Dutton. She will always do my books, which means I don't have to lean on the in-house editors."

The Marlowes' intimate rapport is evident at lunch in their current home, where they finish each others' stories and trade appreciative comments over a splendid meal of poached salmon and generous quantities of wine. They seem comfortably settled in this pretty house on the Connecticut shore, but the writer can't imagine staying put for very long. "The game plan for the near and middle future would be to spend half our time here and half elsewhere. I think if I remained in one place I'd be less interesting to myself and less interesting to my readers. I want to have the newness of experiencing a place for the first time, and I want it to appear in my work; this is very important to me. I love to be on the old road, anytime, anyplace, anywhere: When in doubt, keep moving."

WENDY SMITH
November 18, 1996

BILL McKIBBEN

I't's THE END of the hottest August on record in New York State—
less than an eighth of an inch of rain has fallen—when we head north
out of an infernal Gotham to visit with the environmentalist author
and activist Bill McKibben, who lives in the Adirondacks, about 250
miles away. Behind us and to the southeast, 6000 acres of brush and
pineland are burning on Long Island. On the roadsides, the grass is
baked brown and the shoulders are blighted by inordinate roadkill—
the dry weather has put animals on the move. Later, above Lake
George, a parched hillside will be whitely smoking.

The passage from New York City into the heart of New York State
is measurable in more than miles and dead animals. From the center
of American commerce and culture (so-called), one passes rolling
meadows, once farmed, now pasture for thoroughbreds; the Catskills,
humbly humped to the west, are spotted with hardscrabble towns
amidst a dubious Woodstock and Leatherstocking legacy; Albany,
once an iron-foundry and canal-terminus town, is a jagged architec-
tural morass with an egg-shaped building at its center, an unwitting
symbol of what government, the city's dominant industry, will do.

When the Adirondacks, the oldest mountains in the world, finally
come into view, spruce green with slivers of sunlit lakes to the north
and west, one wonders if this, at last, is paradise. Not so fast. For nothing is as simple as it seems, nor as idyllic.

There is poverty in these Adirondack counties. On the way in, you
pass towns whose names reflect the capital industries that buoyed
them but which have since failed: Mineville, Gloversville, Tan-
nersville, the once-bullish Speculator. Johnsburg, the little hamlet that
McKibben calls home, is half boarded up. But down Garnet Lake
Road, on which McKibben's farmhouse sits, the visitor is eased back
into admiration for a life in nature gracefully carved out. Altogether,

after the four-and-a-half-hour trip, one is left with some of the sour confusions and conflicted feelings that one suspects must bedevil McKibben himself. Does this entire transit spell "the end of nature," as his first book was called, or is this natural splendor amidst straitened community the basis of "hope, human and wild," as his newest book is called?

"This is what the summers of the 21st century will be like," says McKibben, a tall, pale, toothily handsome man who, but for his graying hair, seems even younger than his 34 years. With a teenager's gangly gait, in shorts and T-shirt, he has walked up from the pond behind his house, on which his wife, the writer and editor Sue Halpern, and their two-year-old daughter are sitting on a raft. "This is what we've been talking about for years," he says, shaking hands.

McKibben, indeed, is an interesting mix of hope and despair. On the one hand, the political situation is at its worst, he notes, with the gutting of the Clean Water Act and other environmental rollbacks sponsored by the Republican congress; on the other, he senses that these acts will hasten the circumstances that will make reform a necessity. But it is the sunnier side of McKibben's global view that shines through in *Hope, Human and Wild*, (Little, Brown).

McKibben describes *Hope* as an attempt to "convince myself and others that it is not completely pie-in-the-sky to imagine there could be other ways to conduct ourselves." After *The End of Nature* (Random House, 1989), which sternly rebuked Western society for ushering in the Earth's ruination, such an effort to uplift might seem an about-face. But to McKibben, it is a necessary adjustment. "The point of the new book," says McKibben, "is to counter despair. Environmentalists have become too enmeshed in what is politically possible *right now*." He senses that, after hearing environmentalists cry wolf for so long, the world doesn't so much disbelieve the dire warnings as accept them as pointing to an inevitability. "To destroy the environment has come to be seen as the unfortunate byproduct of progress," he laments. "And to save it is standing in the way." He wants to remind people that there are other solutions.

These are conservative times, no doubt. And as McKibben rows around Garnet Lake ("I feel more comfortable outside, rather than inside talking into a tape recorder") with its undeveloped shoreline ringed with tall white pines, one wonders if he hasn't found a refuge from it all, his own "acre of grass," as Yeats put it. But the oarsman's occasional silent reveries are countered by a bulldog's engagement with the powers that be. "Global-change issues are so huge and so perilous," he says, "that there is no question that we will have to have government deeply involved."

McKibben admits that at the moment, "we are in a sort of short pause between bouts of environmental concern." But he says of the next wave, "We won't have any choice. That's what the politics of the next 50 years will be about; not what Newt Gingrich thinks it will be about."

In *Hope, Human and Wild,* McKibben looks at three different locales—his beloved Adirondacks; Curitiba, a mountain city in Brazil; and Kerala, a community in India. In each of the three portraits, he finds that enormous progress has been made by dint of human imagination and prudent government involvement. Looking over his shoulder at the vaulting ranks of pine (that extend, he says, "all the way to Lake Ontario"), he reminds his note-taking boatmate that 100 years ago the hill was clear-cut hillside, completely logged out. "Now, there are wild deer and moose running around," he says. Reforesting and the protection granted by the Adirondack Park Agency have saved this vista. And, most significantly, it has been the alliance between logging companies, state government and local citizenry that has made it work. The standard-of-living problems, however, remain to be solved.

McKibben insists on being a pragmatist. He is not all zeal and back-to-nature at any costs. In fact, he says, "I love cities, and cities are where the greatest environmental economies can be had, with mass transit, public parks and the like." In Curitiba, a city of 1.5 million people, McKibben found some amazingly deft solutions to the kinds of urban planning problems that have left many another city-center a ghost town. McKibben profiles the efforts there of a gallant mayor, Jaime Lerner, to fend off intentions to cure a snarl of downtown traffic with an overpass that would obliterate the old commercial district. Lerner alone was convinced that a pedestrian mall was the answer. Over one weekend, he ordered city workers to jackhammer the street, put in park benches and plant thousands of flowers. When an automobile club threatened to retake the street, they arrived in the dawn to find the mall covered by long sheets of paper, with dozens of children coloring pictures. "The transformation of Curitiba had begun," writes McKibben. Thanks to more ingenious planning—"five structural axes" bringing cars into and out of the city—the entire settlement of the area has taken on a sensible order and scale. "You're doing a strange archeology," McKibben quotes Lerner as saying. "You can't go wrong if the city is growing along the trail of memory and of transport. Memory is the identity of the city, and transport is the future." Curitiba is now a model for urban planners.

McKibben expects to be attacked from all sides for this book—by environmentalists who don't think optimism is the proper note for the times, and by pro-growth advocates, irked enough by McKibben's former doomsaying to scoff knowingly at his brighter tone. And he knows that, by ranging far afield, to South America and the Indian subcontinent, he runs the risk of being accused of breathlessly bringing back evidence that is deemed irrelevant to North American problems. But McKibben is a veteran activist, a seasoned dissident inured to conflict. "If the world made us completely and utterly happy," he says, putting up the oars for a bit, "there'd be no chance of change." In the crystalline current next to us a good-sized bass holds motionless, as if listening—one of the converted, surely.

There is something Emersonian to McKibben's cast of mind—like Emerson, he focuses on what is natural to Man and what is false in Nature. Both men write prose that rings like oratory—in fact, lay ministering is common to each (Eerdmans has published a book of McKibben's sermons; he teaches Sunday school at the local Methodist church.) McKibben even hails from Lexington, Mass., down the road from Emerson's Concord; and each attended Harvard.

"Lexington, the birthplace of American liberty," muses McKibben. "Maybe that explains my rebelliousness—and my patriotism." Both his parents worked for the *Boston Globe,* and McKibben says he always saw himself as "a newspaperman." But Harvard, he says, "became the end of my education; all I worked on was the *Crimson.*" But that was where the young McKibben's prose was discovered by the *New Yorker's* William Shawn.

"Shawn had come across something of mine in the *Crimson,* and called me. I hung up: I thought it was a *Lampoon* prank. Six months later, he called again. It was April Fool's Day. Then I *knew* it was a prank. But he called again. He wanted me for the Talk of the Town," the famous short, often whimsical front-of-the-book pieces, which, until Tina Brown took over, were just as famously unsigned.

McKibben, 21, moved to New York. He wrote more than 400 Talk pieces and numerous long essays. One detailed where everything that entered his apartment came from, and where everything that left it went. He came to know sewage barges and the source of the oil that

Con Ed buys. To finish the piece, he went for a few weeks to a writers' colony in the Adirondacks and fell in love with the area.

Things were already "turbulent" at the *New Yorker,* says McKibben, in the wake of S.I. Newhouse's purchase of the magazine, and Shawn was concerned about the succession to his editorship. After unsuccessfully courting Jonathan Schell, Shawn asked McKibben to consider the post. But then Shawn was fired and replaced by Robert Gottlieb, and McKibben quit the same day, after five years. "It was the end of a glorious tradition, I could see that," he says now.

McKibben had developed enough contacts to make a go as a freelance writer, and agent Gloria Loomis took him on as a client. David Rosenthal, then at Random (he now runs Villard), bought his first two books, *The End of Nature* and *The Age of Missing Information* (1992), a critical look at American television, but Jim Silberman at Little, Brown showed more enthusiasm for *Hope,* and McKibben moved there on a one-book deal.

All of McKibben's books, in a sense, pursue the same theme, no different than the piece for Shawn on his Bleecker and Broadway apartment—what do we consume, why do we consume it, and what are the consequences? "Does it make sense to have things the way we have them, that's what all my books are about," he says. "Is it desirable? Is something else possible? What I've learned so far is that what is sound and elegant and civilized and respectful of community is also environmentally benign." McKibben looks around appreciatively at the bowl of blue sky above the lake. "The Adirondacks," he says, "are at the epicenter of the recovery."

A late afternoon breeze has come up, tingling the surface of the lake. McKibben turns the boat about and leans in to the rowing toward shore.

MICHAEL COFFEY
November 13, 1995

STEVEN MILLHAUSER

Saratoga Springs, in upstate New York, is perhaps best known as the home of the oldest racetrack in America, where Texans in the obligatory ten-gallon hats and the more genteel traditional horsey set gather each August for the Travers Stakes. But Steven Millhauser's imagination is captured more by structures like the old Batchelor mansion, an elaborately painted and turreted Victorian folly a few blocks off the main drag. "The man who built that was not thinking just of a practical dwelling," Millhauser tells *PW* on a brilliant early spring day. "He was a dreamer."

In seven novels and short-story collections, Millhauser has made a considerable reputation writing about the inner lives of novelists, painters, puppeteers and other assorted inventors. His latest novel, *Martin Dressler: The Tale of an American Dreamer* (Crown), depicts a turn-of-the-century entrepreneur caught up in "a long dream of stone," building an increasingly fantastical series of hotels in a precisely evoked, but oddly ethereal, New York City. His ambitions culminate in the Grand Cosmo, a monstrously rococo pleasure dome that combines elements of the hotel, the department store, the carnival and the museum in its endlessly mutating interiors. This shadow city, "in comparison with which the actual city was not simply inferior, but superfluous," is the dreamer's greatest success, and the businessman's undoing.

But when attention turns to himself and his own creative impulses, Millhauser insists writers are the most boring people imaginable. "I'm assuming everything I say is of no interest whatsoever, and that's what allows me to say it," he warns. "If I thought it was of interest, I'd immediately be silent."

Tall and thin, with graying hair and a gently exacting professorial manner, Millhauser, 52, is disarmingly voluble even when threatening to revert to the public silence he has kept for most of his career. With few exceptions, he has scrupulously avoided interviews—"that means

213

I'm now unscrupulous," he deadpans—and the biographical sheet on file in his publicist's office is revealingly blank. "You know, I was convinced you were going to describe my shirt. So I chose the least noticeable, the blandest one possible," he says of his (heretofore unnoticed) blue and purple plaid flannel.

Millhauser's playful mockery of his own public non-persona belies the persistent melancholy of his artist tales, even as it echoes their mordant wit. His first novel, *Edwin Mullhouse: The Life and Death of an American Writer 1943–1954 by Jeffrey Cartwright,* published in 1972, was a dark elegy for the creative genius of childhood, a portrait of the artist as a 12-year-old boy written by an overly literal, secretly envious best friend. The melancholy stories gathered in collections with names capturing Millhauser's fascination with the fantastic and the outmoded—*The Barnum Museum, In the Penny Arcade, Little Kingdoms*—often returned to the theme of the solitary inventor or artist, stranded both ahead of and behind his own time, gradually fading out of the real world and into the woodwork of the imaginary.

Now, after 25 years of making dreamers his business, Millhauser has made the dreamer a businessman. "I wanted to write about something as different from my earlier stories about artists as possible," he says, having chosen to meet in a coffee shop across from the Adelphi, the only hotel remaining from Saratoga's heyday as a summer playground for the likes of J.P. Morgan, Diamond Jim Brady and Lillian Russell. (Millhauser has lived in this historic town with his wife and two young children since the late 1980s). "And the thing most different from an artist is a businessman, someone who looks at the world practically. Now I have a feeling that as I did this I was secretly turning him into an artist, trying to find the place where his imagination touched mine, because I wanted it to be a sympathetic view. I've always liked the myth of the self-made man in America."

The novel grew out of research Millhauser did for a story called "Paradise Park," a long fantasy on turn-of-the-century Coney Island published in *Grand Street* in 1993. Millhauser had found a historical moment in which time itself seemed out of joint. "The grand hotels, the great department stores," Millhauser says, "always combined the most modern mechanisms—elevators, vacuum-cleaning systems—with deliberate imitations of old-fashioned European features. It's a wonderful contradiction—looking back over your shoulder at something that is passing and also at everything that is aggressively modern in America."

Since the market forces that spectacularly reward and punish such dreamers in stone as Martin Dressler are generally oblivious to novelists of a serious bent, Millhauser has, since the late 1980s, taken four months out of each writing year to teach at Skidmore College. For him, teaching writing is an odd, paradoxical, complicated business, but he throws himself into it. "Writing can't be taught," he insists, "and if you know that it can't you'll suffer much less confusion. But what can be taught is a certain kind of attentive, skillful reading. If you want to write, you absorb literature. And then you can't *stop* writing."

Millhauser recalls wanting to write stories ever since he could read them. "When I was seven years old," he intones, pausing with a mock portentousness worthy of Edwin Mullhouse's preadolescent biographer. "But seriously, I guess I always thought from childhood that I wanted to write. But then many children think that. It has no special meaning."

After finishing college at Columbia, Millhauser took part-time jobs, shuttled back and forth between New York City and his parents' house in Stratford, Conn., and completed numerous stories and a novel. An agent circulated the novel, and while Knopf rejected it, an editor did express interest in seeing his next book. In the meantime, Millhauser enrolled in the English Ph.D. program at Brown, working, over two summers, on the book that became *Edwin Mullhouse*. It was accepted "instantly," he says, by Knopf's Robert Gottlieb in 1971 and published to rave reviews in 1972.

Edwin Mullhouse is a not-so-gentle satire on the savage art of literary biography, which—quite literally, in the novel—murders genius in its very attempt to anatomize it. Jeffrey Cartwright, playing Boswell to the 12-year-old author of a hallucinatory masterpiece called *Cartoons*, documents everything from Edwin's earliest burblings to his schoolyard crushes on his most violent and disturbed classmates. It's a dizzying, uncannily vivid elaboration of what Holden Caulfield memorably dismissed as "all that David Copperfield kind of crap," transplanted to suburban Connecticut of the 1940s. But in the end, our brief glimpse of *Cartoons* suggests that Jeffrey's biography—and the real world itself—is merely a "scrupulous distortion, a specious clarity and hardness imposed on mists and shadows."

While the novel is a wicked indictment of biography's excesses, Millhauser says its mists and shadows are drawn straight from his own past. The book, he says, "has a deliberately implausible premise, which was what released me into being able to write about my childhood at all. I did Zola-like research, interviewing my third-grade teacher to find out exactly what happened. But within that, I invented wildly. The book imitates a certain kind of realistic novel, and pushes more and more toward the extravagant."

Millhauser followed up his debut with *Portrait of a Romantic* in 1977 and *In the Penny Arcade* in 1984, both from Knopf. When Knopf rejected an early version of *From the Realm of Morpheus*, his agent, Amanda Urban, took the book to Morrow, which published it in 1986. But Millhauser, desiring a smaller house that could give him more attention, subsequently went to Ann Patty's S&S imprint, Poseidon Press, which brought out *The Barnum Museum* in 1990. After Poseidon folded in 1993, just as *Little Kingdoms* was being published, Millhauser followed Patty to Crown. "So I've had a checkered past," he laughs.

Asked about connections between his first and latest novels, Millhauser recalls a remark of Patty's. "She asked me how it feels to have written about an artist in the '70s and a businessman in the '90s, goading me. I just laughed. But I do see definite connections between my work, patterns I helplessly follow. I'm attracted to extreme things, and I see extreme things in a deeply practical culture doomed to failure. There's a place where things go too far, become too much of themselves. I seek out that place always. But on a technical level, with Martin Dressler's last hotel, I wanted to stretch the real into the fantastic without actually snapping it."

On the whole, Millhauser is reluctant to discuss openly the tasks he sets for himself as an artist, hewing to a highly articulate, grown-up version of "the maddening evasiveness" that kept Edwin Mullhouse's fictional biographer from "ever penetrating to the heart of things." It's as if he doesn't want to let readers into the innermost chamber, to reveal just how the man behind the curtain is controlling the men behind their own curtains in his stories. "There's something so intimate about my imagination that I don't want to tamper with it."

Asked about the nature of fiction in a rare interview in 1982 with *Contemporary Authors*, Millhauser made a typically firm, and typically evasive, declaration: "Unless a writer is a trained aesthetician, his opinion concerning the nature of fiction is of no more interest than his opinion concerning the nature of the economy." In other words, as one skeptical academic supposedly said of efforts to bring Nabokov (an author to whom Millhauser has been compared) to Harvard in the 1950s: "Why would you hire an elephant to teach zoology?"

While reluctant to identify himself with "the person representing Steven Millhauser in that interview," the author backs up his old disclaimer. "Most writers are not terribly interesting when it comes to describing the nature of what they do. What you learn from a writer, as a rule, is what his passions are. If I wanted to learn how to think about art theoretically, I would not go to a writer. I would go to a philosopher. And then I would find the philosopher dry and dull and I would finally go back to the works of the writer."

But even as Millhauser asserts that artists as people are not interesting, that they have little of value to say about their own work, he finds their creative drive endlessly fruitful as a subject for his own art. "Artists —at least my kind of artist, a person who draws pictures or writes in a notebook—are not terribly interesting if you observe them from the outside. But they're interesting insofar as they represent a refusal to behave the way conventional people behave. What artists do, if they're the real thing, is shut themselves off secretly in a room and ask not to be disturbed while they pursue waking dreams. This is a very curious way of behaving over a lifetime. It's very close to lunacy, in fact."

Does Millhauser really believe himself to be a lunatic? "Yes and no," he says. "It's as if my fear with each new book is that 'Oh, now I've really stepped over the edge. Now they'll know the truth about me, that I'm a screaming madman who spends all day having pictures in my mind and writing them down.' The only comfort a review has ever given me is that feeling that 'Ah, I'm allowed to do this. I can do this again.'"

But in characteristic style, Millhauser can't resist going on, pulling the rug out from under himself a little bit, wriggling out of one statement about his art with another, equally adamant declaration.

"As I say this, something else rises in me, which is the opposite of that—to assert the absolute validity of what I do. I have no doubts about it; I never have. Dreaming is the healthiest possible thing to do. It sounds arrogant, but when I make up these tales, I'm not removing myself from reality. I'm pointing myself absolutely toward the center."

He pauses. "Of course, I'm also aware that this may be a terrible delusion. I'm involved in a very peculiar human activity. But I'll never stop."

JENNIFER SCHUESSLER
May 6, 1996

ALBERT MURRAY

THE SCHOMBURG Library, Harlem's grand institutional collection of Afro-Americana and scholarship, immediately grabs an interviewer's attention upon exiting the 135th street IRT station, setting just the right tone for an interview with novelist and critic Albert Murray. It seems quite appropriate that the Schomburg should be just around the corner from Murray's apartment; it probably comes in handy for him. An enduring symbol of Harlem's legendary role as the center of African American intellectual and creative life, the Schomburg evokes the depth and range of scholarship that characterizes Murray's writing—which encompasses references to the fiction of Ernest Hemingway and Thomas Mann, the painting of Romare Beardon and the music of Duke Ellington.

A bumper crop of Murray's work is being issued by the Random House family. Pantheon is publishing his third novel, *The Seven League Boots*, and a collection of critical essays, *The Blue Devils of Nada*, and Vintage is reprinting *The Hero and the Blues*, his classic critical study of blues and the art of literary fiction.

Murray's wife, Mozelle, a retired New York City public-school teacher, opens the door to a modest, light-filled honeycomb of an apartment that almost seems to be a branch of the Schomburg. Murray's formidable library takes up most of one long wall, photographs of Duke Ellington and Louis Armstrong and drawings and watercolors by Romare Beardon (an old friend and the subject of a typically lucid essay in *Blue Devils of Nada*) are arranged throughout the room. Mrs. Murray disappears into the apartment, which they share with their daughter, Michel, a former dancer with the Alvin Ailey Dance Company. Murray, who turns 80 this year, emerges gingerly but enthusiastically from his study, a simple, neatly arranged desk tucked informally into a corner of the main room.

His hair is grayer than it appears on his book-jacket photographs, and he now uses a cane (the result of an operation for an arthritic knee), but he still looks robust. He's informally dressed in beige jeans and a Champion sweatshirt cheerfully accented by a bright yellow turtleneck.

Murray projects an instantly engaging combination of professorial erudition and down-home joviality. A marathon conversationalist, he effortlessly delivers a tsunamic outpouring of learned, hip commentary on jazz, world literature, literary theory and, of course, the blues, all of it peppered with jokes, quips, snatches of vivid rural Alabama black dialect, wordplay and barbershop trash talk, periodically punctuated by spasms of unrestrained laughter from both author and interviewer, and by judicious sips of bourbon.

Born in 1916 just outside of Mobile, Ala., Murray is the real-world counterpart to Scooter, the "brownskin boy" hero of his first two novels, *Train Whistle Guitar* (Pantheon, 1974) and *The Spyglass Tree*. (Pantheon, 1991). Much like Scooter, Murray was raised in a rural black community in the 1920s, fished and hunted in the rivers around the Gulf and along the bayou, listened to the blues and spirituals, the whistle of freight trains and the tales of Uncle Remus, Br'er Rabbit and life in the briar patch.

In 1939, he graduated from the famed Tuskegee Institute, the traditionally black college founded by Booker T. Washington (his good friend, the late Ralph Ellison, was a distant and impressive upperclassman at the time) and remained there teaching literature until he joined the Air Force in 1943. He retired as a major in 1962, managing, along the way, to pick up an M.A. and squeeze in innumerable teaching and lecturing gigs at a variety of universities around the world. He published his first book, *The Omni-Americans* (Da Capo Press), an acclaimed collection of critical essays, in 1970 at age 54. His 1971 memoir, *South to a Very Old Place* (McGraw-Hill), was nominated for the National Book Award, and he collaborated with Count Basie on the late bandleader's equally acclaimed autobiography, *Good Morning Blues* (Random House, 1985). "For five years," says Murray, "whenever I wrote 'I', I meant Basie."

Train Whistle Guitar introduces the citizens and stories of Gasoline Point, Ala., as seen through the eyes of Scooter and his best friend, Little Buddy Marshall. Murray uses this classic coming-of-age story to provide a literary equivalent of the blues, creating a work rich in what he calls the "idiomatic particulars" of black life and presenting the people, stories, tall tales, folk traditions and music of his own background as a representative example of contemporary human consciousness.

His writing is an effort to create a framework for understanding the depth and power of the black American idiom, Murray explains, "There ain't no U.S.A. that the world loves without us. You can put the spirituals right in there against the stained windows of the great cathedrals without a drop in aesthetic sophistication or profundity. I'm proud of that. I want to stake our claim to that. The world loves what we stylize."

But he is also quick to emphasize that he is not claiming a racially based creative superiority. Great Art, Murray points out constantly, is about mastering an idiomatic style. American culture, he emphasizes, is "incontestably mulatto. Race has no place in the discussion. Americans constantly confuse culture with race. When you deal with culture you're dealing with idiomatic differences and nuances. That's why the black nationalists are so ridiculous. They cannot be idiomatically African. It's precisely the idiomatic particulars that you color the world with."

He's concerned with "extending, elaborating and refining," his Southern black folk tradition into fiction, crafting that experience within the literary traditions represented by Thomas Mann, James Joyce, T.S. Elliot and William Faulkner. "I'm dealing with the blues in the context of the existential problems of life," Murray says. "Life is just particles and waves until we make a story out of it. Until we can get to a metaphor it doesn't mean anything. It's what Joyce called the 'ineluctable modality.' So when I'm talking about the blues I'm not talking about downtrodden people picking cotton in Mississippi. I'm talking about man just like Malraux is talking about Pascal's image of man's fate."

Pointing to shelves crammed with literary classics, Murray says his work is part of a literary "colloquium" of all the best that has been written. "You're adding on. You had Mark Twain, Melville, Emerson, Hawthorne then Hemingway. And we look at these guys differently because each conception is affected by each new statement."

But no matter how abstruse his theoretical foundations, Murray makes it clear that it is the "idiomatic particulars" that bring a work to life. In portraying "the problems of human consciousness in our time," he says, the artist must "never give up the barbershop or the street. The novelist has to take it back to that. Like the musician, once he gets away from human feeling and away from dance, he's just running exercises. If you don't swing, forget it."

Murray's stories are epic, unlike what he calls the "social science fiction fiction" of Richard Wright and James Baldwin he elegantly lambastes in *The Omni-Americans* and *The Hero and The Blues*. "Most of our black writers are not really interested in literature. They're interested in justice, or they're interested in power; not this intrinsic thing of being alive and getting the most out of life whether you have power or whether you have freedom. We can't say all those lives that were spent in slavery were absolutely meaningless. Somewhere they got something. They found earthly salvation either in some formal thing they received or something they brought with them but somehow they had to feel it. That's the basic problem of art."

It is improvisation and "swing"—that elemental sense of motion, time and stylish existential response—that defines the jazz musician's art and ultimately, says Murray, life itself.

"Midway, middle passage, that's where we start swinging. When I talk about swinging, I'm talking about resilience, flexibility. And I'm talking about perpetual creativity. That's American and that's us, grace under pressure—that's what Hemingway said. If you get yourself boxed off into these political categories, you don't get the universality. The blues is going to start—like life, like time— with 1 and 2 and then how many choruses can you swing?"

Like an arranger, Murray transcribes Scooter's choruses, his growth and education, both in the classroom and out. In *The Spyglass Tree*, Scooter leaves behind the timeless patterns, "the also and also" in Murray's lyrical riff of a phrase, of life in Gasoline Point to enroll in a black Southern college very much like Tuskegee. He has accepted the community's "ancestral imperative," that tradition and responsibility (to African American social aspirations and to the world at large) to learn and to make something significant of himself. The new novel, *The Seven League Boots*, follows Scooter out into the world of art and experience: he has graduated from college and, now a jazz bass player, is touring in a big band led by the Bossman, a fictional composite of Basie and Ellington, and his education (as well as ours) continues, illuminating the heroic, almost fairytale-like existence of the jazz musician.

"We are also the heirs to all that European stuff," says Murray. We start out knowing about Bach and Beethoven and all that. Scooter is [an] American extension, elaboration and refinement of that stuff. He has worked it out through the blues, that is his art, his poetry and fiction, his Aristotelian theory. What is an American sonata? You want to talk about chamber music? Well, in America that's an after-hours joint, it's an after-hours combo."

Of course, Scooter's story is very much Murray's story. "Yeah I'm Scooter. I'm working on the next book. He's entering graduate school now." Like Scooter, who learns his craft on the road, under the tutelage of journeymen and master musicians, Murray came late to publishing, spending time in the literary "woodshed" (as jazz musicians refer to practice time), teaching and working to develop his voice. "I was absorbing all this and I didn't think I was good enough. It's like looking up and seeing Michael Jordan and thinking, I can play with him. I didn't have anything to say. I'm coming from a foundation that has been really thought through. You take the challenge of all this stuff. Then when someone asks, why did this old brownskin boy do so and so. You say, 'Man, look at all them goddamn books, that brownskin boy went to school. This is serious stuff.' "

Murray is his own "representative anecdote" of black American life: "I am the ancestral imperative, I'm a role model. I know it. You want Colin Powell? I've done that too." His characters are easily traced to his life but expand and resonate in "the timeless time of the fable."

Murray was an athlete himself (high-school quarterback, captain of the basketball team), and baseball saturates the pages of the first two novels. Murray has written some of the best fictional evocations of the game's sensibilities, and his passages recall both the Negro Leagues and the insistent allure, for small-town boys, of faraway Big League cities. Satchel Paige played for his father's team and appears as the "money" pitcher Gator Gus in *Train Whistle.* Murray's school years, described so memorably in *South to a Very Old Place*, provide the experiential basis for the fictional college life he creates in *The Spyglass Tree.*

Murray's first published fiction, an excerpt from *Train Whistle,* appeared in a literary anthology, *New World Writing* (NAL, 1953) alongside contributors such as Nadine Gordimer and Gore Vidal. He was recommended to the editor Arabel Porter by Ellison. He moved to McGraw-Hill to work with Joyce Johnson, who edited *South to a Very Old Place* and his first novel. He is currently represented by Andrew Wylie after many years with James Brown Associates. By 1985, when *Good Morning Blues* was published, Murray had a new publisher, Random House, and a new editor, Errol McDonald, then at Knopf. When McDonald moved to Pantheon, he took Murray and his long-anticipated second novel, *The Spyglass Tree,* with him—("The schoolboy in me was disappointed," said Murray. "I wanted that Borzoi on my book.")

Much like the jazz musicians he so admires, Murray has achieved a kind of influential obscurity. He's an intellectual's intellectual (he pulls out a folder of photos of himself schmoozing, over the years, with everyone from Kenneth Burke to Robert Penn Warren), cited for his influence by writers as diverse as Stanley Crouch, Walker Percy and John Edgar Wideman, and yet he is not much known among a general readership that would likely embrace his buoyantly lyrical fictional imagination.

Does it bother him? He pauses a beat: "Life is a low-down dirty shame. But I'm not going to cut my throat. I think my books are good. The irony is that they are all very well reviewed, they are not ignored. So I have enough evidence," he laughs, "that I'm not insane. Walker Percy said '*The Omni-Americans* is the most important book on race relations of our time.' So I'm not going to get caught up with that *Fire Next Time* stuff or those guys [rappers] on the cover of the *New York Times* magazine, because those are not representative anecdotes. They are not telling you about the possibilities. One will tell you how to get lynched but he can't tell you how to be a Louis Armstrong. As Ralph [Ellison] would say, it's enough to give the blues the blues. But I'm conditioned to deal with the blues. I really believe what I write so I have to apply it."

CALVIN REID
February 26, 1996

ANNE PERRY

CURRENT NOTORIETY aside, Anne Perry faces a daunting prospect in her five-week, 22-city tour across North America to promote the latest title in her mystery series starring Victorian London policeman Thomas Pitt and his wife, Charlotte. But since August, 1994, when Perry's 1954 conviction for murder in New Zealand was unfurled in worldwide headlines, notoriety can't be set aside.

"There were a few days last week when I woke up thinking I can't go through with this," she admits in the Manhattan offices of Fawcett Columbine. But now, two days after her arrival from her home in Scotland and with the morning's appearance on NBC's *Today* show behind her, the author seems composed—and resolutely upbeat. "I've experienced a great deal of kindness. All of this has been an eye-opener as to just how very good people are."

Perry is no stranger to book tours and publicity. Her two mystery series, both the books set late in the 19th century, featuring the Pitts— the 15th of which, *Traitors Gate*, is recently out from Fawcett—and the five novels, set in London about 40 years earlier, starring former police inspector William Monk and nurse Hester Latterly, have sold more than three million copies in just the U.S. Fawcett, with all 20 titles in print, has toured her rigorously and successfully here before.

The stakes changed, however, when a journalist, researching the sensational 1954 New Zealand murder trial on which the newly released film *Heavenly Creatures* was based, phoned Meg Davis of MBA Literary Agents in London. The reporter suggested that Juliet Hulme, one of the two then-teenaged girls convicted of murdering the mother of one of them, was in fact Davis's client, Anne Perry. Davis phoned Perry for a denial, which Perry did not deliver.

"I have never lied," Perry reiterates on this drizzly February afternoon. "I have told my church, my closest friends, anybody whose business it was. Plenty of people have always known but simply chose not to report it." Lanky and long-limbed, her chestnut-colored hair hanging loose and smooth, dressed in a conservative blue suit, Perry speaks with animation and a cautious candor, weaving her personal history into the story of her career as a writer—"There was nothing else I ever wanted to be."

The first Thomas Pitt story, *The Cater Street Hangman,* was published by St. Martin's in 1979. "I'd been writing historical dramas for 13 years and had enough rejection slips to cover the walls." A new neighbor in Perry's small Suffolk village introduced her to an agent in London. "I sent her the mystery manuscript and, within two weeks, Tom McCormack, who was passing through, bought it.

"I set right out to write the next one," she recalls. "I'd gone so long with nothing succeeding that when something did, boy, I was going to stay with it!" Plotting had been her problem earlier, Perry believes. "A mystery enforces a certain structure on you."

History, "especially British history," has always been a source of fascination, says Perry. Both her mystery series are steeped in period detail, social and domestic, but at the same time possess a pressing immediacy, due to Perry's vivid characterization and to the social issues central to each narrative. The novels revolve around issues that seem to reach all the way through this century and bear insistently on today's world. How does she choose her themes? "Very often it's something I've read in the newspapers," she answers, citing *Traitors Gate,* in which considerations of loyalty and treason, framed against the ethics and politics of colonization in Africa, spark debate—and more—among the cast.

Perry's appreciation for history and narrative took root in her childhood in England, when she was often hospitalized with respiratory illness. "When I was in hospital, I wasn't allowed to read. I survived in my imagination. I just shut my eyes and lived in my head. If you can't read, you have to make your own stories—from what you have read, what you know and what you imagine. History was magic. Those people were totally real to me.

"By the time I was eight, the doctors said I wouldn't live through another English winter." Her parents sent her to stay with a family in the Bahamas. Perry then moved to New Zealand with this family. A year later, her father, a research physicist, took an administrative job at Christchurch University in New Zealand, reuniting the author with her parents and her younger brother. "That was quite an adjustment," says Perry, noting that the members of her family "were nearly strangers by that time.

"Then, I must have been about 11, I was sent to boarding school, which was another major adjustment and not a nice one. I was the new girl, the different one who spoke with a different accent. After a year and a bit, my parents finally took me out."

Isolation and exclusion are thick threads running through Perry's youth. Describing herself as a "natural student," like her father, but no good at sports, unlike her athletic mother, who was also "very attractive, charming, articulate and glamorous," Perry didn't have many friends at her high school. When she was hospitalized again for a few months, the only student who wrote to her daily was a young New Zealander, Pauline Parker, with whom Perry, then Hulme, was later charged with murder.

Early in 1954, back from the hospital, Perry found out that her parents' marriage had unraveled. Her father planned to return to England. Her mother was leaving New Zealand with another man. Told that she and her brother would go with their father, Perry hoped Pauline could come with them. But Pauline's mother wouldn't agree.

In the film *Heavenly Creatures,* the girls' relationship is given a lesbian cast, a suggestion that also figured in their trial. It's an evaluation that Perry dismisses, with anger. She acknowledges the intensity of adolescents' friendships, noting that "they are very strong because you don't want to be alone. But at 15, in those days, we were about as sexually knowing as the average four-year-old is now. I have no reason to suppose that she wasn't as totally innocent in that respect as I was."

Perry says she went along with the plan to murder Pauline's mother because "I really believed that if I didn't do what she wanted, she [Pauline] would take her own life. Now, I would go to somebody else and say, 'This is going to happen, please help.' But I didn't do that. I never hated the woman. I would have done anything to have gotten out of it. I just didn't know how to."

Pauline's mother was killed, hit repeatedly on the head with a brick, while on a picnic with the two girls in a Christchurch park. Perry maintains that she remembers neither that afternoon nor much of the trial that followed. (The girls' role in the crime was discovered in Pauline's diaries.)

"I really don't want to remember," she says forcefully. That stance has been interpreted by some as lack of remorse. One such article in the *New York Times* prompted her U.S. agent, Donald Maass, to write a letter to the editor, noting that "Ms. Perry has repeatedly stated how sorry she is for her part in that 40-year-old tragedy."

"You have to say, I'm to blame," she observes, talking about sin. "I am sorry for that moment. But then you say, now I am going to learn the lessons of it."

And perhaps the fictional exploration of crime and its effects, drawn against a large and distant, perspective-enhancing, moral canvas is Perry's way of pursuing those lessons. Indeed, after last summer's revelations, it's difficult to read Perry's works without being struck by the connections between her authorial concerns and the circumstances of her life.

After the successful publication of her first mystery, St. Martin's issued the next nine Pitt titles, until Perry moved in 1990 to Fawcett, where her works had been released in paper from the start, with what would be the first in the William Monk series. She soon signed with Fawcett for upcoming Pitt stories as well. It has been a good fit; in 1992 Perry signed a handsome contract with Fawcett to write eight books in the following three years. "I think I've become a better writer since I've had a contract with Fawcett, and an editor, Leona Nevler, who believes in me."

In his first appearance, in *The Face of a Stranger*, Monk wakens in a London hospital in the mid-19th century with no recollection of his identity. He gradually pulls together the pieces of his life and, in the process, confronts a man whom he doesn't much like and who may have committed a brutal murder. About Monk, Perry says, "I wanted to explore the situation of having to discover yourself bit by bit, through the eyes of other people. It's not the discovery of the monster within yourself, it's discovering that there are no monsters; there are only people."

Perry is also firmly grounded in the Church of Latter-Day Saints, to which she converted while living in California 25 years ago. "I'd been looking for a long time for what I could believe wholly. I realized my next-door neighbors in northern California, who were Mormon, had something special." Perry struggled, however, with some of the Mormon tenets. "Someone finally said, 'Don't try to work it out in your brain—get down on your knees and pray. If it's true, the Lord will tell you so.'

"I did and He did. I woke up the next morning and just for a few moments the whole room shone with light. I joined the church."

She talks at length about the church. "I have found that it is a complete way of life. It's not a crutch; it requires far too much of you for that. But it gives you a structure in which to grow."

After the trial in August 1954, which lasted only six days, both girls were convicted of murder and sentenced to indefinite terms in separate prisons. Perry was sent to a women's facility, which, she says, is "still reputed to be the worst in the southern hemisphere." The youngest inmate there, she was assigned to hard labor—"scrubbing in the laundry with caustics.

"It was very lonely. I was never visited by anyone I had previously known, except the headmistress of the school I attended before boarding school." Released after serving slightly more than five years and advised to change her name to "something ordinary," she flew to Italy, where she was met by her father, who then drove her to England. For the next "six or seven years," she held assorted jobs in Northumberland before moving to the U.S. where she lived mostly in California. Drawn back to England to help her mother when her stepfather became ill in the early '70s, she stayed on in Suffolk and focused increasingly on her writing.

Her move to Scotland came in 1989. Her mother, now widowed, also lives in the same village. Perry says her greatest worry when news of her past broke was that it would kill her mother, who suffers from a heart condition. But she reiterates that others' responses have by and large been unstintingly supportive.

Does that augur well for upcoming appearances before the public—and the media? "I have just one story to tell," Perry declares. "And that's the truth." But yes, she will be very glad when the issue of her past fades and she can devote herself fully to the business of writing. "I am very lucky. I love what I do and am rewarded for it richly. I just want to get back to work."

DULCY BRAINARD
March 27, 1995

E. ANNIE PROULX

Mention E. Annie Proulx's name and people flash an instant mental map of where she can be found.

Readers who shivered through Newfoundland's stark climate in *The Shipping News* are certain that she must live there. Yet the landscape of failing farms and dilapidated trailers in *Heart Songs* and *Postcards* prove that rural New England is essential to her frame of reference. (Indeed, she lived in Vermont for over a decade.) *Postcards,* however, also plunged across the map of America, as does her new novel, *Accordion Crimes,* just out from Scribner. In this latest work, the whole country serves as her canvas, a vivid mural of ethnic enclaves that includes urban ghettos, prairie homesteads, sharecroppers' shacks and depressed factory towns.

The characters in *Accordion Crimes* are immigrants or descendants of immigrants from Sicily, Germany, Mexico, France by way of Canada, Africa by way of slavery, Poland, Norway. Their stories are connected by a battered green accordion brought to North America by a Sicilian musician who meets a violent end. Thereafter, it is passed from stranger to stranger on an odyssey that encompasses a century of social history.

It turns out that Proulx is as essentially rootless as her many characters in *Accordion Crimes,* as peripatetic as her protagonist, Loyal Blood, in *Postcards.* She knows the country well, having traversed it repeatedly to research her books, and the allure of the unknown continues to pull at her. She has finally settled, however, in a snug, pine-log cabin in a tiny (pop. 100) town in Wyoming.

What is Annie Proulx doing in Wyoming?

This historic old mining town on the edge of the old frontier is exactly right for her, Proulx says. In fact, all her books, with the exception of *Heart Songs,* were written in Wyoming. A grant from the Ucross Foundation, to write *Postcards,* first brought her here, and she realized "what an enormous help the sight lines were, and the room to walk. There's something about being able to shoot your eyes very far ahead. In northern New England, the trees got in the way," she says. "For me, this land is full of ghosts and spirits. It speaks to me more than any other place I've ever been." She could not make a permanent move while her mother was in ill health in New Hampshire. After her death a year ago, Proulx packed up and headed for the wide open spaces.

Elements that might daunt others—the rugged weather, for example—make Proulx exult. On the last day of April, snow still glistens on the mountain peaks that embrace the spectacularly scenic valley, and wind-driven snow squalls animate the air. An outdoorswoman to her solid bones, Proulx counts cross-country skiing among her necessary delights. The details of hunting, fishing and trapping in her books come squarely from her own capabilities and enjoyment. She is a tall, energetic woman who wears her curly hair short and her black-rimmed glasses with sturdy efficiency. She walks in long strides; talks in a torrent that swings between vehemence and exuberance; laughs in great gusts of mirth, mainly at life's ironies; dresses in generic work-clothes. Fashion is probably the only word in the dictionary that does not resonate for her. Writing makes her happy.

The opportunity to settle down has been a belated blessing. The oldest of five sisters, Edna Annie Proulx was born in Connecticut in 1935, but her family moved often, as her father, of French-Canadian extraction, pursued his career as a textile executive. Her mother, whose New England family roots go back to the early 1600s, was an artist who trained Proulx to cultivate an observant eye.

During years of boring jobs (most of which she won't talk about) and three marriages (ditto), Proulx wrote magazine articles and how-to books to support herself, producing "an occasional short story" when she had the time. She finally saw those tales collected in *Heart Songs* (Scribner, 1988). With her two novels, *Postcards* (1992) and *The Shipping News* (1993), Proulx won, in dazzling succession, enough prizes to give her financial stability. But not intellectual complacency.

Proulx's view of life is unsparing, and social questions intrigue her. She knew for some time that she wanted to write a book about immigrants, "about the cost of coming from one culture to another. I wanted to get a sense of that looming overculture that demands of newcomers that they give up their language, their music, their food, their names. I began to wonder: where did our taste for changing our

230

identity come from? Was it the immigrant experience where the rite of passage was to redefine yourself as an American?"

Characteristically, she wrote the outline of *Accordion Crimes* in one afternoon, while still working on *The Shipping News*. She carefully included an "inner private joke" as she does in every book. "I thought I'd have some fun by writing about multiculturalism, but in a way that other people were not." Her book would be serious too, of course. Perhaps most startling is her candid depiction of the deep seated hate and resentment that each ethnic group holds for those of other national origins, religions and races. Proulx was determined to reflect this latent bigotry. "I feel a responsibility to history," she says.

Yet she knew from the beginning that she didn't want to write a historical novel "plodding onwards from 1890 to the present." Her solution was to compose the narrative of four interlinking parts. "There is the one overarching story that covers 100 years" (the accordion's meanderings). "Within that are nine shorter stories," each with a different immigrant group as focus. "Within that, there is an increasing multiplicity of shorter stories of intersecting lives" (members of each protagonist's family, through several generations); and "within that, tiny flashforwards, fiction bites." The latter are parenthetical asides, both tragic and funny, thumbnail sketches that sum up a marginal character's entire life in just a few words, introduce an element of surprise to the narrative and contribute to the "truncated, staccato effect" that Proulx desired.

"Instead of the river of time, you get a lawn sprinkler effect, a kind of jittery, jammed, off-balance feeling that I very much wanted." The characters in these brief sketches succumb to bizarre accidents and grotesque twists of fate. A man is killed by a boar running down a highway; a little girl playing in her yard has her arms sheared off by jagged metal roofing blown from a passing truck. "I wanted this mosaic of apparently random violence to exist within the sense of continuity," she says.

The characters' names are a litany of ethnic heritage: Dolor Gagnon, Onesiphore Malefoot, Hieronim Przybysz, Abelardo Relampago Salazar. She says that she has not stretched credulity. "Just pick up any phone book and you'll find plenty of names that we choose not to see. It's our upbringing that makes us skip over them. They are the names of invisible people."

The settings she created for her ethnic cameos—the wretchedly poor milltown of Random, Maine, the swampy marshland of Bayou

Féroce, La.—were the catalysts to her imagination. The sense of place is paramount in her conception of story. "Everything that happens to characters comes welling out of the place. Even their definition of themselves, and a lot of this book is about the definition of self."

The fine accretion of concrete details makes these fictional places as real as any location on a map. Proulx digs into the research part of her work with the zeal of a hunting dog. "I was an historian before I became a novelist," she says. Though she dropped out of Maine's Colby College in the 1950s, over a decade later she earned her B.A. from the University of Vermont and, in 1973, an M.A. in history from Sir George Williams University in Montreal (now Concordia University); she lacked only the dissertation for her Ph.D when she quit to become a journalist.

To research *Postcards,* her first novel, she went back and forth across America, stopping in all the states where her homeless protagonist worked and lived. "That was my road book," she says. Newfoundland, which she visited on a fishing trip, became the setting of *The Shipping News* after it struck her like a *coup de foudre.* There, too, long sight lines pulled her in, though she found the sea "a distraction." She explored the island and pored over maps, mirroring the eccentric place names with her own inventions. She absorbed the Newfoundland dialect by going to bed every night with a vernacular dictionary.

When she decided to use the accordion as the instrument of fate in *Accordion Crimes,* Proulx was astonished to discover that there were practically no books on its history in the U.S. What she did find was "a huge stack of court cases" involving accordions, the kinds of petty suits that had to do with class and economics, the bickering that often obsesses outsiders in society. Immigrants, whose "continuity is reduced to genes, whose past is rejected, thrown away and despised," were also the people most likely to play the accordion. "It's the immigrant instrument, because it's light, it's small, it's portable and it doesn't get out of tune," Proulx says.

Her research is effortlessly integrated into the story, and only the long acknowledgements section, listing more than 20 accordion scholars and musicians, suggests how widely she pursued information. Among others, she thanks the man who told her how one would hide money in an accordion. The thread that ties the narrative together is the reader's knowledge that the green-button accordion holds $14,000 secreted in its bellows. The final irony of its totally wasted beneficence is a typical Proulx touch.

Among those who contributed information were her eldest son, Jonathan Lang, a sound engineer; her daughter-in-law, Gail, a blues singer; and her son Morgan Lang, a student of ethnomusicology. Another son, Gillis Lang, is a college student. And for the first time in any of her books, Proulx's dedication includes her daughter Muffy Clarkson, never mentioned before even in her official bio. Proulx responds coolly to questions about this belated introduction. "We've lived apart for many years, not through any enmity but through a family situation. I recently rediscovered her. I love her dearly. It seems a good time to include her with her brothers," she says, then segues to another topic. One does not probe further.

Raising her three sons as a single mother was the factor that limited Proulx's ability to produce fiction. Over several years, Tom Jenks at *Esquire* published a number of her stories. After Jenks went to Scribner's, he suggested collecting them into the book that became *Heart Songs*. Proulx was "between agents at the time"—she had a lot of them, she says, until she "got lucky" and connected with her current agent, Liz Darhansoff. When Jenks suggested adding a novel to the contract, "I could have cared less, so I said sure, go ahead. Then I was in the odd position of having a contract for a novel before I ever thought of writing one."

Jenks left Scribner's before the stories were edited, and John Glusman, "one of the best editors I've ever had," handled publication of *Heart Songs*. When Glusman, too, exited Scribner's, Barbara Grossman saw *Postcards* through, and published *The Shipping News* (Proulx has called her "the editor of my dreams") before she left for Viking. Now Proulx is in editor Nan Graham's hands, and she calls herself fortunate again, though she finds the situation somewhat amusing. "All those marvelous editors shifted away and all that remained in place was Scribner's—and even that went through a corporate takeover and the loss of the apostrophe," she comments wryly.

In the flux of editors' departures, Proulx's work has remained constant. *The Shipping News,* the story of Quoyle, a newspaperman of mediocre record who has failed at marriage, livelihood and life until he experiences the thawing of his heart in the unlikely terrain of frost-bound Newfoundland, was greeted by ecstatic reviews. The prizes—among them an NBA and a Pulitzer—began rolling in, and the book sold more than one million copies in hardcover and paper. Proulx now needs a secretary to handle her mail, and she is besieged by requests for speaking engagements.

Meanwhile, *Accordion Crimes* is a BOMC selection, and a tour beckons in June and July—after which, she claims, she is "never going to do it again. The long sustained silences and empty spaces that are necessary to writing are harder and harder to get," she says with a weary shrug.

It is likely that her future books will each consider a new aspect of the world. She has several in her mind at the moment; research materials are already arranged on "project shelves" in her bookcases. Proulx reserves her most scornful opinions for "this very unpleasant trend that one should only write about one's personal experience. That's the worst piece of advice ever given to students. If only people would write about what intrigues them, what they *don't* know, would do a little research, would become questioning as well as observant. That's the pleasure in writing," she says.

For Annie Proulx's readers, the pleasure is reciprocal.

SYBIL STEINBERG
June 3, 1996

MARIO PUZO

Mario puzo makes us an offer we don't want to refuse. After nearly two decades of public silence, he agrees to grant *PW* his first interview in 18 years in order to talk about his masterful new novel, *The Last Don,* due out from Random House, and about the arc of his writing career. So on an early summer day, we travel out to Long Island under a hot, milky sky to sit with him in the second-floor sunroom of his home. Also present is his editor, Jonathan Karp.

"Why did you decide to speak with us?" we ask Puzo after he sets us up with a cold soda.

"I've reformed." After 75 years, Puzo's voice is husky but still sweet with the lilt and rhythms of the Manhattan streets where he grew up. "I figured, give it a try, it'll be a nice experience before I die. Also, I got all these grandchildren, and they don't know that I used to be famous."

Used to be famous? Puzo delights in irony, though he rarely laughs. This stocky man relaxed on a sofa across from us, large, open face topped by thinning gray hair, clad in a pink shirt and white trousers, gripping a big cigar that he never lights, is world famous as the author of seven novels and 10 films—above all, of *The Godfather,* which, 27 years after publication, has sold, according to Puzo, an astounding 21 million copies. Puzo is proud of what these sales mean. He talks about it within our first five minutes together.

"You know how I know how many copies I sold? I got the money. Nobody said I just sold books. I got money. Statistics, they don't mean anything unless you get the money."

The money has bought Puzo a rambling house in a fancy neighborhood, ringed by lawns and tall trees, sided by a tennis court, filled with fine furniture, plush rugs and several huge TV sets. But a fence shields the house from public view, and the computer shining on the desk nearby is used not by him but by his long-time companion, author

Carol Gino. Puzo writes by hand, and at an old typewriter. Instead of servants or a secretary, he employs two of his five children, all now grown. Here, it seems, is a man who cares passionately about money but who doesn't flaunt it.

Money—its lure and power—dominates Puzo's work. "To me," he says, "money is the focus of everything you see people do." It's not too surprising to hear this from a man born to illiterate Italian immigrant parents in Hell's Kitchen, whose father abandoned his wife and five kids when Puzo was 12. "I knew I lived in poverty," Puzo says. "That was one of the things that helped me to write. It was my way out."

The ambition to write his way out carried Puzo through high school. World War II erupted when he was 21, taking him to Germany, where he met and married the mother of his children, who is now deceased. In the late 1940s, Puzo returned to Manhattan for night classes at the New School. "I was studying literature, trying to be a writer," he reminisces. "Since I was a veteran, I got 120 bucks a month for going to school. So I was going for the 120 bucks. But it was a really wonderful education."

During the day, Puzo worked as a federal employee. In his spare time, he wrote *The Dark Arena*, a literary melodrama set in occupied Germany, published by Random House in 1955. The novel received glowing reviews but sank in sales. So did Puzo's heart. Determined to make it as an artist, he began an autobiographical novel, *The Fortunate Pilgrim*. Shortly before its 1964 publication by Atheneum, he quit the civil service to edit men's adventure magazines. A new job, a new book, a new publisher; but, again, strong reviews drew only weak sales. Now Puzo despaired. "I didn't make money on it. When that happens, you get such a feeling of self-loathing. That you've done something valuable but nobody values it. So you despise yourself. And you despise the public."

He saw only one solution, he recalls. "I said, 'well, I gotta write a book that people will buy.'" As he speaks these words, Puzo's hands, always in motion, swoop like birds of prey. Otherwise, he sits nearly motionless. His eyes glint dark and lustrous from behind wide-framed glasses.

The book was *The Godfather*. When Atheneum rejected Puzo's outline, he brought it to Putnam, where, in 1965, editor Bill Targ advanced him $5000. "I'd never heard of so much money in my life," he says. "I mean, it was mind-boggling." More mind-boggling still was the novel's success. At the top of national bestseller lists for much of 1969, its publication year, it became the top-selling novel of the 1970s and, according to Putnam, of all time. It proved a cultural watershed, bringing the Mafia to national attention and spawning generations of mob novels, influencing writers from Elmore Leonard to Eugene Izzi.

The Godfather swept sea changes into Puzo's professional and personal life as well. He acquired an agent, Candida Donadio, who still represents him. He added wealth to fame when Putnam sold paperback rights to Fawcett for $410,000. And he launched his second career, as a screenwriter. "I refused to write the script of *The Godfather* at first," Puzo remembers. "Then the producer, Al Ruddy, came to New York with his wife. They took me to lunch at the Plaza. I was prepared to say no again. But I was charmed by Ruddy's wife, because she had a poodle in her handbag. She opens the handbag and out pops this dog. And that was so charming I said yes."

The two Oscars Puzo has won, for his screenplays of *The Godfather* and *The Godfather: Part II,* gleam on the mantelpiece in his living room. He has scripted eight other films, most notably *The Godfather: Part III,* the first two *Superman* films, *Earthquake* and *The Cotton Club.* Puzo reveals that he's also written a screenplay that was never filmed, based on a Zane Grey novel "like a western *Godfather.*" Michael Eisner, then head of Paramount, rejected it because, Puzo says, he hated the desert. "I don't like sand in a movie," Eisner reportedly told Puzo.

Talking about screenwriting, again Puzo refers to the money. "The writers today," he says, "we're all sorts of dopes. Everybody should rush out to Hollywood and get the easy money." To transform a novel into a screenplay, he adds, "you figure out what the primary story is. All the other stories, you lop 'em off like they lop off the fat on a piece of pork."

His newfound success granted Puzo freedom to publish what he wanted—in 1972, the essays and stories of *The Godfather Papers;* in 1978, still with Bill Targ at Putnam, *Fools Die,* a novel about Las Vegas, Hollywood and the New York publishing industry. Paperback rights sold to Fawcett for a then-record $2.2 million, but the book failed to match *The Godfather*'s sales or influence. Six years later, Puzo returned with *The Sicilian.* Edited by Joni Evans at Linden Press, the novel briefly brought back Michael Corleone of *Godfather* fame in its tale of a Sicilian brigand. It was the top-selling hardcover fiction of 1985, but Puzo's next book, from Random House, *The Fourth K,* a thriller that placed a future Kennedy in the White House, fared relatively poorly.

"I was a young assistant editor at the time," interjects Karp. "That's how I met Mario. I don't think that people got the political irony of it at all." For that, Puzo takes the blame. "I realized from the failure of the book that there are certain rules that you can't break. I broke them with a Kennedy as the hero when I turned him into a guy who would have been a dictator." Puzo himself can charm, and his fierce honesty is part of his charm.

The Fourth K was almost Puzo's last book. In January 1991, its publication month, he nearly died. Already diabetic, he was stricken with heart trouble and underwent an emergency quadruple bypass. Puzo didn't write during the next two years. Instead, he researched a novel on the Borgias but decided not to write it. "The trouble," he explains, "is in showing the Borgia Pope as he was. That would make such an uproar, who knows if you want to get into that? So I went from the Borgia book to writing a Hollywood and Vegas book. And the Clericuzio popped up."

The Clericuzio are the hypnotic dark heart of *The Last Don,* the most powerful Mafia family in the country. Their chief is Don Domenico Clericuzio, whose great age and power are mirrored in two other male characters, a casino owner and a Hollywood studio chief. Each stands nearly above the novel's wild swirl of deals, betrayals, violence; yet each will order the snuffing of a career or a life as necessary. We ask Puzo if his own years and brush with death influenced the book. "I think so," he says. "The character of Don Clericuzio, for instance. The way he can isolate himself from emotion, where he arranges the killing of his own . . . It's something I can do now. You reach a certain age where you're quite capable of great sin."

Puzo's own age becomes more apparent as we continue to speak. He is game to talk as long as we wish, and he's ever ready with ideas and opinions, but his voice loses zest as the afternoon passes. The air in the room, warm when we came in, grows close.

Puzo's maturity elevates *The Last Don,* a novel as grand and complex as any he has written. It embodies a lifetime of experience or interest in Hollywood, Vegas, the mob—and, above all, in money. "I think *The Last Don* is an ambitious book," he says. "All through it I'm trying to show a strict correlation between the criminal persona and an industrial criminal persona. And that the crucial element is money."

It becomes clear as we speak that Puzo's obsession with money isn't about greed. Early in his life, it was about escape from poverty; in middle age, about public validation of his talent. Now, money is a force to be captured in his art—and one that to him raises a moral question. "What is the central thing to most people?" Puzo asks us. "Earning a living, earning your daily bread. If these guys didn't commit these crimes, they'd be at the mercy of employers, they'd be at the mercy of economics. They're asserting their own power over their fate." Yet Puzo bans morals from his fiction. Though he has taken flak for not condemning characters—Don Corleone especially—who act like monsters, he frowns on those who judge their own creations. "If you're a true novelist, your first duty is to tell a story. If you want to moralize, write nonfiction, philosophy, whatever."

What will follow the *The Last Don?* Karp mentions that Puzo recently got a call from Brando, who, Puzo, explains, "wants to be in *The Last Don* if it's a feature film, but he won't do TV." And film rights have been sold to TV, Puzo announces: "The movie business didn't bid high enough."

Puzo has time to write, since he lives alone. But there is the allure of reading, "the only pleasure in life that hasn't disappointed me," and he works in fits and starts. "I'm an essentially lazy writer," he confesses. "A lot of my writing schedule is laying on the sofa, staring up at the ceiling." Still, he has plans. A film of *The Godfather: Part IV* is "a possibility." He's working on a screenplay of Gino's first book, *The Nurse's Story.* He may yet write the Borgia book, and he's contemplating an epic historical about the Mafia. "I write a book about the 700 years of the Mafia, then I drop dead," he jokes. "Everybody's had enough of the Mafia, everybody's had enough of me."

Whether time will rate Puzo as a great writer or less remains to be seen. He has his Oscars but no major literary prizes, no Pulitzer. "I would have loved to have won a Pulitzer," he says. "But if you go back over the books that won, are they read today? I think the test is, do people keep reading them? Now it's, what, 27 years since *The Godfather?* I still get a royalty check from England, for a substantial amount. Jesus Christ, 27 years, selling a book, that's something."

Yes it is, we agree as we rise to leave. Puzo's hand is dry as we shake it goodbye. He has trouble with stairs, he says, so he can't see us out. Downstairs, we admire those Oscars, testament to Puzo's storytelling prowess, to the remarkable life he has led. We flash to *The Last Don*, and we think of how marvelous it is that this writer, age be damned, has once more put that talent and life's wisdom on the page, and this time in fullest flower.

JEFF ZALESKI
July 29, 1996

NANCY TAYLOR ROSENBERG

To HEAR Nancy Taylor Rosenberg describe it, having been stalked by O. J. Simpson is the least of her travails. That's because she was abused by her grandfather, date-raped at college and sexually harassed during her early years as a policewoman.

Not only has she lived to tell the tales, she's used them as background material for three bestselling legal thrillers, *Mitigating Circumstances, Interest of Justice* and *First Offense.* Her own history—and this includes the time she was thrown from a horse, which is also germane to her writing career—is not, however, what she's drawn on for her newest book from Dutton, *California Angel.*

California Angel, which has a first printing of 125,000 copies, is *not* a legal thriller. Its heroine is Toy Johnson, a woman who falls into trances during which she materializes miles away to perform good deeds. Her actions get her in hot water with the law (yes, there's a courtroom scene) before she's discovered to be an incipient angel about to embark on an existence more rewarding than this one.

During an interview in her stately apartment on Manhattan's Central Park South (there's also another home in Laguna Niguel, Calif.), Rosenberg admits that she's a bit apprehensive about her departure from the genre for which she is best known. But she claims that this novel had its own imperative. "I had to write this book from my heart," she says, perched on a regal sofa behind which are sumptuous views of the New York skyline. She's wearing a long skirt with a slit this high, and every so often square footage falls away, revealing a slim leg. She has *very* long auburn hair, but she's not a woman who's continually pushing it from her face. It's just there, commanding attention—like her Italian greyhound, Princess, who lolls nearby on tapestry cushions.

Rosenberg wrote *California Angel* from the heart, she says, because of a young girl named Janelle. Some time ago, Rosenberg, whose charitable work includes a writing class she sponsors at an inner-city school in Santa Ana, Calif., also decided to "adopt" a family she heard about

241

through the class. (How do you adopt a family? "You just do it," she says.) She discovered that the daughter was "the oldest living survivor" of a disease called methylmalonic aciduria. Known more commonly as MMA, its primary manifestation is that protein introduced into the body turns poisonous.

"I was going to see Janelle—she'd been in the hospital—and I think that I wanted an offering," Rosenberg reports in the rushed, soft-spoken, thoroughly determined manner she has when she gets under way. "I wanted something to take to her. She was very ill, wasted away, a wisp of a child. She needed something else. She needed something magical. She needed something that would take away this horrible fear of dying that she lives with."

Suddenly, Rosenberg says, she knew what her offering would be. "The book just came out. I never stopped writing it. I think I slept a few hours a day. I wrote it in around three weeks of nearly 24-hour days." She pauses, muses, "*Fifteen*-hour days are a piece of cake for me." She resumes the barrage. "It was a compulsion. I didn't think about what I was writing. I hope that doesn't show. I really felt inspired. It's like having a fever and you don't know why. And I never feel that way with my thrillers."

It's not that she doesn't get excited about her thrillers, she explains. "If there are parts that are very good, I even get chills when I read them," she admits. But with her suspense novels, Rosenberg feels that she is in command. *California Angel* was unique in inspiration and execution.

The books she is known for—*Mitigating Circumstances* (1993), *Interest of Justice* (1993) and *First Offense* (1994)—are an entirely different breed. The first two of those page-turners sold 100,000 copies each; Dutton projects 150,000 for the third; all were Literary Guild main selections. They made the 49-year-old Rosenberg a household name, one of the few women writing in the male-dominated world of courtroom thrillers. Appearing in quick succession, they, too, seem to have spilled out of her nonstop, evidence of her obsession to indict a legal system that she finds hugely inadequate.

"I like to think I'm putting the justice system on trial," Rosenberg says with a glint that suggests both mischievousness and resolute anger. She happens to be in a unique position. Having worked as a model in her native Dallas between the ages of 14 and 23, Rosenberg, looking for a more serious pursuit, studied criminology at Southern Methodist University. In 1971 she joined the Dallas police department—as one of two women in its ranks—and soon found herself being sexually harassed in a police car. "Who do you call upon when you're being raped by a policeman and *you're* in uniform?" she asks rhetorically. She was so persona non grata that even the officers' wives were unfriendly. "They didn't want a woman driving around with their husbands at 3 a.m.," she says ruefully. Rosenberg moved from Texas to New Mexico and then to California before deciding in 1980 to retrain as a Ventura probation officer.

That's where she became known as "The Angel of Death" for her vociferous objections to the legalities involving the inadmissibility of prior convictions in courtroom proceedings. Rosenberg reasoned that if she could get felons talking about prior illegal activities during pre-sentencing interviews, she could relay the information to judges. "I worked very closely with criminal offenders—the multiple murderers, the multiple rapists," she says. "I wanted to nail those people. I dug and dug and dug. Yes, being a woman helped. I dressed the part—the short skirt, the high heels. Would you say I manipulated them? *Finesse* is what I call it."

Eventually she felt burned out and retired to join new husband Jerry Rosenberg in a video distribution business. That's when the riding accident occurred. "It was like being jerked off the horse and thrown to the ground," Rosenberg recalls. "It was like God said, 'Write, not *ride.*'" Her decision to devote herself to writing was not entirely surprising, because she'd expressed herself that way since childhood. "I wrote all my life," Rosenberg claims. "I was a very troubled child, and I was also a gifted child. The combination made me very dark, and the only real happiness I felt was when I picked up a pen and reinvented my world *beyond* my world."

Rosenberg suspects that her writing was also "a response" to being abused during the summers she and her sister spent with their maternal grandfather. "It was a typical abuse situation where the abuser tells you that if you tell anyone they won't believe you," she says flatly.

So now Rosenberg blends childhood trauma with her police and probation experiences for books in which heroines with very long hair set about rectifying the system's weakness in meting out justice to remorseless perpetrators. In *Mitigating Circumstances*, Assistant DA Lily Forrester takes the law into her hands, gunning down a suspect—the wrong man, by the way—with impunity. Does this mean Rosenberg believes in vigilantism? "I think she should have gotten caught," Rosenberg says. "Self-justice doesn't work."

She herself will not buy a gun. "The odds are if you own one, you're going to shoot yourself in the foot. We've *got* to get guns off the street," she says fervently. "I'd walk through metal detectors all day long if I thought they would help."

The protagonist of *Interest of Justice* is Judge Lara Sanderstone, who also finds the legal system frustrating after her sister is murdered. Probation officer Ann Carlisle does the sleuthing in *First Offense,* which Rosenberg says she wrote "in response to my belief that minorities do not fare well in the criminal justice system. They are definitely given shoddy treatment. Why are there so many blacks on death row? It isn't because they commit all the crimes." (Incidentally, she waited until her third book to make a probation officer her central character because she originally thought "nobody would be interested" in a heroine with that job.)

Rosenberg's career as a writer actually got under way when she was taking Leonardo Bercovici's writing course at UCLA. Having completed a lengthy section of *Mitigating Circumstances,* she mustered the courage to send samples to agents. Among those who responded was Peter Miller of PMA Literary and Film Management. "It was a Sunday morning, and he was in his office, and I liked that," Rosenberg says. Miller auctioned the book, with Dutton making the winning bid, for $787,000. Rosenberg lowers her voice when she talks about money and keeps it there when confiding that the initial deal, which didn't include paperback rights, was renegotiated. Under the new arrangement, Rosenberg will receive three million dollars for a four-book contract that includes paperback rights and terminates with *Trial By Fire* this fall. Now there's a five-book contract for an amount she won't even disclose in a whisper.

And then there are screen rights, since her books seem naturals for further life on celluloid. Jonathan Demme is producing, and Agnieszka Holland is directing, the movie based on *Mitigating Circumstances. Interest of Justice* will be a TV Movie of the Week starring Sissy Spacek.

California Angel has its own deal. For less than her usual? "I won't say," Rosenberg replies, "but the fact that it is a separate deal is a clue." She also says that she loves and respects Michaela Hamilton, her editor, but when asked why there is so much sex in her books—often within the first pages—she arches an eyebrow and sighs, "Editors." Maybe she's even more miffed at contractual expectations placed on her than she allows, because she stresses, "I think writers should have more liberty to write anything that comes to their minds."

Now about the O. J. Simpson stalking—"stalking" is her word. Simpson and the Rosenbergs belong to the Monarch Beach Club in Laguna Niguel. One day, a few years back, she was driving away from the club with one of her daughters and her daughter's chum. O. J. "curbed" them—pulled in front of them. "He wanted us to go to a hotel with him," Rosenberg says of the ensuing conversation. "I looked at him and saw the slits of his eyes and thought, this guy could be violent." Notions about his current predicament? "I think he's guilty, but I think he may have had an accomplice. Little rat that I am, I think it might have been a police officer. The police—they know how to handle a weapon, how to stage a crime scene."

Rosenberg's take on herself? "I'm a huge fan of Dostoyevski, but how many people today can relate to him? I know I'm not Dostoyevski, but maybe I can write a good book because I've lived it."

DAVID FINKLE
January 16, 1995

SALMAN RUSHDIE

To SALMAN RUSHDIE, the *fatwa* is a boring topic, old history. Though the calendar is rolling toward February 14, the sixth anniversary of the Ayatollah Khomeini's death sentence, issued in response to the purported "blasphemy" of his fourth novel, *The Satanic Verses*, Rushdie is gradually resuming a somewhat normal life. In fact, meeting with him in London, one finds him in a remarkably cheerful mood.

The cloak-and-dagger safety precautions that circumscribed the first few years of Rushdie's enforced isolation have largely abated. These days a visit can be arranged, though the meeting place is shrouded by secrecy and reached via a car whose destination is unknown to us when we embark. There is a security check; we are ushered into an office, and about ten minutes later Rushdie himself arrives, accompanied by two security guards. He is in an ebullient, even gleeful mood, announcing (to Caroline Michel, associate publisher at Random/Cape) that his new novel, *The Moor's Last Sigh,* is near completion. "There are about two days of work left and then I've got to read it and then I've got to do a couple of days of fidgeting," he says, with obvious elation.

While he doesn't deny that the death sentence cast a cloak of terror over his existence, Rushdie is eager to plead that his audience not read his life into his work. On the eve of the U.S. publication of his first collection of short stories, *East, West* (Pantheon), he insists that "one can't pick up a book of mine expecting to find a literary version of the *fatwa*. And it's been very important to me not simply to become a manifestation of that event, because that would be a defeat. If all I could do is talk about that and write about that, then I'd be beaten." Unexpectedly, he grins. "And I have this plan *not* to be beaten."

In addition to providing another example of Rushdie's manifest talents, *East, West* illustrates the very dichotomies in his life, situations that he learned to balance in a nimble tightrope act. Having become accomplished at bridging the chasm between his Eastern, Muslim heritage and his cosmopolitan Western existence, Rushdie writes fluidly about both cultures. The volume is divided into three sections: "East," "West" and "East, West"; and, though all the stories are pervaded by irony, those in the third section, which he wrote *post-fatwa,* have the greatest resonance. In "The Courter," the story that closes the volume, the narrator says: "I, too, have ropes around my neck, I have them to this day, pulling me this way and that, East and West, the nooses tightening, commanding, *choose, choose."*

Rushdie himself claims to have come to terms with that choice. Yet the pull of both cultures, while enriching his work, has left him in an uncomfortable limbo. Condemned by most Muslims in Iran and the East and in England itself, Rushdie is also aware that many of his countrymen—including fellow writers—chose to blame him for the *fatwa* and to excoriate him for his "foolhardy" irreverence. His outspoken criticism of the British status quo, most vocally in a *pre-fatwa* 1982 TV speech in which he roundly condemned British police racism, has illuminated the irony of his round-the-clock protection by those very police.

In fact, Rushdie was astonished by the immediate response of much of the British press and political system. "Looking through a journal which I've kept since this thing started, I came across some entries which I'd forgotten about," he says. "Within moments, it seems, of this crisis's beginning, there were people viciously attacking me in the press. Two days after, a columnist was calling me a coward. For what? I suppose for not presenting myself at the Iranian embassy," he says dryly. Several politicians (including former Prime Minister Sir Edward Heath) made venomous statements. While most of the literary community rallied round him, such writers as John le Carré, Hugh Trevor-Roper, Sir Stephen Spender, Germaine Greer and Roald Dahl raised their voices in condemnation.

"It had something to do with the fact that I've been a very vocal critic of the entrenched Establishment," Rushdie admits. "A part of it is that I'm not one of them. It's not so much race, though that had something to do with it. If this had happened to Kingsley Amis, the government might have behaved differently. It's not even to do with class. There is this thing—which everybody denies exists—that runs the country. If you get understood to be anti-Establishment, then if you're in a weak position, and the Establishment is asked to help you out, they say: we don't see why we should. That manifested itself in my case and was responsible for some of the unpleasantness, which has continued.

"It was the one thing I never expected," Rushdie goes on. "That if a writer in England, at the end of the 20th century, were to be attacked in this medievalist way, that the writer would be *abused* for having called down this thing on himself. I did not understand that. I had not anticipated that."

It is all the more remarkable, then, that *East, West* does not strike the reader as the work of a bitter man. Several stories are poignant, others have a comic bent. Only one story, "At the Auction of the Ruby Slippers," carries a real edge of a satirical anger, and that is directed against the greed and paranoia of our culture as a whole. The remaining eight tales illustrate the range and versatility of Rushdie's language and deal with many of his dominant themes: the question of identity, the concepts of home and exile, of family and friendship. Three of the stories are set in India; these were written before the *fatwa;* the next three are Western-based and do not have Indian characters (one, "Yorick," is a parody of Shakespeare; "Ruby Slippers" obviously was inspired by *The Wizard of Oz;* the third features Columbus and Queen Isabella). Two of these were written *post-fatwa*, as were the three stories in the last section, "East West."

The suggestion that the book reflects a compartmentalization of thought and imagination caused, perhaps, by the *fatwa* is denied by Rushdie. He claims that the only changes in the goals of his work and the way he approaches it are those that would have occurred anyway with his own maturation and the changing of his writing style. "I haven't literally sat down and said: how will I make a literary response to those events?"

On the other hand, he acknowledges that "some of the things I've written about have come out of what's happened. Not only in this collection but in *Haroun and the Sea of Stories*. That's an idea I had before all this happened. Just the germ of it. A storyteller who lost the ability to tell stories and in some way his son would help him get it back. But clearly the final shape of that book, with its emphasis on this discussion of language and silence—people who are trying to speak and those who are trying to sew up their lips—clearly was influenced by what happened to me."

So does Rushdie agree with one of his characters, who ruminates that "fictions . . . are dangerous"? Does he deplore the irony that for most writers fiction is liberating, but for him it has become a potential quicksand where he must step warily? Rushdie insists that fiction can be both at once. "Fiction has been dangerous for its authors *always*.

It's also dangerous for the world in the way that's a necessary danger. Without it, you can't change anything, you can't shake things up in people's heads. It's always been dangerous and it will be a sad day when it stops being dangerous. But I don't write with an eye on those dangers. Truthfully, if I thought about that I wouldn't be able to write at all."

Because fiction is "different for each user," Rushdie says he is fascinated and amused by the divergent critical responses to *East, West*. Though the majority of the reviews in England and in the U.S. so far have been favorable, most critics have singled out different stories to praise or disparage. "If you have nine pieces of varied work, no two reviewers will respond to all of them on the same level. And no two critics will ever agree," he finds. "Whereas in a novel, critics, broadly speaking, will tell you what they think about the entity as a whole." The different responses critics have to stories depend on what the reader brings to them, he thinks. "Some like those having most to do with India and don't like the middle section [set in the West]. Martin Amis, for instance, thinks the middle three are the most interesting. That also has to do with who he is." Rushdie is pleased, however, that the stories "do what writing is supposed to do: that is, they go into the reader's consciousness and are in some way completed by the reader."

"One of the things that's interesting about the nature of reading is that you *assume* that your response is universal. If you like something you don't think: I *like* this. You think: this is *good*. In a way, all readers are absolutists."

The word "absolutists" brings him up short; he gives a deep chuckle. "Which is all right in the context of a variegated response," he continues. "If everybody was saying the same things about the same stories, then they might be right."

As it is, the only story whose merits all critics and readers have agreed upon so far is the last one, "The Courter," in which an aging *ayah* (nursemaid) living with a family in Britain is torn between her love for a hall porter and the pull of her homeland. "I had an ayah but she didn't have an affair with a hall porter," Rushdie says. "I wanted to write about being young during the '60s, when it was supposed to be fun and it wasn't; I wanted to compare the narrator's adolescence with this autumnal love affair."

Although he stresses the fact that much in this collection is "autobiographically motivated," Rushdie feels that "when this kind of fiction works, it's because the emotional heart of it is truthful and none of the incidents are." Speaking about his striking story, "The Harmony of the Spheres," he says, "It's true that when I was much younger I had a friend who was beginning to be a writer and who eventually committed suicide. Those things are in common with the character in the story. But just to write down what happened to my friend would not have been a story. The story began to work at the point where the *fictional* relationship between the narrator and the character, which was not our actual relationship, began to develop and have its own life."

About the surprise closing line, which some reviewers have praised and others have deplored as a "trick ending" that diminishes the story, he says, "The final line is *supposed* to knock you out of your chair. I don't usually write stories with punch lines; my stories don't generally lead to some smart little remark. But "Harmony" is constructed to make you think you know what's going on in the story and then to tell you at the end that in fact you *don't* understand what's going on. The narrator seems to understand the world he's in, but in fact it's a different world."

Perhaps the narrator of that story is most like Rushdie himself. Born in India, the narrator has never felt completely at home in England, but having been introduced to the world of the occult by his best friend from Cambridge days, a writer who has become a paranoid schizophrenic, he thinks he has "found another way of making a bridge between here and there, between my two othernesses, my double unbelonging." His final betrayal by this supposed friend brings home the irony of his feeling of safety under the friend's aegis, and might lead a literal-minded reader to believe that Rushdie has been isolated from his *pre-fatwa* comrades and colleagues.

This is not the case. His writer friends in England, notably Martin Amis, Harold Pinter, Antonia Fraser, Julian Barnes and Margaret Drabble, have been unwavering in their support. They and many others are members of the Salman Rushdie Defence Committee, formed under the umbrella of an anti-censorship organization called Article 19. The intellectual communities in Germany and France rallied to his side. And in the U.S., a large coterie of writers, including William Styron, Norman Mailer, Don DeLillo and Paul Auster, have championed his cause, the latter two being among those responsible for the card describing Rushdie's plight that was inserted in books sold on February 14 of last year.

It is their encouragement, plus the easing of the sense of immediate crisis, that has brought Rushdie somewhat out of hiding. "In England in the last year or two I've resumed to a large extent a great deal of an ordinary life," he says. "And that makes a point, I think, which is that it is possible to get past this thing. This is my attitude now: I do not care about the bloody *fatwa*. I'm not interested in talking about the *fatwa*. Iran is just the dullest topic on the planet. I've got books to talk about and to write. In fact, *I'm* abolishing the *fatwa!*" he declaims, with a chesty laugh.

To maintain this stance, Rushdie admits, he does require other people, the public at large, to change their attitudes. He is frequently ticked off when "people treat me as if I'm a walking bomb. People come up to me at parties and ask, 'Should I be standing here talking to you?'" (The fact that he encounters such questions from presumably sophisticated people at his occasional social outings indicates that the *fatwa* decree has not lost its power to terrify. Certainly he is no longer a gregarious habitué of the Groucho Club, where London's literati hobnob.)

Much more of an inconvenience was the "enormous trouble" he had in getting permission from owners of music copyright to quote from their songs, which are an integral part of "The Courter." He cites two or three cases where "we were refused permission to use three or four words." Most egregious was the recent refusal by the owners of the Flintstones copyright to allow him to quote from a song. "Between the British and the American publication we had to remove three lines of text which happened to be from that extremely dangerous movie called *The Flintstones*," Rushdie says, his enunciation slow and scornful. "So readers in the U.S. will not read those lines because somebody, you know, might bomb Fred Flintstone. That's the level of lunacy I deplore.

"But when it happens it hits me in the face as if somebody had slapped me. It feels like a humiliation. I'm constantly saying to people: Look, there is some risk. I've become very good at knowing what it is and how to deal with it. So if I'm doing something—like coming to this room to talk to you today—it's because I have dealt with that risk, that infinitesimal risk of coming to see you."

One problem that Rushdie cannot surmount is the impossibility of returning to India while the *fatwa* exists. His regret is almost palpable. "Not to be able to go to India is like having a leg cut off. I used to go there for months every year. I have friends I haven't seen in years, I have family there. It's a huge loss for me." Getting there safely would be no problem, he feels; it's the emotional volatility of the Indian masses stirred up by extremist fundamentalist politicians that he fears. "If I went, someone would be sure to try to exploit it. They could put a crowd on the street at a moment's notice, someone would fire shots, people might be hurt."

Not being able to go "home" creates a literary problem too. "I could write about India for the rest of my life without ever going there again, because it's just in the DNA. It's where I'm from. Plenty of writers who are exiled go on doing that. That's not the problem. The problem is that I have no desire to become that kind of nostalgist writer. India is changing very fast right now; it's undergoing a great convulsion. I can understand what's going on because I know what Indian people are like and how they react to things. I can imagine it, but I'm not *there*. I don't want to be one of those old duffers looking nostalgically over the horizon to where they used to come from. I'd much rather face the realities of life that I have now."

Though his novel-in-progress, *The Moor's Last Sigh,* is set mainly in India, Rushdie feels he has not in this work experienced any distancing from his subject. "It comes out of an interest in certain changes I know a lot about," he says. "But I cannot envisage myself, after I finish this, putting a major piece of work in India without being able to go there. I can't see setting a 500-page novel there again, unless something changes. That's a forced choice. Beyond that I have the freedom of the imagination. And the choices I'm making are still my choices."

If the *fatwa* has had any subconscious effect on his fiction, it is in the lessons he's learned about human nature, Rushdie says, some of which have been "dreadful"; yet there's another side, too. "If you are faced with so much ugliness of various kinds you find yourself trying to think about the opposite of that, about what human values actually are. Nobody survives an event like the *fatwa* by themselves. They survive it because people stand beside them. And a lot of people have done that for me. Not just people I know. Even people I don't know send me extraordinary messages. My friends have been heroic. You learn that about human nature as well. It's not all bad news." This "rollercoaster ride for the emotions" has freed up his fiction, Rushdie thinks, toward a more directly emotional kind of writing, which he was able to do in some of the later stories in *East, West.*

Explaining the dedication of *East, West* "for Andrew and Gillon," the author himself exhibits a rush of emotions. "That dedication stands for the simple reason that there is nobody who has done more to protect the publication of *The Satanic Verses* than [his agents], Andrew Wylie and Gillon Aitken. And Andrew gets plenty of stick; he gets called names in the press. But the fact is that the two of them did something extraordinary for me for which I'll always be grateful. Which is that they were completely unafraid at the moment of maximum terror. They didn't lock their office doors. They didn't change their behavior one iota. And they demanded that the publishers that we dealt with should do the same. Andrew and Gillon had to save that publication, country by country, where publishers were running scared."

Rushdie says he knows of a publisher who dashed with a screwdriver to remove the company's nameplate from the front door "so they wouldn't get bombed." He says there are cases of publishers moving their desks away from the windows and being unwilling to go out for business lunches because they were afraid. He makes some veiled statements about the way he was treated by Penguin. "There was chaos out there. Because Andrew and Gillon showed no terror at all, they were able to save the publication of the book," he says.

So the conversation has again veered to the *fatwa*. Suppose he were to use the whole melodramatic situation in a novel, we ask, how would he write the last chapter?

"It would have a happy ending, for a start," Rushdie says with a laugh. "But I'd have to write the story as nonfiction. There's no point in making up a novel about it. What's interesting about the story is that it's true. And most of what happened has not been told. I would love to tell the story straightforwardly, without keeping secrets. If only because a lot of people have helped me and at the moment I can't identify them. There are an awful lot of people who come out of it very well, and an awful lot who come out of it very badly indeed. So I would just like to reach a point at which I could stop buttoning my lip and simply tell the story." His voice sinks to a whisper. "About this extraordinary, in some ways dreadful and in other ways quite moving event that happened to all of us."

SYBIL STEINBERG
January 25, 1995

253

Mark Salzman

IF THE UBIQUITOUS appearance of painters, photographers, dancers and writers in high-powered ads can be said to have any significance for our culture, it is that artistic achievement is a marketable commodity, and artists themselves, especially photogenic ones, are valuable properties. Young, handsome and talented, Mark Salzman is an adman's dream, having not only two books to his credit, one of them an acclaimed memoir—*Iron & Silk* (1986), about his life as an English teacher in China—but also a signature hobby: martial arts. Salzman has been known to bring swords to his bookstore appearances and to work swordplay into his readings.

The Gap snagged him for one of its austere, black-and-white magazine ads not long after *Iron & Silk* was published, showing him in black pants and a sleeveless tee, lunging forward with a sword twirled backward in each hand. In 1991, after the release of the movie version in which he starred, Dewar's featured him in its Profiles campaign. Asked in the ad why he does what he does, Salzman replied, "What else do you do with a degree from Yale in Chinese language and literature?"

Based on the impression those ads convey, an interviewer expects to encounter a self-possessed writer with a chic self-image, slightly arrogant perhaps and absolutely sure of his place in the world. Instead, Salzman turns out to be somewhat collegiate in appearance, modest to the point of self-effacement and honest enough to confess that his own moments of self-doubt inspired his newest book, *The Soloist*. Published by Random House, the novel is about a musical prodigy living in Los Angeles.

Settling down to egg-white omelettes and rosemary toast at a small cafe in trendy Oldtown, in Pasadena, not far from his suburban L.A. home, Salzman, now 34, explains that he pursued Chinese studies as a way of gaining a liberal education, hoping, as college students do, to find "answers." "It wasn't a practical degree if you didn't want to be a Sinologist," he says. It did, however, take him to China, where he taught English and studied martial arts from 1982 to 1984, and it did in fact provide him with some answers—but not to all of his questions. After his China sojourn, he still had no idea what to do with his life, so he returned to New Haven and earned a modest living teaching martial arts, meanwhile entertaining friends with stories about his time in China as a "Foreign Devil." That was how *Iron & Silk* was born.

"A friend suggested I write one of the narratives as a short story, and when I did he sent it off to another friend who was an editor. She [Becky Saletan, then newly installed at Random, now at S & S] called and asked if there was more. She was looking for a book to champion, which worked to my advantage. She encouraged me to continue until there was a book, and she had ideas how to structure it in short chapter form. When it came out I felt that writing could be a career, and that I had better get to work."

He had used up all his interesting real-life material, he says, so he decided to turn to fiction. His second book, *The Laughing Sutra* (1991), also used China as a setting. The novel is a parable about a boy raised by a monk who is determined to recover a long-lost sacred scroll called the Laughing Sutra, which has found its way to the U.S. China is in the grip of the Cultural Revolution, and the Red Guard has taken over the country. The boy, now a young man, escapes to America to rescue the scroll for the monk, discovering in the process a new and better life for himself. He then has to decide whether he should return with the Sutra to China and a possibly dismal existence or stay in America, thereby betraying the old man.

"The book explores the question of the boundary between loyalty to yourself and loyalty to those you love," Salzman says. "Anyone with parents knows you find yourself in situations when you do have to make these decisions. And often the sides are so evenly balanced.

"In my writing I love to take real-life situations and say: What if they were much worse? I use fiction as a form of problem-solving." *The Soloist,* he says, looks at the difference between our expectations of what our lives should be and how they actually turn out. How do you deal with not having all your dreams come true?

The main character in the book, 36-year-old Reinhart Sundheimer, is a cello prodigy whose career ends at age 18 when he becomes obsessed by the idea of perfect pitch and can no longer play without distraction. His life crumbles. A call to serve on jury duty opens new doors, but he finds himself the lone dissenting voice in a murder trial. A fellow juror with whom he nearly has an affair loathes him—for his obstinacy, he thinks. He takes on a talented young Korean cellist as a student, and through him Reinhart finally comes to terms with his own talent.

"I wanted to create a character who had a hard time with his dreams," Salzman says. "One of my favorite books is Ishiguro's *The Remains of the Day*. Stylistically it was a very strong influence. It's a nearly perfect book; I was completely knocked out." He gives a pithy summary of Ishiguro's story of a butler who, after a long career of selfless service, suddenly regrets his devotion to duty at the expense of emotional commitment.

"So many people I deeply admire feel they didn't live up to their own ideals, and what I admire is that they can live with that in a dignified way. Both my parents have dealt with that situation. I think my fear is that I won't be able to." He explains that his mother, a concert harpsichordist to whom *The Soloist* is dedicated, decided that she wanted children and put her ambitions on hold while she devoted herself to raising them. "Now that we're all three grown up, she's concertizing. The music world isn't responsive, but she doesn't regret her choices. That's what I admire. Not feeling sorry for yourself." His father wanted to be a painter but became a social worker in order to support a family. "He loathed his career," Salzman says. "He painted at night. Now he's retired and he is painting again. He did it all without whining."

Whatever the source of his sensitivity, Salzman says he finds it easy to come up with dilemmas to explore. The one that currently plagues him has to do with the decision-making process, not necessarily a life-and-death decision like Reinhart's, but one that affects everyday life, including how one does one's work. "As human beings we are gifted with intelligence," says Salzman, laying out the sequence of his thoughts slowly and carefully. "Our intelligence allows us to make informed decisions. To make informed decisions you gather as much knowledge as you can. When you've gained enough knowledge you're confident you can make the right decision. My problem is feeling confident I've gathered enough information. If there's no outside voice telling you you're now capable, when do you stop the research? I can't seem to escape this. It comes up all the time. I feel so burdened sometimes with trying to be rational, although the benefits of accepting the burden are entirely worthwhile. It's deeply satisfying to struggle with a decision, to know you haven't shirked a responsibility."

Not much about the book is based on real life, he says, but he's a bit worried that people will ask him about an episode in which Reinhart is impotent. To deflect his concern, he points out that he's happily married to a documentary filmmaker, a fifth-generation, non-Chinese speaking Chinese American, whom he met at Yale and married five years ago. She was a national champion fencer, and the friend who introduced them thought that they'd have sports in common, which wasn't true. He thought fencing was "shallow," and she thought martial arts were "flaky." "We had a lot to get over," he says. (Since he injured his back from overtraining he has given up all forms of martial arts except Tai Chi, which uses very slow movements.)

One part in the book that is true, he says, besides the fact that he himself plays the cello, is "the bit about the astronaut." Reinhart sits in a box for hours at a time, pretending to be an astronaut in a spaceship. "As a child," says Salzman, "I would sit in a box looking out with a periscope while my mother gave oboe and piano lessons.

"The parents of her students would say, 'Where's your son,' and she'd say, 'In his box.' She was very patient with me."

He grew up in Connecticut by no means a prodigy, though he studied violin at age four, piano at five and cello at seven, settling, finally, on the cello. For a time he entertained the idea that he would be a professional musician, but he found that such thoughts took the fun out of playing. He likes playing casually, for small groups of friends, and with his mother, with whom he plays Vivaldi, Scarlatti, and Jacchini, music he calls "wonderful stuff for cello and harpsichord." When he's alone he plays Bach. "His cello suites don't feel old at all. They're like good Philip Glass. The austerity of it moves me."

He mentions E. B. White as the writer who has had the most influence on his work, citing as his favorite White story, "The Death of a Pig," which describes a man raising a pig for slaughter. "The pig becomes ill and dies, and he's heartbroken. I like his understatement. Ishiguro comes closest to my ideal, though; I'd love to meet him."

Writing *The Soloist*, also a work of understatement, was an enjoyable experience, Salzman says. With a first success behind him and a second book under his belt, he was free to loosen up and stretch his wings. "I've been overwhelmed by the acceptance I've had, particularly because I know so many writers who've worked harder over more time and haven't had attention. I feel lucky. If *Laughing Sutra* had been first, it would have been harder. How do you convince a publisher you're worth the risk? China, at the time of *Iron & Silk*, was very interesting to people. If I had been teaching English in Venezuela it wouldn't have had the same appeal."

Salzman acquired his agent, Eric Ashworth at Ashworth and Donadio, in much the way he acquired his editor: through the intervention of a friend. "I've had nothing but good experiences with agents and editors," he says. After Ashworth's recent retirement, Neil Olsen at Donadio took over as agent, and Random's Joe Fox is now his editor, unnamed but thanked in the acknowledgements of *The Soloist*. "I wanted to name him but he sent a letter saying he doesn't think editors should be identified," Salzman says. "The idea persists that writers exist in a vacuum. They're geniuses and no one dares touch their work. I benefit enormously from my friends and editors and my wife, who reads all my drafts. It would be great to be a completely independent genius. That not being the case, I'm more than glad to acknowledge help."

In general, Salzman doesn't seek the company of writers, he says, preferring to spend time with people who think about things outside his realm. He enjoys living near Caltech, where a cult has grown up around the late physicist Richard Feynman. "You get to meet people who knew him and can hear all the hilarious stories about him." He's a big fan of science books, too. Recent reading includes *The Third Chimpanzee* by Jared Diamond and Stephen Jay Gould, "of course."

His working habits are not consistent, Salzman says. He tries to write five days a week; two to three hours at a stretch constitutes a good day for him. He will go for weeks working in the morning, then will shift and work in the afternoon. After 5:00 p.m. he hikes, reads, daydreams.

"I've always been a big daydreamer," he says. "My fantasies for myself are outlandish. I could never live up to my expectations as a kid. I wanted to cure cancer. Actually I can't complain at all. Things have worked out better than I could ever have expected."

The future holds more books, but he doesn't know yet what the next will be. He's getting used to the difficult, unproductive period between finishing a manuscript and seeing completed copies in the stores. "This time I played the cello and didn't even make an effort to write," he says. "My wife worried that I wasn't writing, but I know now that I will."

SUZANNE MANTEL
January 17, 1994

CATHLEEN SCHINE

"I WOULD HAVE NEVER said I was a novelist until very recently," says Cathleen Schine. "I had so many friends who said, 'I'm a novelist. I'm working on a novel and there are four main characters and they're all ME' and of course they'd never finish."

Now 12 years after the publication of her first book, *Alice in Bed*, and with her fourth novel, *The Love Letter,* due out from Houghton Mifflin, Schine is finally beginning to admit she's a novelist.

Schine's apartment on Manhattan's Upper West Side is certainly the kind one imagines for a writer. Aside from a husband, two children and two cats, it houses wall after wall of bookcases. Every surface is covered with mementos—three pairs of brass shoes (one tarnished, two of more recent vintage), numerous pictures of her family (and one of Toscanini). Copies of the recent German translation of her third novel, *Rameau's Niece,* are stacked on a ledge, an LP of *Götterdämmerung* is propped on the floor.

Schine moves a bit hesitantly, with something of the "thudding ephemeral quality" she ascribes to Helen MacFarquhar, the tart bookseller heroine of *The Love Letter.* It's the result of her year (in the early 1970s) in the hospital and two subsequent hip replacement surgeries. The other result of that year was the largely autobiographical *Alice in Bed.*

Margot Hentoff, an old family friend and, at the time, an editor at the *Village Voice,* had been intrigued by Schine's story of her medical misadventures and suggested she write about them for the *Voice.* "She was enormously helpful, but, while I was writing it, she'd say 'save this for the novel.'" In fact, Schine began writing her novel almost immediately after finishing the *Voice* piece. "I was too naïve to know that it was difficult. I wrote one page a day—I had nothing else to do and that was my job. I knew nothing about writing a novel, which I think, reading *Alice in Bed,* perhaps you can see. It's really 365 one-page sections."

Schine also didn't know it was supposed to be hard to get a first novel published. A friend suggested she submit the manuscript to agent Candida Donadio. Donadio called Schine, saying in a deep voice, which, in Schine's imitation, sounds like an elderly Hungarian, "I go for it."

Donadio, who is still Schine's agent, sold *Alice in Bed* to the first editor she tried, Vicki Wilson at Knopf. John Updike praised it in the *New Yorker.* There were three printings. And a paperback.

It was all a surprise for Schine, whose career musings to date had vacillated between being a medievalist and being a retail clothing buyer. Born in Westport, Conn., in 1953, her first taste of writing had been the "really icky poetry" she wrote in high school—some of which she has integrated into *The Love Letter.* In 1971, she went to Sarah Lawrence "in order to write poetry. But the minute I got there, I was too embarrassed and stopped writing."

Instead, she decided to study medieval history, transferring to Barnard for its larger research facilities. But, she says, almost her entire career there was a blur. Stricken with colitis, she spent most of her sophomore year in a painkiller-induced stupor. "I don't remember anything," she says.

Schine was also taking cortisone, which sometimes has a side effect called aseptic necrosis of the hips ("basically that means they get inflamed and disintegrate"). After the year in the hospital, Schine and her new plastic hips transferred once again, this time to the University of Chicago to continue graduate work in medieval history.

Schine began to believe that she wasn't cut out to be an academic. "I just wasn't good enough. I didn't have the *sitz-fleisch.* I went to Florence, where I was supposed to study paleography. But it was beautiful outside and I'd get all itchy and bored. I'd run out and buy shoes.

"To be a good historian you have to remember a lot of stuff and it has to make a pattern." But, she says, "I have a terrible, terrible memory." That characteristic of Margaret Nathan in *Rameau's Niece* is, she admits, "hideously autobiographical."

It's true that Schine is bad at dates, trying hard to approximate the years of her various college tenures and confessing that she doesn't remember the exact anniversary of her marriage to David Denby, film critic at *New York* magazine. She knows it was 1981: "Someone needlepointed a footstool for us with the date on it. But it broke. The only way to find out the date would be to dig through the closet and find the pieces."

Schine's marriage was followed by two children. Max, born in 1983, and Tommy, born in 1987. She had started working on *To the Birdhouse,* but that book would take seven years to see publication. "I thought, The world can wait for a second novel by me, but I'll never get another chance to be with my little children."

Like *Alice in Bed, To The Birdhouse* portrays Alice Brody and her family members. But this second novel had a more arduous publishing history than its predecessor. "It had been a long time and everyone had forgotten about me," Schine claims. Vicki Wilson at Knopf didn't want the novel, and it went to nine different publishers before landing with Michael di Capua at FSG.

After *To The Birdhouse* was published, Schine's position had changed. With both boys in school, she gave up her odd journalistic writing to focus on her next book. By this time, she was also ready to leave the Brody family behind. "Michael was very important to me," says Schine. "He gave me the confidence to take myself more seriously. So I took a risk, in my own very small way," she says, remembering that, while writing *Rameau's Niece,* she had to repeat to herself: "'dare to be pretentious.'" She decided to make her heroine an academic. But, she says, "I was sick of reading about struggling, bitter academics. I thought, Let's make her someone who accidentally had a big success. It'll be very funny. She'll be baffled."

When a friend suggested Margaret write about something in the philosophical/pornographic tradition, Schine jumped at it. "I started reading John Locke. I was thrilled because he's all about the senses, and if you have the idea of sex on your mind, it's all about sex. I thought: desire, and the desire to know—these are the same things on some level. It was a very exciting realization. It made all the 18th-century stuff wonderfully sexy, but it also made all the searching and yearning and erotic, emotional material much deeper."

Although the project started under di Capua, the two came to a parting of ways. When di Capua left FSG for HarperCollins, Schine decamped to Ticknor & Fields, and John Herman, whom she describes as "smart and sane."

Her academic heroine's adventures with infidelity and New York intellectual culture were compared to works of David Lodge and Kingsley Amis. Both the *New York Times* and the *VLS* touted it as one of their favorite books of 1993, and it was a finalist for the 1992–1993 *Los Angeles Times* Book Prize.

A review in the *New Yorker* called *Rameau's Niece* "that rare comic novel—a warm comic novel," an assessment Schine no doubt appreciates. "I don't think anyone would consider what I write satire in the traditional sense. I had wanted *Rameau's Niece* to be a satire of a certain intellectual set of New York life, but I couldn't do it because you really need to be angry in a certain way that I'm not. But also for satire you need to have a sense of the way things ought to be and how they've fallen away."

If, for *Rameau's Niece,* she dared "to be pretentious," for *The Love Letter* she says, she had to "dare to be romantic." "I thought, You know what you like to read, you like to read comedies, but you also like real, heartfelt, earnest romance. It's dangerous to be earnest, but now's the time to try."

Her reading tastes are based in the 19th century—George Eliot, Dickens, Trollope. And Jane Austen. Before sitting down to write, she reads *Emma.* "One of the things that's so wonderful about Emma is that, at some level, she's an unsympathetic character and yet you're completely sympathetic to her throughout. Those kinds of characters really interest me—deeply flawed characters who you take to your heart.

"I didn't really know how to write a novel," Schine adds. "I'd read *Emma* and then say 'Oh, *that's* what you do.' Periodically I read *Pictures from an Institution* by Randall Jarrell, which is the funniest book ever written, on the off chance that maybe I'll be able to steal some stylistic details. That's my goal in life: to successfully appropriate something from that book."

Another change of editor awaited her for *The Love Letter*: when Herman left after a shakeup at Ticknor & Fields, the book came of age under Janet Silver at Houghton Mifflin. "She's the first editor I've ever had who is my age—we have the same childcare problems and get the same sinus headaches. She saved my life."

Having started writing, Schine came quickly to a crisis. "I'd get Helen to the bookstore and then I had no idea what she was supposed to do." Schine went to Manhattan's Three Lives bookstore for an apprenticeship. "I think 'work' should be put in quotations," she says. "I tried to work but it's very physical in a way I didn't expect. They all go to chiropractors and I can see why. Then again I have these problems with my hips and I can't squat and I can't bend down and I was using a cane. I was hopeless, completely useless."

Nor did she go there every day. "Occasionally, I had to actually write." After the scattershot time spent with *To the Birdhouse,* Schine had actually been able to sit down in a tiny office in her apartment and write *Rameau's Niece.* But with *The Love Letter,* her husband was at home writing his own book, [his paean to the classics, *Great Books*]. "I said to a friend of mine whose husband is also a writer, 'He doesn't do anything, he doesn't say anything. He's very respectful and quiet.' And she said, 'Yes, but it's like having a bad fluorescent lightbulb buzzing above your head.'"

So Schine made a deal with a cousin who had just gotten a job in publishing and lived in the Village. "When she went to work in the morning, I'd go down to her studio and, in return, I'd help her with the rent. She had a portrait of Virginia Woolf above her desk. So that was the room of my own, only it belonged to someone else."

Both the academic setting of *Rameau's Niece* and the bookstore of *The Love Letter* had allowed Schine to give free rein to her love of books, mentioning old favorites and recent influential reads. "I had to be careful because sometimes there were lists of books that were there simply because I loved them."

In a way, it's a convert's passion. As she admits, at the time of her marriage, "I'd read nothing. I'd read Colette and Dostoyevski in high school and all this medieval philosophy, but really nothing else. I had read or tried to read Derrida before I'd read any literature. It was a waste of time: once you figure out what these people are saying, it's not very much. It's not that it's untrue, it's just a sort of small truth, whereas novels are full of big *and* small truths—and are much more fun to read.

"I think sometimes of what Groucho Marx said: 'I wouldn't want to belong to a club that would have me as a member.' The fact that literature was something that I loved and that I could read easily made it seem as if it wasn't worth pursuing. It seemed like it was cheating," Schine muses. One can only be grateful she decided to cheat and join the club.

MARIA SIMSON
May 8, 1995

JIM SHEPARD

An ordinary life gradually takes on the dimensions of a nightmare; the situation is not unusual in a novel. But in Jim Shepard's compelling *Kiss of the Wolf*, (Harcourt Brace) the tale has a jolting impact because the protagonist's actions—she accidentally runs a man down on a dark road at night and never tells the police—are so at odds with her moral integrity. What's more, Joannie Mucherino's 11-year-old son is a passenger in the car, and she must cope with the effects of her behavior on him while fending off the advances of a sinister, misogynistic would-be lover—the wolf of the title.

To move from the book's impeccably rendered lower-middle class neighborhood setting to Williamstown, Mass., the picture-pretty college town in which the author lives, is a dislocating experience. His icing-pink, white-columned house looks as if it were wrenched from the pages of *Gone With the Wind.* "We rent—does that help?" he quips when we remark on the contrast between art and life.

Shepard is the author of three highly respected previous novels: *Flights* (1983), about an adolescent boy who proves himself by stealing and flying a plane; *Paper Doll* (1987), which centers on a group of heartbreakingly young airmen facing death in WW II; and *Lights Out in the Reptile House* (1990), an examination of individuals trapped in a brutal, fictional totalitarian society.

A slender, quiet-spoken man of 37, Shepard has taught at Williams College for 11 years. He writes at home, in his upstairs study, where he's currently working on a novel based on the life of F. W. Murnau, director of the classic vampire film, *Nosferatu;* posters from the film decorate the walls. We talk in the living room, where Shepard's two dogs settle in as well. We're interrupted occasionally by Shepard's two-year-old son Aidan, who periodically enters to sit on his father's knee.

Williamstown is a substantial remove from Shepard's background. He grew up Catholic in Bridgeport, Conn., where he was born to an

264

Italian mother who arrived here when she was 10 years old after her father "had a run-in with the Fascist Italian regime."

His maternal relatives dominated Shepard's youth. "My dad is half-Italian, half-Irish, but he had only one brother, whereas my mother's side was large enough to provide me with 29 first cousins." The experience of growing up Catholic among his Italian kin was what powered his first novel, Shepard says, and provided setting and material for the current one.

"Individual responsibility versus passivity is an issue I grew up with. It was always being raised in both implicit and explicit ways by my education in a Catholic school, and by family, too. As I look over my four books, I realize that the issue of passivity as it relates to responsibility—the way in which not doing the right thing can become actively doing the wrong thing—is something I've become more explicit about. That kind of passivity is one of the ways at getting at how good people can end up doing bad things. I consider all my protagonists good people, people who wouldn't want to hurt anybody. What I'm interested in is how just that can become a *justification* for hurting people."

All his books seem "very Catholic" to Shepard. "One of the things the nuns drill into you in benign and not so benign ways is that *all* your actions have consequences and usually the consequences are ethical ones. The negative part is if you're always measuring activity in ethical terms, you tend to have a large capacity for guilt. The good part about it is that those people who have been raised Catholic, and who were paying attention, are very rarely thoughtless people. I think it makes for characters who are very often dealing with surprisingly large thematic issues without seeming like they've been educated at the Sorbonne. The challenge, of course, is having them put it into their own language."

Although there were no precedents in his family, Shepard always nursed a desire to write. At Trinity College in Hartford, Conn., however, his desire to write fiction was initially discouraged by the teacher of the writing workshop in which he was enrolled. "Because I had no history of hoping someone was really going to like my work, it wasn't particularly devastating to me. I thought it might be a private act, writing," Shepard recalls.

But he persevered, and a story he did for the workshop's fiction section changed everything. "I wrote in a completely different way. It was voice-driven—something that came to me in the middle of the night—and I squatted on my little bedroom floor and wrote half-naked and was very excited about it." The same professor who had previously belittled his efforts suggested that he send it to the *Atlantic*. "I went from feeling I didn't belong in the class to being told I had written something good enough to publish." The *Atlantic* didn't take that piece but encouraged him to show them other work. A month later the magazine accepted another story. "I had a four-week struggle to publish," Shepard says, wryly. He was 19 years old.

After earning a Masters degree at Brown, Shepard joined the faculty at the University of Michigan. "The idea of myself as a professor was burlesque—I thought it quite silly for a long time. Charlie Baxter has a great phrase for it: he calls it 'the fraud police.' It took me quite a while to realize that the fraud police weren't going to come into my classroom and carry me out. The first year, I taught a class on Hitchcock and Kubrick that had 200 people; you got a T. A. for every 15 or 20 people, so I had this army of teaching assistants in the front row, all of whom were 10 years older than I was. They would stare at me, like 'Who is this kid?'"

Given what most publishers are willing to pay for most fiction, "especially if you're not John Irving or Stephen King"—Shepard thinks that teaching is the best financial hedge for a writer. "It's a wonderful way of having an irregular life, which is what most writers would like in terms of what hours you have to put in when. It's also a superb way of training yourself to be a better reader, which is what you have to do to be a better writer anyway. Even if I were a zillionaire, I think I would work out some sort of thing where I taught half the year."

At Michigan Shepard met novelist Ron Hansen, and the two have remained close friends, each the only reader of the other's work before submission to a publisher. The two men are currently co-editing a new short-story collection, *You've Got to Read This: Contemporary American Writers Introduce Stories That Held Them in Awe,* for HarperCollins.

Initially Shepard was represented by Liz Darhansoff; he is now a client of Peter Matson, at Sterling Lord Literistic. His first editor was Robert Gottlieb at Knopf, whom he praises for his "savvy editorial suggestions. I sent my first novel to him on a Wednesday and he called me the following Monday and said that he liked it." Gottlieb edited *Flights* and *Paper Doll* before he "was spirited away by the *New Yorker,* which left me to be binked across the table at Knopf like a poker chip to whomever showed some enthusiasm. Or maybe it was the lowest person on the totem pole."

Decamping to Norton for *Reptile House,* Shepard enjoyed working with Gerry Howard, whom he praises. But the novel received what Shepard terms "a horrifying review" in the *New York Times,* after which, he says, the house drastically cut the budget for publicity. "The reviewer said essentially, 'Who cares about any of this stuff?'" Shepard feels that the negative assessment stopped most other papers from considering the book. "That meant that Norton really was in no position to do the fourth book. I was back on the market." He ended up happily with Harcourt and Pat Strachan, whom he calls "a wonderful editor."

Despite his peripatetic path, Shepard knows that he's been lucky in working with some of the best editors in the business. "I've never had an editor who wasn't helpful. While I recognize that as a breed they are becoming less and less editors and more and more marketers, that hasn't been true in my case. I've dealt with literary editors who've said, 'I'm going to do the best I can to market this book, *and* I'm going to make it the best book I can.' Pat, especially, has been astute at both."

Nabokov and Joyce are the writers Shepard credits as most important to his work, although Kafka had a large influence on *Reptile House,* as did Coetzee. "Joyce had a *huge* effect in terms of how profoundly I could redeem my background. When I was much younger, it was Hemingway and Salinger. As an Italian kid growing up in Bridgeport, it was important to me to discover that you could do literature in those voices; you didn't have to sound like Henry James. To read something like 'Just Before the War with the Eskimos' or *Catcher in the Rye* was to realize that just to be faithful to the voices around you held the possibility of great meaning."

Shepard has an extraordinary ear for voice, which he utilizes to fascinating effect in *Kiss of the Wolf* in the character of Bruno. As Shepard points out, Bruno's appearance follows that of three other characters who are, in effect, feeling sorry for themselves. "His response is, 'You have a problem, too bad, my condolences, *deal* with it'—a kind of Darwinian ruthlessness.

"One of the things that interested me in Bruno as a character is that he is a particular kind of—I don't want to say Italian male—but certainly a kind of radical misogynist I knew. It was a kind of misogyny that understood that you were going to absorb a certain amount of humiliation just because of the pecking order, and you were going to take that rage out on somebody farther down the line. I have known people like Bruno and have been entranced by their speech. I suppose anybody who's powered by emotions as powerful as humiliation or rage is intrinsically interesting as a fictional character because they're just so energized.

"I am fascinated by the problem of evil, the issue of evil. I would call Bruno an evil figure. But I'm fascinated by evil figures in the context of the possibility of good. One of the reasons Bruno stands out is that everybody else in the novel—although they're not particularly successful at it—is trying to work towards helping one another."

Despite their bleak settings and situations, Shepard does not think that his novels are downbeat. "Often our index to how bleak a work is has a lot to do with where the final characters are left. I'm more than willing to register that it's a lot bleaker than people would expect from chatting with me at dinner, but I'm not ready to call it unrelentingly bleak."

He says that he chooses to write about people whom he fundamentally admires, "people who are essentially good but who get themselves into bad positions. I care about them a lot, so it doesn't seem to me that I'm dealing with a horrifying moral vacuum or people who are incapable of redemption. The redemptions that I'm interested in are redemptions that happen to the characters themselves while they're still in the here and now. They might be small, but they're not unimportant."

Shepard tells his students that one of the principal responsibilities of the writer is to persevere. "Persevering in the writer's case is really more a matter of persevering with your own limitations rather than persevering with the world. The day-to-day failure is, of course, the failure upstairs in your study that no one else knows about. That confrontation with your own limitations—your ability to perceive, to understand and to get it down on paper—is so much more devastating day-to-day. There's so much confrontation with your own failure and so much anxiety that it keeps even the most spectacular egos in check."

Shepard himself is refreshingly modest. Perhaps it's his perception of his own limitations that makes his characters so vulnerable and human.

AMANDA SMITH
January 31, 1994

MONA SIMPSON

Mona Simpson's three novels are unsparing portraits of daughters neglected by incompetent parents. At 39, the tables have turned and the novelist is a parent herself, sharing her capacious Upper West Side apartment with her son, Gabriel, who is almost three, and her husband, Richard Appel. Three years ago, in a coincidence as improbable as it is apt, Appel abandoned his job as a federal prosecutor to write full-time for the TV series *The Simpsons*—a family that would make even the most dysfunctional household seem copacetic by comparison. "It's great for me," quips Simpson. "I get the stationery, put a caret in the title and write 'Mona.'"

Clad entirely in black, her angular face animated by luminous blue eyes and just a little over five feet tall, Simpson has the place to herself on the September afternoon that she sits for an interview. Gabriel, it turns out, is with a babysitter after being up most of the night with a cold. "He may trudge in any minute," she warns.

At a time when many writers are recording their lives in literary memoirs instead of disguising them in fictional form, Simpson's books are refreshing reminders of the emotional resonance and disquieting candor that a good novel can still convey. In her debut, *Anywhere but Here* (Knopf, 1987), its sequel, *The Lost Father* (Knopf, 1992), and her latest, *A Regular Guy,* (Knopf) Simpson dissects the same, bitter family plot: each of the three novels portrays a flaky mother, a daughter's struggle to win back an absent father and a family gripped by wanderlust and the allure of the West. In each case, Simpson reworks this motif with such bravura and authority that readers have long suspected that her books have to be based on lived experience, whether she admits it or not.

In *A Regular Guy*, Simpson trains her gaze on the decline and fall of a flamboyant young biotech tycoon, Tom Owens, and his daughter, Jane di Natali. Rejected by Owens before her birth, Jane is reared in a commune by her shaggy and increasingly desperate mother, who, when Jane is 10, teaches her to drive a rusty truck over the Sierra mountains to the opulent California suburb where Owens lives. As critics have observed, Owens bears as sharp a resemblance to Simpson's real-life brother, Steven Jobs, the brash young co-founder of Apple Computers, as he does to the deadbeat fathers of her previous two novels. But Simpson, whose cheerful voice turns abrupt and self-conscious when faced with questions that she deems too personal, declines to address their similarities, preferring not to discuss her family at all.

As traffic roars by on Riverside Drive, details of Simpson's childhood gradually emerge over coffee and a plate of freshly baked chocolate chip cookies. Green Bay, Wis., where Simpson attended the same public school as the children of the Green Bay Packers, certainly resembles the fictional Bay City, Wis., where the first section of *Anywhere but Here* is set. Ann August, the heroine of that novel, is uprooted from Bay City when her highly neurotic mother, Adele, abandoned by Ann's father, absconds to Beverly Hills in a stolen car. In fact, Simpson's parents separated when she was 10, and she spent her teenage years in L.A. "The move in *Anywhere but Here* is totally true," she admits. "It's probably the truest thing in the book. It's what sparked it."

In 1979, after earning a B.A. in creative writing at Berkeley, Simpson dabbled in various Bay Area jobs, working as an acupuncturist's assistant ("I didn't know a thing about it. I'd turn the needles sometimes, that's all") and writing features for the *San Francisco Chronicle,* the *East Bay Express* and other area newspapers.

Simpson eventually left the west coast to enroll in the graduate writing program at Columbia University. She wrote poetry there, then switched to fiction, placing pieces with journals like *Ploughshares, Iowa Review* and the *Paris Review,* where she became an editor after earning her M.F.A. in 1983. Her salary at the *Paris Review* covered her rent but little else. "During my tenure they finally broke down and gave us health insurance," she remembers with a grin.

Struggling to pay off college loans, Simpson lived on 100th Street and West End Avenue in the same building as her friend, novelist Jonathan Dee. "I had this great landlord who was sort of a guardian angel of writers on the Upper West Side," says Simpson. She lived there for several years, eventually moving into a bigger apartment as compensation for editing her landlord's granddaughter's college entrance essay.

It was a short story that James Atlas fished out of the slush pile at the *Atlantic Monthly* that finally put her on the inside track. He didn't publish it, Simpson recalls, but sent it to Amanda Urban at ICM. "She called me out of the blue and took me to a very fancy lunch. I remember I didn't yet have a New York coat and it was snowing. She had a fur coat."

Four years later, Simpson says, she sent Urban a manuscript of *Anywhere but Here,* which had begun to germinate at Columbia, under the guidance of Elizabeth Hardwick and Richard Price. Urban sold the novel to Ann Close at Knopf for $15,000. Shortly thereafter, subsidized by a Guggenheim grant, she quit her job at the *Paris Review* to take a teaching fellowship at Princeton. It was a heady but confusing time, Simpson recalls: "Publishing any first novel is a very strange experience," she says. "If you're long into your 20s or 30s, [a writer] feels partly like an impostor. Your parents are making excuses for you. And then to actually have a book come out, it sort of quantifies it, there's something there that wasn't there before."

Anywhere but Here defied the laws of publishing gravity for a literary first novel, selling 25,000 copies in hardcover and close to 200,000 in paperback. The free-wheeling odyssey of capricious and pipe-dreaming Adele August and her precocious, long-suffering daughter struck a nerve with readers, many of whom were riveted by the novel's opening scene, in which Adele stops on a desolate road, forces Ann out of the car and drives off, ostensibly never to return. She eventually comes back and offers to take Ann out for ice cream. "When I did readings, I often read from the beginning of the book," says Simpson. "So many people would come up and say 'How did you know that I did that?' or 'That happened to me.' After that book a lot of people confided in me."

Critics found the raw emotion and sprawling complexity of *Anywhere but Here* a welcome contrast to the trendier fiction of the mid-1980s, be it the urban psychodramas of Jay McInerney and Bret Easton Ellis or the dirty realism of Ann Beattie and Raymond Carver. "It was less clear at the time that [minimalism] was what we were in the middle of," Simpson reflects. "In a funny way I did consider myself a minimalist. I thought my unit, in that book especially, was the line, almost more than the paragraph or the scene. I *was* influenced by writers like Raymond Carver in that book. But I think a lot of influences were invisible."

Five years in the writing, the sequel to *Anywhere but Here* opens when Ann, in her late 20s, is flunking out of medical school in New York. She has assumed her birth name, Mayan Atassi, and grown obsessed with finding her father. When they meet, after 500 pages of detours and dead ends, it's a crushing disappointment.

Asked if writing *The Lost Father* was cathartic, Simpson grows standoffish. "All the books are consoling in their ways to me," she says. "I'm not as affected by the plot. I get more consolation and satisfaction from a paragraph that's just right." While she bristles at questions about her parents, Simpson acknowledges "a lot of the feelings and themes in *The Lost Father* were close to my life, but not the details."

Pressed to acknowledge just how much of her work is autobiographical, she finally blurts out with a nervous laugh, "Twenty-five percent," then hastily changes the subject. "What I'd finally say about truth and autobiography," she says, "is that all writers are probably trying to get at some core truth of life, at some configuration that is enduring and truthful. I just haven't found the truth to be my vehicle. It seems sort of disorganized and repetitive and cluttered with randomness and meaningless avenues. That's not to say I don't exclude something because it happened. Some true things do have a certain resonance and vibrancy, but lots of them don't and lots of them benefit from a complete change."

Over the years, Simpson has taken stabs at nonfiction but she hasn't liked the results. "I've tried in very small forms, not to write a memoir, but a few [autobiographical] essays, and they've been disastrous. I published one about my grandmother redecorating her house in 1950 and everyone in my family called in with outrage at my inaccuracies."

A Regular Guy, edited by Gary Fisketjon at Knopf, simmered for years before it was published. "It was longer, and I actually had two characters who collapsed into one," she explains. "It also took me a while to find the third person." Some of the early reviews have criticized Simpson's decision to abandon the intimate, first-person narrative of her first two novels for a more decorous third-person. Harping on the similarities between Owens and Steven Jobs, critics like Michiko Kakwan in the *New York Times* have argued that Simpson's tale of a family unit splintered by class and self-interest might have been more vivid in her familiar first-person voice.

While the novel sacrifices the immediacy of the previous two for a more fastidious, emotional detachment, the use of the third person in fact grants Simpson a more ecumenical view of the murky questions of illegitimacy, creativity and commerce that are its focal point. Such critics also overlook the fact that Owens, like any character, is a composite.

Owens's finickiness, Simpson admits, comes from her. "I'm a vegetarian but I'm not as good as Owens. I would like to be that rigorous but I'm not." Perhaps on some level a metaphor for Simpson's own anxieties about youthful success, Owens also smacks of Kary Mullis, the iconoclastic, boyish Nobel laureate who made a fortune from his discovery of P.C.R., a device for reproducing DNA.

Simpson doesn't deem her three novels a trilogy. Nor did she set out in her new book to recast the same story and the same rag-tag family featured in her previous two. "It's true that I haven't written a war novel or something," she shrugs. "But what else is there but families?" Since the art of the novel "is a little bit old," she adds, "there is a sense now that it is intriguing to write about some of the more modern forms of the family that are extreme. But actually I'm interested in the more subtle things, too. I think it would be a fascinating novel to start out where Jane Austen leaves off, to start at a wedding and portray a relatively uneventful, happy marriage. It's a novel I would read."

Involved in various M.F.A. programs in the past, Simpson, who was named one of *Granta's* best young American novelists on the basis of the first chapter of *A Regular Guy,* now teaches in the fall semester at Bard College. She'll spend the rest of the year in Los Angeles. She works at home most days. As the long intervals between novels suggest, however, she has a penchant for multiple drafts and endless rewrites. She has spent the entire summer working on one short story. Writing novels, she says, is "very stabilizing. You can pretty much work every day. There's always something to do in it."

Gabriel hasn't materialized as the afternoon winds down and Simpson prepares to return to her work. The vicissitudes of parenthood are clearly a welcome distraction from the more predictable work of writing. "The nice thing about books is that you can revise them," she says with an abashed smile. "Whereas Gabriel is only one once. I've probably made like 10,000 mistakes and he's not even three years old. You can't go back. You can't throw it out if it's not working. You can't go back and put it all in a different voice."

Reading Simpson's fiction, however, one can't help thinking that she *has* gone back, and that finally, what gives her three novels their unnerving power is her determination to revisit in fiction events that have proven intractable in real life.

JONATHAN BING
November 4, 1996

JOHN UPDIKE

"*I*N THE BEAUTY OF *the lilies Christ was born across the sea*—this odd and uplifting line from. . . 'The Battle Hymn of the Republic' seemed to me to summarize what I had to say about America." Thus muses John Updike in his 1989 memoir, *Self-Consciousness*. The phrase obviously continued to resonate for him; he has used it—with some trepidation—("Does anyone know that song anymore?") as the title of his new novel, a four-generation saga called *In the Beauty of the Lilies* (Knopf).

A literary detective need not look far to find more presentiments of the newest Updike opus. Elsewhere in *Self-Consciousness*, Updike writes about his grandfather, Presbyterian minister Harley Updike, who abandoned his ministry under somewhat clouded circumstances, probably a combination of fatigue and "the stain of unsuccess," which was euphemized as "a throat affection," in his 1923 obituary in a Trenton, N.J. newspaper. For a time, however, Harley's wife had replaced him in the pulpit, with more natural ability for the task than the hapless clergyman himself evidently possessed.

That story became "part of family mythology, a kind of blot on the common vitality of the Updike clan," the author says jocularly, citing the germination of his saga. In the novel, the fictional Rev. Clarence Wilmot loses his faith, but the relationship with God continues to allure and confuse his descendants, a progeny whose beliefs range from troubled agnosticism to what Updike, extemporizing with gleeful wit, calls "triumphant self-confidence and prayerful chutzpah." Three generations after the minister's anguished renunciation, his great-grandson succumbs to crackpot fundamentalism and self-sacrifice in a Waco-like fiery inferno. Updike says that in his book he has attempted "to make God a character," although in ways that illuminate the spiritual emptiness of American life.

Updike has become a literary icon by depicting—with discerning insight and sometimes salacious fidelity—the angst of the suburban

American Protestant middle class in the latter part of the 20th century. To date he has produced enough work to fill columns of print in *Contemporary Authors:* 17 novels, nine collections of short stories, six volumes of poetry, five books of essays and criticism, four books for children, and other sundry works. Indeed, one could speculate that his productivity is as vigorous a reflection of the Protestant work ethic as was any 19th-century WASP's confidence that the deity would reward unstinting effort. And the honors Updike has earned—two Pulitzer Prizes, the National Book Award, the American Book Award and the NBCC Award, among others—are perhaps the most visible manifestation of a life spent in earnest pursuit of God's grace and favor.

He has used clerical figures in previous works, but even when his characters are mundanely middle class, God is omnipresent, generally in the epiphanic moments that illumine the murk and morass of ordinary life. This is the bedrock of our national character, Updike feels. "Some sense of religious mission is part of being an American," he says. "America itself is a kind of religious concept. The Puritans came here to make a perfect land, to get away from the dirty old European mess. And many later immigrants arrived here with hearts full of hope. So you don't have to force the theme of religion on an American novel. It's very much there, either its presence or its absence."

The four generations that *Lilies* depicts, he says, are meant to allude to the biblical line from Abraham to Isaac to Joseph and his brothers. "One of the traces left by my Sunday school education was being haunted by that particular saga, and the notion that we are members of our ancestors. I wanted to give an American version of that sense."

An earnest statement, that, but not the way Updike delivers it, with an amused gleam in his eyes, lively under undisciplined brows. And not the way he renders it on the page, where the trajectory of one family's rise and fall, each generation swept along on currents of social and ethical turmoil, is conveyed with narrative brio. Updike anchors each decade with brand names, domestic trivia and a pageant of movie history; one of his themes here is that traditional religious models have been replaced by Hollywood's pervasive icons. As in his other works, Updike's gift for exact, metaphorical observation binds matters of the soul to the ephemera of daily life.

Certainly, Updike's preoccupation with metaphysics does not confine him to a cloistered existence. The author and his interviewer are enjoying tea in a bastion of WASP refinement, Boston's Ritz Carlton Hotel. (Tea is Updike's invariable beverage; the medicine that controls his psoriasis forbids alcohol.) He has driven in from his home in nearby Beverly Farms, which he shares with his second wife. Sporting a tweedy jacket and rep tie, his silver hair molded to his head like a sleek cap, he is engagingly unpretentious, often couching his more serious concerns in urbane wit and self-mocking candor. In the hushed, deferential atmosphere of the Ritz—massed flowers in stately urns, a harp trilling in the background—he exhibits little of the elegiac irony common to his 60ish protagonists in stories in *The Afterlife*, published two years ago.

Intimations of mortality always have been central to Updike's work, however, so it is not surprising when he reflects that his characters' sometimes self-destructive behavior is rooted in a "refusal to settle, which is a positive thing. You want to feel alive when you are alive," he says, referring to protagonists who indulge in adultery, break out of stifling marriages and cause pain to blameless spouses and children—in a restless search for a transcendence that religious faith has somehow failed to provide. Nevertheless, "there's a lot of capacity for guilt left in the old religious corpse," Updike says, and there are personal echoes here: he too extricated himself from his first marriage and household in 1976, and many of his characters trod autobiographical turf. "We're all feeling guilty, and rightly so. Those men in *The Afterlife* are rueful to find themselves 60, but I don't think they would give back their lives."

Most of Updike's male characters use sex to sublimate their inchoate spiritual yearnings. In *Lilies* the character who indulges in sex with lusty abandon is Essie Wilmot, who resolutely uses her body to get from Paterson, N.J., to Hollywood. Reinventing herself as Alma DeMott, she enjoys sexual promiscuity without a soupçon of guilt.

"There is a lot of me in Alma, of course," Updike admits. "I too was raised in a small town and went to the movies and plotted to get out. But she's much more attractive than I was and she seems more precocious sexually." The slight stutter that accompanies his more audacious statements adds unwitting emphasis here.

"I've long been interested in the private life of movie stars," he continues. "Americans in this century have looked to movies for a lot of what they used to get from religion. We've used movies as models of how to live, how to make our lives come out right." The energy and luck and looks that movie stars project seem to him to be emblematic of our national fascination with perfectibility, and a kind of endless yearning that is never satisfied.

Also inherent in the American character is the sense of emptiness brought about by religious expectation, Updike thinks. "Just the fact that you're mortal is frightening enough. There's a kind of despair in the air now; the Oklahoma bombing was a despairing act." The Christian Right "is trying to wag the tail of the Republic these days," while organized churches are "just treading water," he suggests.

Updike himself is far from the treading-water stage. The autobiographical references in both his fiction and non-fiction attest to a determination, partly nurtured in the Lutheran church of his youth, to make his life count. Winning a scholarship to Harvard allowed him to escape from small town oblivion in Shillington, Pa., where he was born in 1932, during the Depression. His father was a high school math teacher; his mother wrote unpublished novels. ("She lived a lot of her life clawing at the glass, trying to get into print," Updike muses.) After graduating summa cum laude, he accepted a fellowship at Oxford's Ruskin School of Drawing and Fine Art with the vague idea of becoming a graphic artist.

Then the *New Yorker* beckoned. The magazine had accepted several pieces he wrote before graduating from Harvard; "I was industrious and sent them more." He came home from Oxford to a staff job at the magazine, "exactly where I wanted to be. My dreams began to come true at about the age of 22," he acknowledges. "It was only after about five years that I began to think of stretching my horizons, to try to write a novel." He and his first wife left New York for Massachusetts, where he wrote full-time and they raised four children.

Updike had singular luck in another respect, his career-long affiliation with Knopf. Though a volume of his poetry, *The Carpentered Hen,* had been issued by Harper & Row in 1958, his first novel, *The Poorhouse Fair,* was accepted by Knopf editor Sandy Richardson— who was fired six months afterwards, Updike says, with a bemused shake of his head. Updike then fell under the avuncular care of Alfred Knopf himself: "He was very cute to me, very indulgent, kind of wise at the right moments." By the early '60s, Updike had effected a switch to Judith Jones, who has been his "terrific" editor since *Rabbit, Run.*

Somehow throughout those years "the moment to acquire an agent never came. I'm increasingly quaint in this way," he says, with a wheezing laugh. "The importance of having an agent is something that has happened since I began. Knopf has acted in many ways as my agent— selling foreign rights and what little movie deals are done. I've also tried not to get greedy. One reason you stay with a publisher is that you're not hopping around to get another hundred thousand dollars added to your advance."

Knopf has just rewarded that loyalty, and acknowledged the best-selling track record of the Rabbit books by reissuing them in a one-volume, 1516-page Everyman edition. "It makes a handful, doesn't it?" Updike asks, flashing his wide smile. "I was thrilled at them wanting to do it because I was raised on the Everyman editions and the Modern Library and the Oxford classics. To be in a kind of revived Everyman feels very good." Especially since, perhaps, the Rabbit books have brought him his greatest popularity and financial satisfaction. "It's almost as though I'm two authors; I'm the guy who writes the Rabbit books and then I'm the guy who writes all those other things," he says, mindful of the irony.

But preparing the new edition has given the famously fastidious author a busy year. "I reread them all and tried to bring them all into line." Resolving such questions as Rabbit's son Nelson's birthday and the correct spellings of topical references was a wearisome occupation. "I'm the kind of writer who likes to put in brand names but I don't seem to know them exactly right so there are a lot of small errors in those books," Updike says. He also hopes "to give the ideal reader an opportunity to read them all through and see if there is a kind of mega-novel here, a single story about aging in America.

"My whole year has been spent either rereading the Rabbits or trying to get *Lilies* through the press. Plus all those book reviews . . . I've felt that I'm a one-man word glut," Updike says with a semi-abashed grin. And more seriously: "It has felt a little much like I'm not giving myself the dreaming space you need to advance or grow. I've not had enough of the kind of leisure that an artist really needs. You may think that at 63 I've no right to grow any more," he challenges, eliciting the obviously expected vehement denial. "But I really don't feel that I'm finished yet," he says. "I'd like to produce a few more surprises."

SYBIL STEINBERG
January 8, 1996

DOROTHY WEST

To be called "the last surviving member" of any group is not a designation one plans for—or necessarily desires. Generally it means that one is a curiosity, a relic of a forgotten era. Yet Dorothy West, indeed the last surviving member of the Harlem Renaissance, is having her own private renaissance, and that is a different matter entirely. At the age of 87 West saw the publication from Doubleday of her second novel, *The Wedding*, in January of this year; it was a BOMC selection. (Her first novel, *The Living is Easy*, appeared in 1948.) Around the time of her 88th birthday, Doubleday is issuing *The Richer, the Poorer*, a collection of stories, sketches and reminiscences culled from a lifetime of work.

West says that she is "lucky, very lucky," that America has rediscovered her work. "All this didn't have to happen. But it's made me think about my age. Oprah Winfrey [who has optioned *The Wedding*] has three projects ahead of mine. I don't know whether I'll be alive when she gets to me," West muses. This doleful possibility contradicted by her wide smile.

West is a tiny woman, slightly bent with age. Vivacious, a charmer with a gamine smile, she dots her conversation with a disarming refrain: "Oh, do you really think so?" She is, in truth, a chatterbox, but a delightful one. Stories tumble out of her at a dizzying rate, rarely achieving closure before she veers into another subject altogether. Even so, she manages to touch on most of the important events of her life.

Born and brought up in an upper middle class black family in Boston, West has lived full time on Martha's Vineyard since the 1940s, in a small A-frame cottage reached via a dirt road. The house is one of seven or eight built around a grassy green space, obviously the inspiration for the elite enclave called The Oval in *The Wedding*. If it is indeed far less formal than its fictional counterpart, West herself perfectly fits the image of the quintessential black bourgeoisie: her accent is richly Bostonian, and her interest in class and breeding remains a focal point of her life as well as her writing.

By the time she was born, her father, who had been freed from slavery at age seven, had become a successful wholesale produce dealer— the only black man to have an establishment in the Boston Market. "The gifts he had given me were endurance and strength of will," West writes in *The Richer, the Poorer.* Her mother, to whom the book is dedicated and who is evoked in several of the reminiscences, was the major influence: a beautiful woman who set high standards for her daughter, instilling self-confidence and pride.

The family lived in an elegant, four-story house, and although Dorothy was an only child, the rooms were filled with extended family. The Wests were also among the first families to own a vacation home in the black community of Oak Bluffs on Martha's Vineyard.

At age 10 West won acceptance to the prestigious Girls' Latin School; her short stories began appearing in the Boston *Post* when she was 14. Three years later she went to New York to accept second prize for a story called "The Typewriter" (included in *The Richer*) from *Opportunity* magazine. She shared the prize with an older writer—Zora Neale Hurston. While attending the Columbia School of Journalism, she became the youngest member of the group of black writers and artists that was later dubbed the Harlem Renaissance: the likes of Langston Hughes, Wallace Thurman and Countee Cullen.

Several heady years followed. West toured with Du Bose Hayward's *Porgy* (she stayed with the Paul Robesons when the show moved to London) and later went to Moscow to participate in a (never made) film about racism in America. Eventually, West took a job with the New York welfare department, where she made jolting acquaintance with the impact of poverty on the lives of the city's black residents. The stories she wrote at that time—several of which are included in the new book—explored the issues of race and class; most were first published in the Sunday edition of the *New York Daily News.* In 1934, West used her small savings to start a quarterly literary magazine, *Challenge,* but, dissatisfied with the quality of the submissions from younger black writers, she closed it down in 1937. With Richard Wright, she then launched *New Challenge;* its leftist political slant made her uneasy, however, and she folded it a short time later. The Harlem Renaissance was truly over.

The optimism and intellectual ferment of that time have no current counterpart, in West's opinion. Asked whether she considers the popularity of such black writers as Toni Morrison and Alice Walker a comparable phenomenon, she dissents vigorously. "No, there can never again be a period like ours. Now people are more sophisticated. We were young, naïve and poor. Today's writers live in a different world."

One summer in the 1940s, West made her annual pilgrimage to the Vineyard, started writing *The Living Is Easy* and never returned to the mainland. Her house bears evidence of her preoccupations. "I'm a writer. I don't cook and I don't clean." In the tiny living room, seven chairs and a small sofa are set helter skelter; pushpins pierce their upholstery, securing memos and letters; piles of papers and books occupy every surface. The glass front of the credenza is scotchtaped with notes three deep, and more papers bristle from the desk's every cranny. An adjacent room holds dozens of boxes of the papers that will go to Radcliffe.

Originally published by Houghton Mifflin (and now back in print from the Feminist Press), *The Living Is Easy* is the story of a tempestuous marriage between fair-skinned Cleo Judson, who is obsessed with moving up in the world, and her dark-complexioned husband, an unassuming businessman. West was forthright in describing how successful blacks considered themselves superior to their uneducated brethren—and to uneducated, uncultured white people, too. Yet she viewed their false values and social pretensions with irony, satirizing their desire to "live white."

The book was well received, and West was elated to learn that the *Ladies' Home Journal* was planning to serialize it. "I was going to get what at that time was a lot of money. But weeks went by before my agent [George Bye] called again. The *Journal* had decided to drop the book because a survey indicated that they would lose many subscribers in the South," she comments wryly.

West's confidence was shaken. She started another book and didn't like it. She began mulling over the plot of *The Wedding*, a multigenerational story of a family whose marital alliances achieve the acme of 1950s black respectability: light complexions, financial stability and social standing. But she feared that the climate was not right for a work about her small stratum of the black population.

Her career in limbo, West had to find other means to support herself. She began a long association with the Vineyard *Gazette*, first as a billing clerk, and eventually as a contributor. In the acknowledgments to *The Richer*, she calls it "a relationship that has brought [me] nothing but joy."

281

The impetus to finish *The Wedding* slowly leaked away during the '60s, in part because of the emergence of the Black Panthers, West says. "I hated them! They scorned the upper middle class. I wanted to write about people like my father, who were ambitious. But people like him were anathema to the Black Panthers, who said that all black people are victims. Every time I turned on the TV there was a black person making a fool of himself. It was a discouraging time."

She was afraid that her book would be scorned by both black and white critics and readers. "I had a suspicion that the reviewers, who were white, would not know how to judge my work in that prevailing climate. In fact, if I had brought the book out then, white people would not have accepted it," she declares.

Then Jackie Onassis entered West's life. West did not contact her directly; the idea horrifies her. "She was an Islander, you know; my manners would not allow me to approach her." Onassis heard about the novel through a third party, and a working friendship commenced. "Mrs. Onassis came every Monday to talk about the chapter she had picked up the week before. She was like me; she liked to learn. I'd ramble on in my way and she would say to me, 'Dorothy, you must put that in the book.'"

Onassis died before the book was finished. West still misses her Monday visits. "One day I told her that I hated my name. And Mrs. Onassis said, 'I hate my name, too.' And *this* fool didn't ask her why or what name she would have rather been called! I'll always regret that," West says wistfully.

Though nuances of skin pigmentation are tremendously important to her upwardly mobile characters, West insists that color never mattered to her. "In my family we come in every conceivable color." Including her cousins, who lived in her extended household: "We had a blond boy; I was brown; my cousin Helen was pink and gold; cousin Eugenia was a creamy olive. My mother was golden-skinned."

Yet color undoubtedly played a bigger part in her youth than she will admit. Perhaps it even influenced her decision to become a writer. Enrolled in school when she was four, she overheard other kindergarteners say to her light-skinned cousins: "Why do you want to play with that nigger?"

West claims the jeering of less well-bred children never hurt her. But since she wanted to spare her cousins from having to defend her, she remained indoors whenever possible, saying that she preferred to use the time to write. "I've never been on a skate or on a sled. I'm glad

I did not go out so they [her cousins] could have a good time," she says without a trace of self-pity.

Perhaps in those years she began idealizing a future in which the races mingle. At the end of *The Wedding*, Shelby, who is marrying a white man, says: "Color was a false distinction; love was not." West obviously feels that so-called miscegenation is a positive goal.

Her parents' and grandparents' generations never admitted that they had white blood, "though they have some of the bluest blood in America." West does. In the reminiscence called "The Purse," she writes that "the master's red hair [was evident] in her [maternal grandmother's] bouncing braids." She says, "My father's eyes were bright blue; he had quite a lot of white blood. I think there is something about mixed blood that is good for blacks."

West knows that hers is not a "fashionable" theory, but she feels she has earned the right to speak out. And then after her vision of races mixing in harmony and mutual benefit, she tells another story. "The last marriage proposal I got [her first was from Countee Cullen] was from a light skinned man—he was almost all blueblood. But I knew I couldn't have children. A doctor in New York suggested I consult the best gynecologist of the time, in Boston. And that man came to the door of the waiting room and said to me: 'There are enough black people in the world. Why do you want to have another black baby?'

"I walked for an hour after that. I couldn't go home. That became my dark secret. I never said a word about it until I saw Anita Hill on television and people said they didn't believe her story because she had never told anyone about it at the time. Well, I never did either. But I'm telling it now."

For a woman who fervently believed that class, education and deportment could conquer racism, it had to be a searing experience. West claims that it was not. "You can't be sorry for yourself. I'm happy that I can leave this message: color is not important. Class is what matters. It always will."

And Dorothy West is an author who would define class not as financial standing or social position but as respect—for oneself and for the aspirations and differences of others.

SYBIL STEINBERG
July 3, 1995

TOBIAS WOLFF

THE LITERARY FORM of choice for Tobias Wolff is the short story, and by all accounts he has mastered it admirably. His work has been widely praised and duly recognized with honors including the O. Henry Prize, the PEN/Faulkner Award and the Rea Award. He has also edited *The Vintage Book of Contemporary American Short Stories* (Vintage) and guest edited *The Best American Short Stories 1994* (Houghton Mifflin).

But it is with two volumes of memoirs, *This Boy's Life* (Atlantic Monthly Press, 1988) and his new *In Pharaoh's Army: Memories of the Lost War,* (Knopf) that Wolff is reaching what is undoubtedly a much wider audience. His first memoir became the basis of a 1993 coming-of-age movie of the same name starring Ellen Barkin and Robert De Niro, while the second enjoys the unusual distinction of being chosen as a finalist for the National Book Award two weeks before its official publication.

The experiences recalled by *In Pharaoh's Army* barely take the author through the age of 22, leaving the 27 succeeding years of his life largely unexamined. "That may be so, but this is going to be my last memoir anyway," Wolff insists good-naturedly as he sits for an interview in his comfortable house not far from the campus of Syracuse University, where he has taught literature and writing since 1980.

He sits at ease in his third-floor study, a converted attic that has been soundproofed and paneled in pine. The room is spacious and spare. The walls are mostly bare, the exception being a framed poster from the film of *This Boy's Life* autographed by the principals. Two windows overlook a quiet, residential neighborhood, but since his desk faces a corner wall, they provide no distraction while he is working. He and his wife, Catherine, a clinical social worker, have three children: Michael, 15, Patrick, 14, and Mary Elizabeth, 5.

Because a writer's life is sedentary, the former Army officer who once took pride in his "command presence" keeps fit and lean by working out on an exercise machine that dominates the middle of the floor, and by taking a daily swim in the university pool. "These have been inwardly exciting times for me, probably the most meaningful of my life," he notes. "But as you can see, they are quiet, and they don't lend themselves to the kind of narrative treatment that [my] earlier years do."

Central to Wolff's work ethic is his insistence that his memoirs demand just as much artistry as his fiction and just as much effort to develop. "I did a lot of rewriting on this book, and that is because I intended it as a literary work," he says pointedly.

In Pharaoh's Army picks up the trail of young Wolff's journey toward manhood in 1965, when he is 18 and at loose ends after being asked to leave prep school for his failing grades; he is fearful that he will face harm from a malicious shipmate if he remains aboard a Coast and Geodetic Survey ship about to sail for the Azores. Rosemary, the peripatetic mother Wolff profiled so splendidly in *This Boy's Life,* now receives only passing attention—living in Washington, D.C., she offers no resistance when her son announces his intention to join the Army.

Arthur Samuels Wolff, meanwhile, the absentee father of the earlier book—and the shadowy "duke" in older brother Geoffrey Wolff's 1979 memoir, *The Duke of Deception*—reappears more sharply focused. He enters the story at crucial times, just before Tobias goes off on a combat tour to Vietnam in 1967 and after he returns in 1968, when the two men achieve a degree of rapprochement.

A quintessential con man who spent time in jail for various fraudulent activities, such as passing bad checks, "Duke" Wolff died in 1970. In an odd way, he had inspired his son's decision to join the Army. "I knew I wanted to be a different kind of man, and I had made a more or less conscious attempt to separate myself from him," Wolff says. "But at the end of his life we accepted each other in a way that we never really had before."

At the outset of *In Pharaoh's Army,* the Tobias Wolff we encounter is a soldier eager to take part in the defining event of his generation. "One of my pleasures was to learn I was hardy and capable," he writes, qualities that earn him an appointment to Officer Candidate School. Trained as a paratrooper, he volunteers for Special Forces and learns to speak Vietnamese. But once "in country," he becomes an adviser to a Vietnamese battalion in the Mekong Delta, spending his tour on the fringes of combat. Readers in search of riveting battle scenes will have to look elsewhere; of far greater moment is the maturation of Tobias Wolff. The immature lieutenant who arrives in the war zone returns

285

home as a man ready to spend four years at Oxford University (1968–1972) and to begin his life as a writer.

"What the two memoirs show in different ways is someone who's unformed and trying to find a place in the world," Wolff observes. In his next breath, he again stresses his conviction that *In Pharaoh's Army* is *not* a sequel to *This Boy's Life.*

"I'm a really different person in the new book. I see it as a story about a young man going off to war, and the kind of moral transformations that take place." Because Wolff never intended to write an encyclopedic account of his military service, he was not hindered by the fact that he never kept a journal. "I'm glad I didn't take notes, because what is essential in that experience is exactly what would have stayed with me. I remembered what I needed to remember," he says.

As a youngster who had been on the move from state to state with his mother during the 1950s, Wolff began at an early age to believe he could one day become a writer. While a student at Concrete High School in Concrete, Wash., he often wrote papers and essays for other students and felt especially rewarded once when a classmate told him his material was so good he should think about doing it for a living.

His brother Geoffrey stayed with their father after their parents separated, but he encouraged Tobias' aspirations during their periodic telephone conversations, and—later on, when they got to know each other better—by furnishing him with books to read. In addition to *The Duke of Deception,* Geoffrey Wolff's work includes a biography of Harry Crosby, a collection of essays and three novels. Tobias dedicated *In Pharaoh's Army* to him, with the phrase, "For my brother, who gave me books."

Once out of the Army, Wolff was more determined than ever to fulfill his dream of writing; he set aside two to three hours every day to write, even while enrolled as a full-time student at Oxford. When he returned to the United States, he worked at a variety of jobs, including a six-month stint as a cub reporter for the *Washington Post.* "I was a lousy reporter, and nobody tried to talk me out of leaving," he says. "The best job I had at this time was waiting on tables in San Francisco. I wrote three novels, one of which, I am embarrassed now to say, was taken in England by Allen and Unwin." He is unwilling to divulge the title of that book. "It does not represent my mature work and I don't want anybody to read it," he explains. "Most people's juvenilia doesn't get published, but mine did. Blessedly it died, but it had the virtue, at least, of making me feel that somebody else in the world thought I was a writer."

The sales of that book also served to buoy his spirits. "I wasn't just a waiter anymore, but a waiter who wrote books that somebody else might even publish." During his San Francisco period, Wolff began taking graduate courses at Stanford University, and earned an M.A. in English in 1978. It was during this time as well that he became "captivated by stories." He recalls, "I found stories better suited to my particular gifts at that point. I liked everything about them—the power, the directness, the unity of impression, the ability they have to conjure up a whole world in a few pages and then get something going indelibly in a reader's mind. The novel, on the other hand, implies a kind of stability, a steady fund of experience, a certain place in which one stays for a while. Because of the very nomadic and very fragmentary life I led as a child, perhaps, there was something in my own experience that lent itself to an appreciation of the story, which has a very momentary nature."

Soon, his dedication began to be rewarded with acceptances by magazines. "The first story I sent out was called 'Smokers,' and it was bought by the *Atlantic Monthly*. That was in 1976; a few months later they took another story called 'The Liar.' Pretty soon I had stories in *Vogue* and *TriQuarterly*." A 1981 collection of Wolff's stories, *In the Garden of the North American Martyrs*, was followed in 1984 by *The Barracks Thief*, a 101-page novel that was inspired by his military experiences and won the PEN/Faulkner Award. *Back in the World*, a second collection of stories, was published in 1985. He is working on a new collection of stories, *The Night in Question*, that he hopes will be ready sometime next year.

Having published five books with four different publishing houses (Ecco, Houghton Mifflin, Atlantic Monthly Press and Knopf), Wolff has worked with his share of editors over the years. "I have been extremely fortunate in my editors. At Ecco, I had the benefit of Daniel Halpern's sharp eye, his ability to image a story in different ways. My next book was edited by Nan Talese at Houghton Mifflin. She was an enthusiastic reader, brimming with ideas and encouragement. *This Boy's Life* and *In Pharaoh's Army* went through the hands of Gary Fisketjon. Gary is a remarkably painstaking, hard-working editor. When I get my manuscripts back from him, every sentence has some mark of his reaction. Nothing is demanded; everything is suggested."

In addition, Wolff says that he and his brother Geoffrey exchange manuscripts when they are in their final stages. "We do a lot of line-by-line editing of each other's work, and it's totally honest. It's fairly ruthless, as a matter of fact, but we also let each other know what we've done right." Wolff's agent of the last 14 years has been Amanda Urban. "Binky is a great friend and a tireless advocate for writers. Once I give a manuscript to her, I relax."

If there is a thematic connection between Wolff's stories and his two volumes of memoirs, he believes it is his continuing interest in relationships and domestic life. "That sense of kinship is what makes stories important to us," he writes in his introduction to *The Vintage Book of Contemporary American Short Stories.* "Family life has always been great theater, and always will be, like war." Wolff says he hopes readers will identify a consistency of "tone, feeling and atmosphere" in his books and feel a "certain quality of moral intention" in them that is "characteristic and definitive."

The writing, meanwhile, has its own agenda, and when a story is ready, it is ready. "I work every day, at least six hours a day," he says. "Sometimes the pace is glacial. It takes me about three months to get a story to the point where I really like it. When I am working at the top of my form, I see things differently, and there's an excitement that comes when things become clear to me that were not so clear before. I can think of no other word for what happens than revelation."

NICHOLAS A. BASBANES
October 24, 1994

BIBLIOGRAPHY

(Books currently in print by interviewed authors)

SHERMAN ALEXIE

The Business of Fancydancing, Hanging Loose, paper, 1992
The First Indian on the Moon, Hanging Loose, paper, 1993
Indian Killer, Grove Atlantic, 1996
The Lone Ranger and Tonto Fistfight in Heaven, HarperPerennial,
      paper, 1994
Old Shirts and New Skins, Univ. of California, paper, 1993
Reservation Blues, Grove Atlantic, 1995; Warner, paper, 1996
The Summer of Black Widows, Hanging Loose, 1996

JULIA ALVAREZ

Homecoming, Plume, paper, 1996
How the Garcia Girls Lost Their Accents, Algonquin, 1991; Plume,
      paper, 1992
In the Time of the Butterflies, Algonquin, 1994; Plume, paper, 1995
The Other Side, Dutton, 1995; Plume, paper, 1996
¡Yo!, Algonquin, 1997

STEPHEN AMBROSE

Band of Brothers, Touchstone, paper, 1993
Crazy Horse and Custer, Anchor, paper, 1996
D-Day, June 6, 1944, Simon & Schuster, 1994; Touchstone, paper,
      1995
Eisenhower, Touchstone, paper, 1991
Halleck, Louisiana State Univ., paper, 1996

289

Nixon, Touchstone, paper, 1988
Pegasus Bridge, June 6, 1944, Touchstone, paper, 1988
Rise to Globalism, Penguin, paper, 1993
Undaunted Courage, Simon & Schuster, 1996
Upton and the Army, Louisiana State Univ., paper, 1993

RUDOLFO ANAYA

The Adventures of Juan Chicaspatas, Arte Publico, paper, 1984
The Anaya Reader, Warner, paper, 1995
Bless Me, Ultima, Warner, paper, 1994
The Farolitos of Christmas, Hyperion, 1995
Heart of Aztlan, Univ. of New Mexico, paper, 1988
Jalamanta, Warner, 1996; Warner, paper, 1997
Maya's Children, Hyperion, 1997
Rio Grande Fall, Warner, 1996; Warner, paper, 1997
Tortuga, Univ. of New Mexico, paper, 1988
Zia Summer, Warner, 1995; Warner, paper, 1996

RICK BASS

The Book of Yaak, Houghton Mifflin, 1997
The Deer Pasture, Norton, paper, 1996
In the Loyal Mountains, Houghton Mifflin, 1995
The Lost Grizzlies, Houghton Mifflin, 1995
The Ninemile Wolves, Ballantine, paper, 1993
Oil Notes, Southern Methodist Univ., paper, 1995
Platte River, Houghton Mifflin, 1994; Ballantine, paper, 1995
The Watch, Norton, paper, 1994
Wild to the Heart, Norton, paper, 1990
Winter, Houghton Mifflin, paper, 1992

CARL BERNSTEIN

Loyalties, Simon & Schuster, 1989; Touchstone, paper, 1990
(—with Marco Politi)
His Holiness: John Paul II and the Hidden History of Our Time,
        Doubleday, 1996
(—with Bob Woodward)
All the President's Men, Touchstone, paper, 1994
The Final Days, Touchstone, paper, 1994

DORIS BETTS

The Astronomer and Other Stories, Louisiana State Univ., paper, 1995
The Sharp Teeth of Love, Knopf, 1997
Souls Raised from the Dead, Knopf, 1994; Touchstone, paper, 1995

LARRY BOND

Cauldron, Warner, paper, 1994
The Enemy Within, Warner, 1996; Warner, paper, 1997
Red Phoenix, Warner, paper, 1990

JIMMY BRESLIN

I Want to Thank My Brain for Remembering Me, Little, Brown, 1996
Mark Rothko, Univ. of Chicago, 1993

ANDRÉ BRINK

An Act of Terror, Vintage, paper, 1993
A Chain of Voices, Penguin, paper, 1983
A Dry White Season, Penguin, paper, 1984
Imaginings of Sand, Harcourt Brace, 1996
On the Contrary, Little, Brown, 1994

A.S. BYATT

Angels and Insects, Vintage, paper, 1994
Babel Tower, Random House, 1996; Vintage, paper, 1996
The Game, Vintage, paper, 1992
Imagining, Vintage, paper, 1997
The Matisse Stories, Random House, 1995; Vintage, paper, 1996
Passions of the Mind, Vintage, paper, 1993
Possession, Random House, 1990; Vintage, paper, 1991
Shadow of the Sun, Harcourt Brace, paper, 1993
Still Life, Scribner, paper, 1997
Sugar and Other Stories, Vintage, paper, 1992
Unruly Times, Trafalgar Square, paper, 1990
The Virgin in the Garden, Vintage, paper, 1992

JAMES CARROLL

An American Requiem, Houghton Mifflin, 1996
The City Below, Houghton Mifflin, 1994
Memorial Bridge, Houghton Mifflin, 1991; Ivy, paper, 1995
Mortal Friends, Beacon Press, paper, 1992

ANA CASTILLO

Loverboys, Norton, 1996
Massacre of the Dreamers, Univ. of New Mexico, 1994; Plume,
        paper, 1995
The Mixquiahuala Letters, Anchor, paper, 1992
My Father Was a Toltec, Norton, 1995; Norton, paper, 1996
Sapogonia, Anchor, paper, 1994
So Far from God, Norton, 1993; Plume, paper, 1994

MICHAEL CHABON

A Model World and Other Stories, Morrow, 1991; Avon, paper, 1992
The Mysteries of Pittsburgh, HarperPerennial, paper, 1989
Wonder Boys, Villard, 1995; Picador, paper, 1995

BERNARD CORNWELL

Battle Flag, HarperPaperbacks, paper, 1996
The Bloody Ground, HarperCollins, 1996
Copperhead, HarperPaperbacks, paper, 1994
Crackdown, HarperPaperbacks, paper, 1991
Killer's Wake, HarperPaperbacks, paper, 1990
Rebel, HarperPaperbacks, paper, 1994
Sharpe's Battle, HarperCollins, 1995; HarperPaperbacks, paper, 1996
Sharpe's Company, Penguin, paper, 1987
Sharpe's Devil, HarperPaperbacks, paper, 1993
Sharpe's Eagle, Penguin, paper, 1987
Sharpe's Enemy, Penguin, paper, 1987
Sharpe's Gold, Penguin, paper, 1987
Sharpe's Honor, Penguin, paper, 1990
Sharpe's Regiment, Penguin, paper, 1987
Sharpe's Revenge, Penguin, paper, 1990

Sharpe's Rifles, Penguin, paper, 1989
Sharpe's Siege, Penguin, paper, 1990
Sharpe's Sword, Penguin, paper, 1987
Storm Child, HarperPaperbacks, paper, 1992
Waterloo, Penguin, paper, 1991
The Winter King, St. Martin's, 1996

BRAM DIJKSTRA

Cubism, Stieglitz and the Early Poetry of William Carlos Williams,
    Princeton Univ., paper, 1989
Defoe and Economics, St. Martin's, 1987
Evil Sisters, Knopf, 1996
Idols of Perversity, Oxford, 1986; Oxford, paper, 1988

MARK DOTY

Atlantis, HarperCollins, 1995; HarperPerennial, paper, 1995
Heaven's Coast, HarperCollins, 1996; HarperPerennial, paper, 1997
My Alexandria, Univ. of Illinois, paper, 1993

RODDY DOYLE

The Barrytown Trilogy, Penguin, paper, 1995
Brownbread and War, Penguin, paper, 1994
The Commitments, Vintage, paper, 1989
Paddy Clarke Ha Ha Ha, Penguin, paper, 1995
The Snapper, Penguin, paper, 1992
The Van, Penguin, paper, 1993
The Woman Who Walked into Doors, Viking, 1996; Penguin, paper,
    1997

RIKKI DUCORNET

The Complete Butcher's Tales, Dalkey Archive, 1994
Entering Fire, City Lights, paper, 1987
The Fountains of Neptune, Dalkey Archive, 1992; Dalkey Archive,
    paper, 1993
The Jade Cabinet, Dalkey Archive, 1993; Dalkey Archive, paper, 1994
Phosphor in Dreamland, Dalkey Archive, paper, 1995
The Stain, Dalkey Archive, paper, 1995

ANNIE ERNAUX

Cleaned Out, Dalkey Archive, 1990; Dalkey Archive, paper, 1996
Exteriors, Seven Stories, 1996
A Frozen Woman, Seven Stories, 1995; Seven Stories, paper, 1996
A Man's Place, Seven Stories, 1992
Simple Passion, Seven Stories, 1993; Ballantine, paper, 1994
A Woman's Story, Seven Stories, 1991; Ballantine, paper, 1992

CONNIE MAY FOWLER

Before Women Had Wings, Putnam, 1996
River of Hidden Dreams, Putnam, 1994; Fawcett, paper, 1995
Sugar Cage, Washington Square, paper, 1993

MARSHALL FRADY

Jesse: The Life and Pilgrimage of Jesse Jackson, Random House, 1996
Wallace, Vintage, paper, 1996

MAVIS GALLANT

Across the Bridge, Random House, 1993; Carroll & Graf, paper, 1994
The Collected Stories of Mavis Gallant, Random House, 1996
Overhead in a Balloon, Random House, 1987
The Pegnitz Junction, Graywolf, paper, 1984

OLIVIA GOLDSMITH

The Bestseller, HarperCollins, 1996
The First Wives Club, Pocket, paper, 1996
Flavor of the Month, Pocket, paper, 1994
Marrying Mom, HarperCollins, paper, 1996
(—with Amy F. Collins)
Simple Isn't Easy, HarperPaperbacks, paper, 1995

WINSTON GROOM

Better Times Than These, Pocket, paper, 1994
Forrest Gump, Pocket, 1994; Pocket, paper, 1994
Gone the Sun, Pocket, paper, 1996
Gump and Company, Pocket, 1995; Pocket, paper, 1996

Gumpisms, Pocket, paper, 1994

Shrouds of Glory, Grove Atlantic, 1994; Pocket, paper, 1996

RON HANSEN

The Assassination of Jesse James by the Coward Robert Ford,
     HarperPerennial, paper, 1997

Atticus, HarperCollins, 1996; HarperPerennial, paper, 1997

Desperadoes, HarperPerennial, paper, 1997

Mariette in Ecstasy, Burlingame, paper, 1992

ROBERT HASS

Field Guide, Yale Univ., paper, 1973

Human Wishes, Ecco, paper, 1989

Praise, Ecco, paper, 1979

Sun Under Wood, Ecco, 1996

Twentieth Century Pleasures, Ecco, paper, 1985

SEAMUS HEANEY

The Cure at Troy, Farrar, Straus & Giroux, 1991; Noonday, paper,
     1991

Death of a Naturalist, Faber, paper, 1969

Door into the Dark, Faber, paper, 1972

Field Work, Noonday, paper, 1981

The Government of the Tongue, Noonday, paper, 1990

The Haw Lantern, Farrar, Straus & Giroux, 1987; Noonday, paper,
     1989

North, Faber, paper, 1985

Preoccupations, Noonday, paper, 1981

The Redress of Poetry, Farrar, Straus & Giroux, 1995; Noonday,
     paper, 1996

Seeing Things, Farrar, Straus & Giroux, 1991; Noonday, paper, 1993

Selected Poems, 1966–1987, Farrar, Straus & Giroux, 1990; Noonday,
     paper, 1991

The Spirit Level, Farrar, Straus & Giroux, 1995

Station Island, Farrar, Straus & Giroux, 1985; Noonday, paper, 1986

Sweeney Astray, Farrar, Straus & Giroux, 1984; Noonday, paper, 1985

Sweeney's Flight, Farrar, Straus & Giroux, 1992

URSULA HEGI

Floating in My Mother's Palm, Random House, paper, 1991
Salt Dancers, Simon & Schuster, 1995; Touchstone, paper, 1996
Stones from the River, Touchstone, paper, 1995

ANDREW HOLLERAN

The Beauty of Men, Morrow, 1996; Plume, paper, 1997
Dancer from the Dance, Plume, paper, 1986
Nights in Aruba, Plume, paper, 1984

KAZUO ISHIGURO

An Artist of the Floating World, Vintage, paper, 1989
A View of Pale Hills, Vintage, paper, 1990
The Remains of the Day, Knopf, 1989; Vintage, paper, 1993
The Unconsoled, Knopf, 1995; Vintage, paper, 1996

THOMAS KENEALLY

Bring Larks and Heroes, Penguin, paper, 1989
The Chant of Jimmy Blacksmith, Penguin, paper, 1983
Confederates, HarperPerennial, paper, 1987
A Family Madness, Touchstone, paper, 1993
Gossip from the Forest, Harvest, paper, 1985
Ned Kelly and the City of Bees, Godine, paper, 1994
The Playmaker, Touchstone, paper, 1993
A River Town, Doubleday, 1995; Plume, paper, 1996
Schindler's List, Simon & Schuster, 1994; Touchstone, paper, 1993
Season in Purgatory, Harvest, paper, 1985
To Asmara, Warner, paper, 1990
A Victim of the Aurora, Harvest, paper, 1985
Woman of the Inner Sea, Plume, paper, 1994

JAMAICA KINCAID

Annie, Gwen, Lilly, Pam and Tulip, Knopf, 1989
Annie John, Farrar, Straus & Giroux, 1985; Plume, paper, 1992

At the Bottom of the River, Farrar, Straus & Giroux, 1983; Plume, paper, 1992

The Autobiography of My Mother, Farrar, Straus & Giroux, 1995; Plume, paper, 1997

Lucy, Farrar, Straus & Giroux, 1990; Plume, paper, 1991

A Small Place, Plume, paper, 1989

MICHAEL KORDA

Charmed Lives, Avon, paper, 1981

Curtain, Warner, paper, 1992

The Immortals, Simon & Schuster, 1992; Avon, paper, 1993

Man to Man, Random House, 1996

GUS LEE

China Boy, Plume, paper, 1994

Honor and Duty, Knopf, 1994; Ivy, paper, 1995

Tiger's Tail, Knopf, 1996

JIM LEHRER

The Last Debate, Random House, 1995

White Widow, Random House, 1996

MARK LEYNER

Et Tu, Babe, Vintage, paper, 1993

I Smell Esther Williams and Other Stories, Vintage, paper, 1993

My Cousin, My Gastroenterologist, Vintage, paper, 1995

Tooth Imprints on a Corn Dog, Crown, 1995; Vintage, paper, 1996

BARRY LOPEZ

Arctic Dreams, Bantam, paper, 1996

Crossing Open Ground, Scribner, 1988; Vintage, paper, 1989

Crow and Weasel, North Point, 1990; HarperPerennial, paper, 1993

Desert Notes, Avon, paper, 1990

Field Notes, Knopf, 1994; Avon, paper, 1995

Giving Birth to Thunder, Sleeping with His Daughter, Avon, paper, 1990
Northwest Passage, Aperture, 1996
Of Wolves and Men, Scribner, paper, 1978
The Rediscovery of North America, Univ. Press of Kentucky, 1990;
      Vintage, paper, 1992
River Notes, Avon, paper, 1990
Winter Count, Avon, paper, 1993

ROBERT MacNEIL

Burden of Desire, Dell, paper, 1993
The Canadian Feeling, Penguin, paper, 1996
Eudora Welty, Univ. of Mississippi, paper, 1990
The Voyage, Doubleday, 1995; Harvest, paper, 1996
Wordstruck, Penguin, paper, 1990

STEPHEN MARLOWE

The Death and Life of Miguel de Cervantes, Arcade, 1996
The Lighthouse at the End of the World, Dutton, 1995; Plume,
      paper, 1996

BILL McKIBBEN

The Age of Missing Information, Plume, paper, 1993
The Comforting Whirlwind, Eerdmans, paper, 1994
The End of Nature, Anchor, paper, 1990
Hope, Human and Wild, Little, Brown, 1995

STEVEN MILLHAUSER

Edwin Mullhouse, Random House, paper, 1996
Little Kingdoms, Simon & Schuster, 1993
Martin Dressler, Random House, 1996

ALBERT MURRAY

The Blue Devils of Nada, Pantheon, 1996
The Hero and the Blues, Vintage, paper, 1996
The Seven League Boots, Pantheon, 1996
South to a Very Old Place, Vintage, paper, 1991

The Spyglass Tree, Vintage, paper, 1992
Train Whistle Guitar, Northeastern Univ., paper, 1989

ANNE PERRY

Ashworth Hall, Crest, paper, 1997
Belgrave Square, Crest, paper, 1993
Bethlehem Road, Crest, paper, 1991
Bluegate Fields, Crest, paper, 1986
Cain His Brother, Fawcett, 1995; Ivy, paper, 1996
Callander Square, Crest, paper, 1986
Cardington Crescent, Crest, paper, 1988
The Cater Street Hangman, Crest, paper, 1985
A Dangerous Mourning, Ivy, paper, 1992
Death in the Devil's Acre, Crest, paper, 1987
Defend and Betray, Ivy, paper, 1993
The Face of a Stranger, Ivy, paper, 1991
Farriers' Lane, Crest, paper, 1994
Highgate Rise, Crest, paper, 1992
The Hyde Park Headsman, Crest, paper, 1995
Paragon Walks, Crest, paper, 1986
Pentecost Alley, Crest, paper, 1997
Resurrection Row, Crest, paper, 1986
Rutland Place, Crest, paper, 1986
Silence in Hanover Close, Crest, paper, 1989
The Sins of the Wolf, Fawcett, 1994; Ivy, paper, 1995
A Sudden, Fearful Death, Ivy, paper, 1994
Traitors Gate, Fawcett, 1995; Crest, paper, 1996
Weighed in the Balance, Fawcett, 1996; Crest, paper, 1996

E. ANNIE PROULX

Accordion Crimes, Scribner, 1996
Heart Songs and Other Stories, Macmillan, paper, 1995
Postcards, Scribner, paper, 1997
The Shipping News, Scribner, paper, 1994

MARIO PUZO

The Dark Arena, Crest, paper, 1977
Fools Die, Signet, paper, 1979

The Godfather, Putnam, 1969; Signet, paper, 1983
The Last Don, Random House, 1996

NANCY TAYLOR ROSENBERG

California Angel, Dutton, 1995; Signet, paper, 1996
Finding Fact, Dutton, 1997
First Offense, Dutton, 1994; Signet, paper, 1995
Interest of Justice, Signet, paper, 1994
Mitigating Circumstances, Signet, paper, 1993
Trial by Fire, Dutton, 1996; Signet, paper, 1996

SALMAN RUSHDIE

East, West: Stories, Pantheon, 1995; Vintage, paper, 1996
Grimus, Overlook Press, 1982
Haroun and the Sea of Stories, Penguin, paper, 1991
Imaginary Homelands, Penguin, paper, 1992
The Jaguar Smile, Penguin, paper, 1987
Midnight's Children, Avon, paper, 1982
The Moor's Last Sigh, Pantheon, 1996
The Satanic Verses, Viking, 1989; Consortium, paper, 1992

MARK SALZMAN

Iron & Silk, Vintage, paper, 1989
The Laughing Sutra, Vintage, paper, 1992
Lost in Place, Random House, 1995; Vintage, paper, 1996
The Soloist, Random House, 1994; Vintage, paper, 1996

CATHLEEN SCHINE

Alice in Bed, Plume, paper, 1996
The Love Letter, Houghton Mifflin, 1995
Rameau's Niece, Plume, paper, 1994
To the Birdhouse, Farrar, Straus & Giroux, 1990; Plume, paper, 1996

JIM SHEPARD

Battling Against Castro, Knopf, 1996
Kiss of the Wolf, Harcourt Brace, 1994; Harcourt Brace, paper, 1995

Lights Out in the Reptile House, Avon, paper, 1991
Paper Doll, Knopf, 1986

MONA SIMPSON

Anywhere but Here, Knopf, 1986; Vintage, paper, 1992
The Lost Father, Vintage, paper, 1993
A Regular Guy, Random House, 1996; Vintage, paper, 1997

JOHN UPDIKE

The Afterlife and Other Stories, Knopf, 1994; Crest, paper, 1995
Assorted Prose, Knopf, 1965
Bech is Back, Knopf, 1982
Brazil, Knopf, 1994; Crest, paper, 1995
The Carpentered Hen, Knopf, 1982
Centaur, Knopf, 1963; Crest, paper, 1987
A Child's Calendar, Knopf, 1965
Collected Poems, 1953–1993, Knopf, 1993
The Coup, Knopf, 1978
Couples, Knopf, 1969; Crest, paper, 1985
Facing Nature: Poems, Knopf, 1985
Golf Dreams, Knopf, 1996; Crest, paper, 1997
A Helpful Alphabet of Friendly Objects, Knopf, 1995
Hugging the Shore, Knopf, 1983
In the Beauty of the Lilies, Knopf, 1996; Crest, paper, 1996
Marry Me!, Knopf, 1976; Crest, paper, 1983
Memories of the Ford Administration, Knopf, 1992; Crest, paper,
     1993
Midpoint and Other Poems, Knopf, 1969
A Month of Sundays, Knopf, 1975; Crest, paper, 1985
Museums and Women and Other Stories, Knopf, 1972
Music School, Knopf, 1966
Odd Jobs: Essays and Criticism, Knopf, 1991
Pigeon Feathers and Other Stories, Knopf, 1962; Crest, paper, 1986
The Poorhouse Fair, Knopf, 1977
Problems and Other Stories, Knopf, 1979
Rabbit Angstrom: The Four Novels, Knopf, 1995
Rabbit at Rest, Crest, paper, 1991
Rabbit Is Rich, Knopf, 1981; Crest, paper, 1982

Rabbit Redux, Knopf, 1971; Crest, paper, 1985
Rabbit Run, Knopf, 1960; Crest, paper, 1983
Roger's Version, Knopf, 1986; Crest, paper, 1987
S, Knopf, 1988; Crest, paper, 1989
Self-Consciousness: Memoirs, Knopf, 1989; Expression, paper, 1990
Telephone Poles and Other Poems, Knopf, 1963
Too Far to Go, Crest, paper, 1982
Trust Me, Crest, paper, 1988
The Witches of Eastwick, Knopf, 1984; Crest, paper, 1985

DOROTHY WEST

The Living Is Easy, Feminist Press, paper, 1995
The Richer, the Poorer, Doubleday, 1995; Anchor, paper, 1996
The Wedding, Doubleday, 1995; Anchor, paper, 1996

TOBIAS WOLFF

Back in the World, Vintage, paper, 1996
The Barracks Thief, Ecco, 1993
In Pharaoh's Army, Knopf, 1994; Knopf, paper, 1995
In the Garden of the North American Martyrs, Ecco, paper, 1996
The Night in Question, Knopf, 1996
This Boy's Life, HarperPerennial, paper, 1990